Friedel's Conversations with the Dead

Friedel's Conversations with the Dead

The Fascinating Story of Friedrich Jürgenson, Pioneer of EVP

Anabela Cardoso and Anders Leopold

www.whitecrowbooks.com

Friedel's Conversations with the Dead

Copyright © 2023 by Anabela Cardoso. All rights reserved.

Published in the United States of America and the United Kingdom by
White Crow Books; an imprint of White Crow Productions Ltd.

The right of Anabela Cardoso and Anders Leopold to be identified as the authors of this work has been asserted in accordance with the Copyright, Design and Patents act 1988.

No part of this book may be reproduced, copied or used in any form or manner whatsoever without written permission, except in the case of brief quotations in reviews and critical articles.

For information, contact White Crow Books by e-mail: info@whitecrowbooks.com.

Cover Design by Astrid@Astridpaints.com

Interior design by Velin@Perseus-Design.com

Paperback: ISBN: 978-1-78677-230-5

eBook: ISBN: 978-1-78677-231-2

Non-Fiction / Body, Mind & Spirit / Parapsychology / Afterlife & Reincarnation

www.whitecrowbooks.com

ACKNOWLEDGEMENTS

A sincere word of appreciation is due to Carl Michael von Hausswolff and the Jürgenson Foundation, the institution he founded to honour and preserve the work of Friedrich Jürgenson, the great pioneer of the electronic voices. The remarkable archive would have been lost without his generous and enlightening initiative.

It is true that Friedel opened the world of direct transcendence to humanity, in which no intermediaries are necessary but without Carl Michael's decisive action the world would not have become fully aware of the bridge between dimensions that Friedel constructed with so much love and labour that allows the marvellous direct communications we enjoy today.

Heartfelt thanks are due to Tom Ruffles, author and a distinguished member of the Society for Psychical Research, and to Chris Jensen Romer, dedicated psychical researcher, who supported my work from the very beginning with enthusiasm and concrete advice.

Also, to my dear friend Carlos Fernández, author and publisher, who has accompanied me from the very first day I entered the unending quest about life and death through ITC research. He has been unfailingly beside me with his friendship, help and expert technical advice, which I value immensely.

Last but not least to my publisher Jon Beecher, for his unwavering patience and understanding and for his wise guidance.

This book is the result of an intimate collaboration between all of us who took part in it with dedication and love for Friedel and his pioneering mission toward the new way aimed at changing the prevailing human paradigm that he so fervently desired.

CONTENTS

ACKNOWLEDGEMENTS V
FOREWORD 1
PREFACE 5
INTRODUCTION 11
A BRIEF PRESENTATION OF EVP 11
1. SCIENTISTS WHO RESEARCHED THE VOICE PHENOMENA 19
2. BEFORE THE VOICES 35
3. THE FIRST SIGNS 43
4. FIRST CONTACT 57
5. SWEDISH TV PERSONALITY, ARNE WEISE 75
6. RECORDINGS ON NEW YEAR'S EVE 89
7. THE WORLD PRESS PUT IN THEIR PLACE 111
8. THE SCIENTIFIC TESTS 133
9. FRIEDEL ANSWERS QUESTIONS 151
10. SURREAL MESSAGES: FRIEDEL'S INTERPRETATION OF THE "HITLER" MONOLOGUE 161
11. FRIEDEL AND THE POPE 173
12. FRIEDEL ON LIFE ON THE OTHER SIDE 191
13. PICTURES FROM THE OTHER SIDE 207
14. OTHER RESEARCHERS OBTAIN GOOD RESULTS 215

15. FRIEDEL'S AND ANDERS LEOPOLD'S JOINT RECORDINGS 225
16. THE VOICE PHENOMENA SPREAD ALL OVER THE WORLD 243
17. RECORD AND LISTEN 265
REFERENCES 273
PHOTO CREDITS 275
NOTES 279

FOREWORD

My first encounter with Friedrich Jürgenson's work was in 1964 at the hairdresser's in my hometown, Linköping. Being a devoted Beatles fan my mother forced me to have a bi-monthly haircut, and my only pleasure in that was waiting for my turn while glancing through the magazines in the waiting area. One of the magazines was the weekly *Saxons*, and apart from gossip and trivialities they published articles on paranormal topics.

Friedrich Jürgenson was something of a celebrity at the time as a result of his widely publicized first press conference on Electronic Voice Phenomena in 1963. Subsequently, Saxons published his first book, *Rösterna från Rymden* (The Voices from Space) in 1964.

Jürgenson's fame spread throughout Sweden and he remained well known until his passing in 1987. His final appearance in the Swedish media was in January 1985 when he was the subject of the popular television show Här Är Ditt Liv, a Swedish version of the American TV series, "This Is Your Life."

As Jürgenson's work became known in Sweden and elsewhere, he attracted students and followers such as Konstantin Raudive, Claude and Ellen Thorlin and Lizz Werneroth, who were keen to replicate his findings, and were performing their own experiments with the "voices" and writing about them. Raudive was the most well-known, particularly after his book was published in German under the title *Unhörbares Wird Hörbar* (The Inaudible Becomes Audible) in 1968, and in English titled *Breakthrough: An Amazing Experiment in Electronic Communication with the Dead* in 1971.

Anders Leopold Elmqvist (1937-2021) was a close friend of Jürgenson for more than 20 years. He worked primarily as a journalist for the evening-paper *Aftonbladet*, and covered Jürgenson's press conferences and the two became friends until Friedel's passing.

In the late 1980s Anders Leopold (as he later called himself) became known in Sweden as one of several private investigators who in 1986 investigated the assassination of the Swedish Prime Minister, Olof Palme.

Friedel's Conversations with the Dead is Leopold's personal tribute to Friedrich Jürgenson's, life and work, and the first oeuvre to do so.

I am a visual and sound artist, and in the late 1980s I took an interest in EVP, which led me to Friedrich Jürgenson's archive in 1999. During that time I discovered the work of George W. Meek and his Metascience Foundation, and also Raymond Cass, Michael Esposito, Leif Elggren and later Marja-Lena Sillanpää and Anabela Cardoso.

When I was informed by my father-in-law, the Swedish actor Sven Lindberg, that Jürgenson had lived in Höör, south Sweden, and that Jürgenson's life-comrade Märta Annell still lived there, I decided to go and visit her together with my wife Marietta. That visit was in the early winter of 1999, and, as a result, Märta gave me Jürgenson's archive, because she didn't know what to do with it, and, when Jürgenson's son who lived in Israel, came to collect Jürgenson's belongings after his passing, he wasn't interested in the archive.

In early 2000, artist Carsten Höller and I drove down from Stockholm to Höör and collected all 1000 quarter inch tapes, notebooks, press clippings and photographs. I then founded the *Friedrich Jürgenson Foundation* in order to find a home for the archive. The archive was shown in art exhibitions in Stockholm, Göteborg and Frankfurt during 2000 to 2004, and then with the assistance of Peter Weibel we found a home for it in the ZKM art and media museum in Karlsruhe, Germany, where it remains to this day.

Jürgenson's "best of" voices together with the now famous black and white photograph of Jürgenson showing himself on Claude Thorlin's TV set on the day of Jürgenson's funeral, has been widely presented in contemporary art exhibitions in Berlin, New York City, Seoul and elsewhere.

A CD was produced and released by P.A.R.C / Ash International in London and his autobiographical book *Sprechfunk Mit Verstorbenen* was translated into English and published by Firework Edition in 2004.

In 2004 a small house in Chiang Mai, Thailand was erected with the name: The KREV Jürgenson Star House.

Thanks to a thorough translation and rewrite by renowned ITC/EVP researcher Anabela Cardoso, this book is now available to English speaking readers.

The legacy of Friedrich Jürgenson lives on.

Carl Michael von Hausswolff, Stockholm 2023,
artist, composer, curator and chairman of
the Friedrich Jürgenson Foundation.

PREFACE

The book

In the summer of 2020, I was contacted by a Swedish journalist named Anders Leopold via a Swedish friend of mine. Anders had been a close friend of Friedrich Jürgenson, the founder of Electronic Voice Phenomena (EVP) who is considered by many to be a pioneer in contemporary paranormal investigation, and someone whom I've had a profound interest in since I began my research in EVP and Instrumental Transcommunication (ITC) in 1998.

Anders published a book in 2014 titled *Min vän på andra sidan: boken om Friedrich Jürgenson som upptäckte röstfenomen från en fjärde livsdimension* (My friend on the other side: the book about Friedrich Jürgenson who discovered the voice phenomena from a fourth dimension of life).[1]

My friend had been a member of the *ITC Journal* Editorial Team for many years and, knowing of my interest in Jürgenson's work and his fascinating life, had suggested he contact me.[2]

The book had been published in Sweden, but Anders knew no one with the proper knowledge of the field to translate and publish it in English. He was very keen on having the work translated and revised because he knew that the English version could open the door to the worldwide knowledge of a major figure in the history of humanity, his dear friend Friedel, the builder of the "bridge" between the two worlds as he himself referred to his work.

I accepted the task with great emotion and love for someone who albeit being 'on the other side,' I feel as close to my heart and soul as if he lived with me. I did not know then that the job would be colossal, but, even if I had known, I would have accepted it just the same. For some reason unknown to me, Friedrich Jürgenson has been my guiding light since the beginning of my ITC work. Thus, the forthcoming joy of learning intimate details of his personal, as well as his artistic life, was an incomparable reward for the work, the difficulty of which, however, by far exceeded what I had expected.

Besides the already problematic issues regarding the language and the length of the text, the fact that Anders Leopold died suddenly of a cardiac attack when I was in the middle of the book, greatly increased the difficulties and the toil as one can easily imagine.

Nonetheless, despite the exhausting labor it meant to me, I celebrate the task with elation and gratitude. Before his death, Anders Leopold entrusted me with the job dearest to his heart, a job I hope to have accomplished to his satisfaction after his death. Thus, here is our common work—Anders Leopold provided the facts, the dates and the citations and I rewrote the text based on the Swedish original.

This is a book not only about the multifaceted Friedrich Jürgenson, his adventurous life, his joys, his toil and his hardships, but also about the unbelievable discovery of the door he opened to humanity—the direct communication between our Earthly dimension and the next one, via electronic devices. A discovery announced as early as the nineteenth century by the French educator and Spiritist Allan Kardec (1804 – 1869).

I hope that readers who are familiar with my work, ITC followers and the public in general, will enjoy the vivid and witty descriptions of Friedrich Jürgenson's personality, his intelligence, sensitivity and charismatic life throughout many countries and cultures. With unbounded friendship, which in no way affected his judgement, critical sense and righteousness, Anders Leopold tells us about a renaissance man born in the twentieth century.

A man of great culture and artistic value, an atheist cherished by two Popes, Friedel, as he was affectionately known, unwittingly discovered the electronic voices of the dead in a remote forest in Sweden, in his magical Nysund, one of the most harmonious and beautiful places I have seen in my life.

However, and before we get into the book proper, perhaps we should ponder the reasons why this man and his astounding findings have been, more often than not, relegated to the boundaries of "fertile imagination" and "inconsequential labor" by some parapsychologists. It is a strange but true situation.

The renowned twentieth century parapsychologist Professor Hans Bender[2], a brilliant scientist who conducted and witnessed many of Friedel's tests, stated about the voices, "This is the most important discovery in the history of parapsychology!" A discovery that happened in Sweden and not in the English-speaking countries from which the majority of parapsychologists originate. Perhaps one of the reasons why most of those renowned parapsychologists have not yet recognized Jürgenson's contribution to the field is that the works were, and still are, published mainly in German and Italian, and thus ignored by English speaking scientists.

I cannot be sure but I notice some similarity with Hans Bender who was one of the major contributors to parapsychology, but, despite this, is not mentioned as frequently as he should be outside of Germany.

In any case, to show disdain for Jürgenson and his work in the name of rigor and experimental control as some have done, is actually a product of combined ignorance and arrogance, and it renders a bad service to humanity and to the study of anomalous phenomena of whatever kind. The bias it introduces in an area that should be unprejudiced, free and open minded, is detrimental to the advancement of individual self-knowledge and to the expansion of human consciousness. Instead of rendering parapsychology more prestigious, it limits it, which is less appealing to the public, who are often eager to learn and get involved in a field that so many have experienced even if rarely under controlled conditions.

Moreover, few experiments in parapsychology have been as controlled as Professor Bender's tests of Friedrich Jürgenson's voices. There are no excuses for an attitude of neglect toward a discipline that many think provides the best evidence of consciousness surviving bodily death.

In a later chapter the reader will have the opportunity of evaluating the descriptions of the tests carried out by Professor Bender. Detailed reports were published at the time in the "Zeitschrift für Parapsychologie und Grenzgebiete der Psychologie," a prestigious German scientific publication.

Friedrich Jürgenson publicly identified humanity's main problem: "I recognized that all our anxieties and miseries could not be eliminated until we had incontestably solved the problem of death." After his discovery he devoted the rest of his life, career and reputation to the noble aim of trying to shift the prevalent paradigm in a generous, open-minded, and universal way. We owe him immense gratitude.

Anders Leopold's account of his friend's extraordinary life, of his torments and joys, is detailed, knowledgeable and thoroughly honest.

I have not seen a better biography of the man who is the beacon of all knowledgeable ITC operators, although, regrettably, still little known to many practitioners and the general public.

The recordings

Some of the audio examples selected by Anders Leopold are difficult or impossible to interpret because they are partially, or totally damaged. They are copies of the originals, as he tells us in the book, but the main problem is the rather primitive recording medium used: the reel-to-reel tapes of the 1960s, which deteriorated over time.

Furthermore, most of the anomalous voices received by Friedrich Jürgenson (FJ) came through radio programs and/or radio music and that circumstance renders their auditory perception even more difficult. Also, in some musical examples, the original song was replaced by the anomalous utterances while the music remained—A similar situation has happened in my own experiments (see *Neuroquantology* 2012, Sept., Vol. 10, Issue 3, pp. 492-514).

When listening to the audio recordings, we must bear in mind that Jürgenson was endowed with excellent natural hearing capability, was fully trained in music, and spoke several languages. These conditions surely contributed for his choice as the herald of the novel way of communication between our world and the next dimension.

When we listen to these fantastic recordings miraculously preserved that Anders Leopold called 'impossible' but we now know are possible, we should recognize that they represent the first anomalous electronic voices in the world recorded en masse that consequently initiated EVP and ITC: an unprecedented feat, which shouldn't be marred because of the quality of some of the recordings. If there were only one, it would be one of William James' so-called White Crows, evidence that not all crows are black, but fortunately there are many.

Anders published 37 voice examples in his original Swedish book. Because some of them are indeed of difficult or impossible comprehension and would require a lot of time and concentration from the readers of the English version, I have identified the most paradigmatic and clearest voices in the text proper. However, all thirty-seven audio clips can be found on the ITC Journal website which might appeal to ITC purists.[3]

I believe that if the reader listens to the labelled ones only, however, they still suffice for the proper understanding of the amazing pioneering work of FJ as early as the 1960s, and of all the barriers he had to overcome to finally attain the recognition of the electronic voice phenomenon by the international and the scientific communities of his time.

It is a feat unmatched in our days when, regrettably, ITC and EVP seem to have lost prestige due to the misuse, sometimes unwittingly, that many have made of this remarkable tool, which allows individual access to the next dimension of life in an objective and repeatable way—a joy within reach of all people, as Friedrich Jürgenson ardently desired.

In the audio examples, Anders Leopold's voice introduces the recording and Jürgenson's voice describes the situation and the content in German. Naturally, this represents an added difficulty for the English readers, but the book proper contains detailed descriptions of the recordings, as well as of the circumstances around their reception, in English.

Professor Hans Bender participated in, listened to and approved many of these audios; some of them he sent to the Max Planck Institute in Munich for testing and confirmation of FJ's and his own interpretations. There were few, if any, anomalous phenomena subjected to such tight scrutiny at the time.

Even the Vatican, with their all-encompassing scientific knowledge, (including parapsychology) and Paul VI, the Pope of Jürgenson's time, supported and confirmed the relevance and the authenticity of the voices. This and other amazing circumstances described in the book will transport readers to the inconceivable world of Friedrich Jürgenson, Friedel to his friends.

INTRODUCTION

A BRIEF PRESENTATION OF EVP

One can perhaps date the paranormal phenomenon that we know as EVP to the beginning of the 1900s when the Russian ethnologist Vladimir Bogoraz (Waldemar Bogoras) visited a shaman in Siberia. A shaman is a person who states that while in trance he travels to other worlds. Bogoraz brought a phonograph[4] to record the shaman in the altered state of consciousness where he would travel to the world of the spirits. The only thing we know about this historic EVP recording is that Bogoraz claimed that strange voices were intermingled with the shaman's voice (Bogoras, 1975).

In the 1940s, in the United States, photographer and medium Attila von Szalay recorded strange voices on a wire recorder during spiritualist séances. It appears that these voices were mixed with the medium's voice. When the tape recorder was developed, he continued his experiments with his colleague Raymond Bayless. In 1959 they published their results, but their work received no attention. On June 12, of the same year another artist, Friedrich Jürgenson, recorded his mother's voice on tape. She had been dead for five years: this date marks the birth of EVP. In 1963, Friedrich Jürgenson held his first international press conference and was featured in the media worldwide.

My friend, Friedel

Harry Friedrich Jürgenson was born on Feb. 8, 1903, in the Russian city of Odessa. Sixty-one years later, we met one day in May 1964, when the magical lake by his country house Nysund (in Mölnbo, about sixty kilometers south of Stockholm) reflected the colors of the setting sun. Birdsong, which he claimed gave him the first message from his since long deceased mother, swept over the surface and returned as an astral echo.

I am a journalist, and at the time I was working for the well-known Swedish newspaper, *Aftonbladet*. And he was the man who claimed to have had contact with the dead through a tape recorder.

We remained close friends until October 15, 1987, when he went over to the other side, to what he called "life in the fourth dimension."

This versatile and complex person who, with immense charisma and joy of life devoted himself to the opposite of life—death—discovered what in parapsychology is called EVP, Electronic Voice Phenomena. In other words, electronically mediated contacts with another dimension of life via tape recorder and radio. Continued research led this discipline to be known as ITC, Instrumental TransCommunication, which includes contacts via computers, TV and telephone: i.e. contacts with live intelligent beings in another dimension who, under certain circumstances, can reach us.

In this book I wish to introduce readers to the fascinating story of Friedrich Jürgenson's life and the so-called spirit voices as well as his artistry, which granted him the honor of painting several portraits of two popes. Furthermore, he obtained the permission of the Vatican to make excavations in Pompeii and documented this with three films; he was granted the difficult authorization to film a papal audience and much, much more. Friedel, which we his friends called him, also published three books, about the voice phenomena, which were translated into several languages.

In this account of my friend's life and work, I will try to remove some of the doubts about historical figures who have long been dead and yet, under very strange circumstances, try to contact us, the living. You will read some of the testimonials from people who, without the slightest hesitation, believe that they heard a dear loved one from the other side, beyond death.

The man you will meet was a philanthropist, philosopher, artist, archaeologist and uncompromising in his beliefs. He tolerated no cheating, no tricks, no quackery; he earned no money from his discovery in spite of great offers, and he always refused to allow a cult to be created around him. Nothing of what he did was based on faith, spiritualism, or mediumship. My friend was modest and unassuming. He radiated spontaneous warmth, kindness, understanding, knowledge, ethics, and humility.

He described to me, late one night, in his sometimes cryptic way, that we live in a dimension limited by time and space. He said, "people think that this dimension is the only reality available—something that we can take in with our senses—but this dimension reflects what lies beyond time and space. We are bound by our time but in the universe exists no time. We see stars that have been extinct for millions of years, and, in spite of it, the light reaches us. Other researchers and scientists, such as C. G. Jung, Sir Oliver Lodge, Professor J. B. Rhine and Professor C. D. Broad, revealed that man is able to exceed the limit of the physical body's five known senses."

Friedel held his first press conference on June 14, 1963, and his first book *Rösterna från rymden* (The Voices from Space) appeared in the spring of 1964, a few months before another international press conference. The meeting with the international press resulted in scores of articles in major newspapers, mainly in Germany, England, Italy and the United States, while the Swedish media remained quite uninterested. Some newspapers were serious, others, mainly the Swedish ones, simply made a fool out of him. When the book was published, there was increased interest in Friedel and his spirit voices.

Naturally, he was hurt by the way the Swedish press treated him. Below I reproduce a letter to the editor, which Friedel wrote in June 1963 after that first press conference. He felt a strong need to explain himself, but no Swedish newspaper published his article.

Thus, my friend Friedel, I herein publish your letter with great appreciation:

> The articles published in Sweden regarding my tape contacts with a higher level of existence have brought about a lively echo in the world press. As this matter concerns the most pressing issues of our existence, and the numerous interviews I have given did not exhaust the subject, I find it necessary to emphasize some important points.
>
> Firstly, I want to clarify the following: I neither belong to a political party, a religious sect, a secret alliance, nor any "ism" of modern times.

I have no intention of founding a new movement or to stand as leader of a newly formed sect.

My only intention is to divulge, through the publication of a book, the events that happened to me over the course of four to five years, and the visits by scientists, psychologists and psychiatrists, sound engineers, writers, and others who were interested in the demonstration and explanation of my tapes. This can lead to joint research with new recordings, which in turn could lead to new discoveries and make today's unpredictable transcendent contacts to be viewed objectively and correctly. These newly opened perspectives cannot yet be assessed.

Without a doubt, these interventions from a higher plane of survival are, in my opinion, the greatest and most significant event of our time, an event which, naturally, also requires commitment from our side. Through this insight into the higher planes of life, or the life in a fourth dimension, the question of death and supernatural phenomena will be resolved. And we can, perhaps for the first time, understand the genuine meaning of all ethics, beyond the limitation imposed by dogma. Undoubtedly, we can understand through this method the issue of life and death and look at it in a new way and understand the evolution of humanity. These contacts are not only the key to the truth of existence, but they also show the way to a life beyond space and time. I would like to point out that an objective recorder cannot be influenced by subjective desires and feelings. It automatically and objectively records what really exists.

I firmly believe that through the research, the term "supernatural" will be dissolved, for all phenomena in this dimension are subject to natural laws that are still unknown to us. If the connection could be extended, it would mean that the public could participate and be convinced. We all know that life is fragile and that we are constantly under the threat of death, which is the only certainty for us. Until today, it was not possible to demonstrably solve the riddle of death, and we have not the correct understanding of life to be able to reveal its secrets where you least expect it. The question now is: are we prepared to face life's deepest secret with an open mind, or should we, burdened by the past, continue to hide its bright core with a black veil?

Friedrich Jürgenson, Mölnbo,
Nysund, June 1963.

During the spring of 1964, *Aftonbladet* decided to publish a story about this remarkable man. I and my photographer, Jerry Windahl, visited Friedel. We were the newspaper's team for central Sweden; our editorial office was not far from Mölnbo and eventually we extended our work to Italy and Rome, where we followed Friedel in his work for the film he made about Pope Paul VI.

Friedel and I contacted each other and that grew into a warm friendship for the next twenty years. In my opinion, his first book had been a bit of a rush job and I encouraged him to develop his material and the events that occurred during the first half of the twentieth century in a new book. I tried not to influence him in any way, even if our conversations were later reflected in the book *Radio and Microphone Contact with the Dead*, which was published in 1968. Already in the preface to the new book, he clearly stated his aversion to the attempts of other people to influence him. He wrote:

> Some of my friends have earnestly tried to dissuade me from leaving my subjective experiences to the public, and instead urged me to stick to the objective tape recordings. By hiding my inner experiences, I would come unscathed from everything and significantly increase my good reputation in the world. But when I, by a twist of fate, happened to come in contact with something really outstanding, which, due to its nature, is capable of solving the most important questions of our existence, personal concerns started losing their importance. It is my deepest conviction that a cropped truth, like a candle without a wick, does not fulfil its function. For this reason, it seemed to me legitimate to present my experiences in their entirety to the public even though I, therefore, would greatly expose myself.

When it came to Friedel's absolute conviction that the voices came from dead people, he could not help but notice my doubts. I liked the theory that scientists (such as Dr Nils-Olof Jacobson) suggested of the existence of an unknown subconscious power, a kind of psychokinesis, i.e., that we use unwittingly to produce the phenomenon. At the beginning, even Prof. Hans Bender leaned in that direction. Friedel, of course, vigorously rejected this when he, and others who recorded without his involvement, identified voices from relatives and close friends who had died several years before. He told me: "Anders, when you get to hear and recognize a voice, and immediately identify it as someone who was very close to you in life, then you will be convinced." *Maybe*, I thought to myself.

I will close this introduction by forwarding an extraordinary message allegedly received from Friedel. The recipient of this message was Adolf Homes from Rivenich in southern Germany, a world-leading researcher of EVP and ITC. Since 1988, Homes continued Friedel's EVP research with radio, computer, TV, and telephone contacts with what appears to be beings from another life dimension. After his death on October 15, 1997, he apparently contacted his friend Friedrich Malkoff (who continued with ITC research) several times.

As a guarantee that this really happened, scientists often refer to Professor Ernst Senkowski[5] (1995). He is the scientist who devised the term "Instrumental TransCommunication" in the 1970s. He published the now classic book *Instrumentelle Transkommunikation* in 1995, which is undoubtedly the major work on ITC and EVP.

On October 13, 1994, Adolf Homes sent a videotape to Ernst Senkowski explaining:

> At 8 o'clock I had a very peculiar feeling. As in a kind of trance, I took my old VHS camera, put it in front of the TV in the living room and started both, with the TV on an empty channel. As soon as I started the camera, a picture was visible on the TV. It seemed to show Friedrich Jürgenson. The image lasted 23 seconds and it was in orange.
>
> At the moment when the picture appeared, I heard a loud knocking in the next room, where the computer is and where we make our recordings. I was, nevertheless, seated and tried to produce an audible contact by calling Friedrich Jürgenson. This attempt did not succeed. After about eight minutes I stopped because I did not hear anything. When I went into the room where the computer is, I saw a text on the screen. Keyboard and monitor had switched themselves on. The computer was turned off because the floppy drive was broken. I filmed the screen with the camera, and it showed the following:

Here, Friedel is making contact

> Dear humans. As is known to you, we are in a position to enter into your structure at choice. I send you repeatedly a projection of myself but with your appearance [the appearance known to you]. The time indication [on the video-camera] is not correct for you.

The projection is in the quanta of no space-time since 17.1.1991. Each [one] of your and of our thoughts has its own electromagnetic reality that does not get lost outside of the time structure. Not only our so-called transcontacts, but [also] the consciousness of the universal whole (des Gesamtuniversellen) is to be understood [as] purely mental/spiritual and in principle creates all physical and psychical forms. From this point of view, we too are still humans. This collective undertaking creates all forms. These, in their turn, represent illusions because they change. Many of us are in a position to adopt [a] physical shape. Please transmit my message to all men. This says to you F. Jürgenson."

(Senkowski, 1995; Cardoso, 2017, pp. 47-49;
ITC Journal 39, 2010 pp. 35-61).

1

SCIENTISTS WHO RESEARCHED THE VOICE PHENOMENA

I will start by introducing some of the personalities who participated in recordings with Friedrich Jürgenson, and who seriously and objectively researched the voice phenomena.

HANS BENDER (1907-1991) was one of the world's most renowned parapsychologists. He created one of the premier research institutions in parapsychological research, the Institut für Grenzgebiete der Parapsychologie und Psycho Hygiene at the University of Freiburg.

Bender and his team traveled around the world exposing charlatans, quacks, and fanatical occultists who not only through their manipulations injured parapsychology, but also diminished its acceptance as science. Bender visited Friedel several times during the 1960s and I could talk to him, both officially in interviews but also off the record. He took several of Friedel's tapes to Freiburg and to the Max Planck Institute in Munich for testing. Bender said that his interest in Friedel's recordings derived from the fact that he was absolutely credible. In May 1970, Bender and his team travelled to Friedel's country house Nysund, in Mölnbo, for several days of recordings and tests using new technological instruments. It became one of the most sensational recordings in Friedel's lifetime, scientifically conducted with German thoroughness. Throughout this book I will return to these sessions. A speech spectrogram performed at the Max Planck Institute demonstrated beyond doubt that the phenomenon existed.

After having known Friedel for six years and having written several articles about him and the voices, I could finally run a headline in *Aftonbladet*, stating "This is a proof that the voice phenomena, the so-called spirit voices, exist" and an image of the speech spectrogram was also published, as we will see.

Bender was known for his great restraint when it came to publishing research in parapsychology. He told me that he felt it was like walking around on a minefield where any misstep could mean the end of the parapsychological research. Here he was completely unbridled, and his main comment was: "This is the most important discovery in the history of parapsychology!" Later, he published an article about the speech spectrogram in the journal *Zeitschrift für Parapsychologie und Grentzgebiete der Psychologie*. He wrote: "This recording (May 4, 1970) was for me clear evidence that alien[6] voices exist and are likely to have a paranormal origin. It also points to the situation that we can establish some sort of contact with another life dimension."

The recording was tested later by Dr. Jochem Sotschek, head of the German State Telegraphic and Electronic Institute, who determined that the voice he heard on the tape said exactly what Bender and his team claimed. Hans Bender did not take the decisive step to add that those were voices from dead people who lived in another life dimension, trying to get in touch with us, the living, under difficult conditions.

JOHN BJOERKHEM (1910-1963), M.A. and PhD in theology, was a pioneer in Swedish parapsychology and hypnosis research. He conducted several high-profile experiments on deep hypnosis with the intention of facilitating the recall of the memory of apparently forgotten events in the life, and maybe in a previous life, of the subject with the help of hypnosis. The results were quite astounding. He could move his subjects farther and farther back in time. They described in childlike terms how, for example, they experienced the first day of school, usually with a completely different shrill voice. There were those who went back even further and began to talk as young children and there was someone who cried like a baby. The transition to parapsychology occurred when he had the idea of making a nineteen-year-old student go into the past and during the hypnosis transported him around twenty-five years back in time. The student replied, confused, not as a child but as an adult, in Finnish, a language he did not know a single word of. To a direct question, he claimed that he was a Finnish fisherman.

John Bjoerkhem visited Friedel on several occasions during the early 1960s. They made recordings and he explained his conclusions to me. A short summary is below:

> I am now convinced that these voice phenomena exist and that Friedrich Jürgenson, although not through any manipulation but in an indescribably complicated way, which he could not master, got the voices on the tape. Also, I have come to know him as an honest person. My conclusion after the experiences I had with him, is that if just a single extra word gets into the tape in a quiet room, we have evidence of the voices' existence. We do not need more empirical evidence because in this type of tape recording every subjective element is excluded.

ARNE WEISE (1930 - 2019), a very popular Swedish TV celebrity, was also a celebrity with regard to the voice phenomena. The recordings in which he participated at Friedel's home shook him, not least because he put a question to the unknown voices and got an answer. Those recordings are perhaps the most impressive in Friedel's collection of about 6000 recordings over twenty-five years.

Both he, Friedel, and I regretted that he could not participate in the popular Swedish TV show *This is Your Life* in 1985 when Friedel was the subject. Weise was a friend of Friedel's before the voice phenomena came into the latter's life and they did several radio programs together, including one about Pope Pius XII. And right after *This is Your Life* I got in touch with him by telephone, in Los Angeles. He regretted that he could not participate in the program because, if there was something he really wanted to make people understand, it was that Friedel had total credibility even if his interpretation [of the phenomenon] was inconsistent with Arne Weise's.

In a letter to me of May 27, 2013, while I worked on this book, Arne Weise said the following, briefly, about his experiences with Friedel and the recordings he participated in:

> Friedel made it immediately clear to me that he was sure of being in contact with living beings in another life dimension. Actually I became nervous when voices directly addressed me. I heard many of Friedel's recordings, but probably, what struck me were the utterly clearest

voices, which to me were a little scary. I am baptized in Swedenborg's teachings and they say clearly that here on the Earth we shall live and we should not keep on trying to get in touch with the other side. So, I have asked myself why I, of all people, met him and became involved in these strange events. It was a tremendous responsibility that Friedel took on when he reached people who had lost their loved ones and convinced them that they could contact them in another life dimension—although he was very careful about this situation.

Friedel was an extremely complicated and versatile person who had been through so much and gained quite a different experience from other people. He was an interesting and exciting man that I liked. He stayed away from those who tried to make money off him and his discovery. That says a lot about his honest intentions.

KONSTANTIN RAUDIVE (1909-1974), PhD, was born in Latvia, studied at the Sorbonne and earned a doctorate in Salamanca. He translated Cervantes' books into Latvian. When he read Friedel's first book, *Rösterna från rymden* (The Voices from Space), his whole life changed, as he himself avowed. He was so fascinated that on his wife Zenta Maurina's advice he visited Friedel in Sweden. We could say that, in a way, he was one of Friedel's followers. He made many recordings, wrote books, and recorded discs. I did not meet Raudive but followed his progress and what he wrote about his voice research. This is one of his comments:

> We now have evidence that the soul lives on after death. Instead of just faith, we have ensured that this is demonstrable by objective physical facts. We have, in an acoustic physical way, established contact between life before and after death, and this may one-day lead to the answer to the eternal question: "Where? Where are we going to?" Death might come to be seen as part of a continuous line of development. I reject completely the hypothesis of the unconscious mind as a dead end in the research. It explains the soul phenomenon but says nothing about how the soul operates in relation to the universe.

Konstantin Raudive died in 1974. In July 1988, the couple Maggy and Jules Harsch-Fishbach of Luxembourg, the most famous ITC researchers in the world, received a pre-announced message on their TV screen, which was videoed. It was a greeting from Raudive as we will discuss later in this book.

SCIENTISTS WHO RESEARCHED THE VOICE PHENOMENA

TORBERN LAURENT (1896-1981) was professor of telegraphy and telephony at the High School of Technology in Stockholm. He was internationally known for his work with the filter theory and frequency transformations. He tested Friedel's recordings and was a guest at Nysund where he participated in the recordings on several occasions. He also tested Friedel's hearing and declared that it was extremely sensitive, which sometimes led to the situation that Friedel heard voices which other people had great difficulty in hearing. Laurent averred in an interview with me on New Year's Eve, in 1965:

> From where these strange sounds and voices available on the bands come, I do not understand. It is very strange, and I am prepared to say that I personally experienced the phenomenon. In the current situation it is very difficult to pinpoint what is behind it.

NILS-OLOF JACOBSON (1937-2017), medical doctor, psychiatrist, and author of a number of articles, books, and reports on the topic of life after death. He wrote the following in a paper called "ITC and Science."

> I came into contact with the electronic voice phenomenon (EVP) in 1969. I have personally experimented quite a lot over the years, receiving many voices that I consider clearly paranormal but the content of the messages has been meagre—usually one to three words, sometimes relevant to my questions—but often with no obvious meaning. Also, I received two telephone calls from the late ITC pioneer Konstantin Raudive in the spring of 1994.
>
> I have been active in parapsychology for a number of years. Scientists active in parapsychology are very anxious about their scientific credibility and acceptance among their colleagues. They believe that they know, from the sum of all their experiences, that a thing such as ITC is of course impossible.
>
> If I claim that ITC is possible, they ask me to demonstrate it. This I cannot do, as I have not myself been able to take the quantum leap from EVP to ITC. Then they ask me to take them to another person who can demonstrate it to their satisfaction, while they are applying all kinds of controls to exclude any form of deception. If such a scientist is actually admitted to an experiment, nothing is likely to happen and the scientist will go home and write a paper that it was, of course, a case of self-deception or a hoax.

In the current situation, interested scientists cannot do much more than study the results presented by lay experimenters. But this is of no interest to the greater scientific community. If I tell my colleagues that some people in Luxembourg and Germany claim to have two-way instrumental contacts with the spirit world, and that I believe this to be true, my colleagues would only laugh at me. I would lose my scientific credibility if I have any left after all my activities in parapsychology, which in itself is suspect to scientists.

Scientists are only interested in what can be proved or disproved in the conventional scientific way. That is, if I claim to have a phenomenon that is not yet accepted within the "official" worldview, I have to provide some proof that it exists. Ideally, it should be possible for other scientists to repeat the occurrence of the phenomenon. If I have no proof, I cannot ask to be taken seriously.

So this is my situation as a physician and scientist interested (and personally believing) in ITC. I can think of two possible outcomes in the development of ITC that I would consider positive:

1. Scientists such as myself will eventually be able to get two-way contacts for themselves. Then we could write from our own personal experience, and also put questions to the other side that would be of interest to science. In this way, ITC could slowly be known and accepted within science.
2. Or, many new ITC stations and bridges would open, so that ITC would become more and more common among lay people. Then, it would not matter what science says because more and more people know that ITC is real. Eventually, science would be forced to deal with the phenomenon.

Either of these scenarios would provide the necessary impetus to bridge science with ITC (ITC Journal, 1, p. 61-62).

Furthermore, Nils-Olof Jacobson is reported as having written the following about the phenomenon that he personally experienced with positive results:

We can speculate about many explanations. In some cases, we can imagine psychokinesis, as how we unconsciously produce this phenomenon. But that is no explanation, rather only a label we put on something we do not understand. Perhaps we, by an unknown form of psychokinesis, can create a kind of "phantoms," which then live their own lives. Some of these stories are in the esoteric literature. Everyone must decide whether these explanations seem reasonable and adequate. Maybe "aliens" are involved. Maybe there are parallel worlds. Maybe there is life after death. Maybe everything is connected in the universe, beyond space and time limits. We easily believe that the part of the reality we see is the only true reality.

We have no reference for this publication, but Anabela Cardoso corresponded extensively with Nils-Olof Jacobson and he confirmed the ideas above, although in his opinion the results of his many experiments in ITC support the life after death explanation rather than any other.

Dr. Jacobson's most famous work *Liv efter döde?: om parapsykologin, mystiken och döden* (1971) was translated into several languages. The English translation, *Life without Death?* was published in 1974.

ANABELA CARDOSO is the most active person in the present day research of EVP and ITC. Anabela, a former diplomat and philosopher, is from Portugal. Besides her many publications and lectures, she has written three books on the electronic voices: *Electronic Voices, Contact with Another Dimension?* (2010); *Electronic Contact with the Dead, What Do the Voices Tell Us?* (2017); *Glimpses of Another World, Impressions and Reflections of an EVP Operator* (2021). She is also responsible for the international magazine *ITC Journal*.

In the years 2008 and 2009 she undertook a comprehensive EVP research project under controlled conditions, which was carried out at the Faculty of Engineering of the University of Vigo, Spain. Several voice experimenters participated in the project, which took place under tight control and yielded positive results (see *NeuroQuantology*, 2012).

Cardoso's project emulated and confirmed Dr Konstantin Raudive's controlled experiments in England before the publication of *Breakthrough*, when the voice tests were carried out at a professional laboratory of Belling and Lee at Enfield, England. The laboratory was completely shielded against electromagnetic waves. Peter Hale, Britain's leading expert in the shielding of electronic frequencies, was the highest technical supervisor of the project. A series of EVP voices was captured. In a letter to Colin Smythe, the British publisher of Raudive's book, Hale wrote: "From the results we got on Friday, I can conclude that something happened that cannot be explained in physical terms."

EVP after Friedrich Jürgenson

Starting at the end and with the purpose of informing my readers about the importance of his discovery, I will discuss what happened to EVP after Friedrich Jürgenson. It was not a one-off, something that was born and died with Friedel, which, therefore, could be seen as yet another manifestation of spiritualism, mediumship, occultism, clairvoyance, etc., or even hysteria or mental illness. Instead, EVP spread all over the world and developed into what is now called ITC (Instrumental Transcommunication). Tape recorders, radios, computers, and TVs are recipient appliances, objective instruments that cannot be influenced by emotions and desires. EVP and ITC experiments are taking place in many countries by individuals and groups, sometimes under strict scientific conditions which exclude fraud, and they claim that they have been able to prove the existence of a fourth life dimension, which, under certain circumstances, we can connect with.

Dr Nils-Olof Jacobson wrote a good summary of what happened after Friedel's breakthrough:

> The oldest known examples of ITC direct radio voices in Europe (if not the world) come from Marcello Bacci and his group in Grosseto, Italy. They regularly received EVP since 1971 and later they received the Direct Radio Voices (DRV), which emanate directly from the radio speakers. As a result of the language barrier, Bacci's results are almost unknown to us, but, on the continent, they are aware of them.
>
> In Germany, Switzerland and Austria there are different groups, since the 1970s, working with EVP. The German Verein für Tonbandstimmen-Forschung was formed in 1975 and has had up to 1,500 members (1999). Several groups have periodically reported electroacoustic voices and ITC, but these phenomena have ceased for some time, and only tape voices have been reported.
>
> Prominent names in this context were Hans-Otto König, Klaus Schreiber, and Peter Haerting. Klaus Schreiber also claimed that he got images from another dimension on TV, but his results remained controversial for some[7].
>
> In 1979, the Americans D. Scott Rogo and Raymond Bayless published the book *Phone Calls from the Dead* in which they discuss some 70 cases.
>
> In the United States, George Meek and William O'Neil worked with EVP in the seventies. In 1977, O'Neil reported a brief ITC contact

with an American doctor who had died five years earlier. In 1980-81, O'Neil recorded many contacts via ITC with a physicist, George Jeffries Mueller, deceased in 1967. Long conversations could be achieved. Mueller's voice was initially "robot-like" but gradually became a little more alive. Towards the end of 1981, the contact ceased, which Mueller had warned about.

For a couple of years in the early eighties, Manfred Boden in Germany received messages that he thought were from the spirit world, partly on a computer and partly on the telephone.

In the village of Dodleston, on the border between England and Wales, lived the teacher, Ken Webster. In 1984-86, he received on a simple computer with a writing program, about 300 messages from a messenger who called himself Tomas Harden and said he lived in Webster's house in the sixteenth century. The language was ancient English, which corresponded well with the stated time. Ken, his fiancée Deb and Tomas Harden had a strange exchange of letters on historical, religious, and other issues, and a sense of friendship developed between them. The dialogue was disrupted by another group who called themselves 2109, that wrote contemptuous comments on the computer in poor modern English. They claimed to be a group of disembodied beings in space (not in the "realm of the dead") and claimed to have started the events as an experiment with time. The contact ended in March 1986, as 2109 had warned about.

Maggy and Jules Harsch-Fischbach lived in Luxembourg; she was a teacher, and he was a civil servant. Maggy became interested in EVP in 1985 and wanted to try recording. Since Jules was not interested, she started on her own in June 1985. After five days she recorded weak voices in several languages; the couple was also multilingual. Eventually Jules became interested, and they started working together. The weak voices gradually became clearer.

In April 1986, they recorded the first electro-acoustic voices. Konstantin Raudive had passed away in 1974. Maggy was fascinated by his work with EVP and believed he wanted to continue similar work wherever he would be. She called him often during her recording attempts. After a while, a throaty voice arose which became increasingly familiar. And then it identified itself as Konstantin Raudive. Other voices claimed to be deceased relatives and acquaintances. The contacts developed into regular lectures by Raudive over philosophical and religious themes. A childlike, synthetic, robot-like voice opened and closed the contacts. He said they could call him The Technician and informed that in the world beyond he was responsible for the Project Kindergarten, as he called the ITC attempts to communicate with the Earth.

As for the couple Harsch-Fischbach (H-F), their contacts developed into something that even for Friedel approached science fiction. They were also subjected to much criticism and gradually withdrew from public view. Eventually, they received both still images and short movie clips and instructions from their communicators to improve the sound quality of the messages. The group of communicators identified themselves as living in a dimension after death. They called it the "third level."

One of these communicators intervened in various other contexts. She informed that she was a scientist and called herself Dr Swejen Salter. And so, dear reader, I ask again, is it science fiction? It looks like it but actually all this happened. Dr Salter reported that she lived a physical life on a planet called Varid, which would be a parallel world to the Earth. She had died in 1987 in a traffic accident, when she was 38 years old. Maggy had the first contact with her in the New Year of 1988. During a few years, Maggy and Swejen had contact by telephone and radio several times a week. Their conversations could be up to ten minutes long. Swejen informed that she belonged to a group called Zeitstrom (Timestream) and that they lived in a planet called Marduk, which could not be found in our time structure. Marduk meant "River of Eternity", which flowed back to its source. She and other communicators avowed that parallel worlds exist.

Nils-Olof Jacobson in his history of the field, reports that in 1986, the couple H-F sought contact with like-minded people and formed an association for ITC studies. They called it the Cercle d'Etudes sur la TransCommunication du Luxembourg (CETL).

I transcribe below some additional thoughts on the voice phenomena published by Nils-Olof Jacobson[8] on his website:

> The Group Zeitstrom receive numerous requests for contact with deceased relatives through the H-F. Maggy and Jules H-F enter the calls on their computer. Some people get answers, most do not. The Group Zeitstrom emphasize that they have an overview of only a small part of [their] planet. They can only contact people who choose to stay nearby. There are many other areas on the planet where people can stay according to their interests and desires. However, nothing

else has been published about how it is feasible to make contact with like-minded people.

According to Zeitstrom, the third level may seem like a science fiction world, with a development further forward than our own, but not as further forward as we can imagine is possible. It is strange to see photos from computer halls and read that they are flying with balloons. All levels of development seem to exist simultaneously, side by side, but then it is the same with us, here. At the same time, the environment has a dreamlike nature. Swejen Salter complains that the new worldviews on the Earth make her planet unstable. The ongoing interaction between the worlds is emphasized in the texts. An idea of the next world is perhaps best summed up in a letter by Senkowski: "The third level seems to be a dream world that is less stable than ours. We dream of them, and at the same time they dream of us. The term 'different interaction' is more useful to describe the trans contacts than the idea of 'independent parties' in a transmitter-receiver model."

The H-F's main support was Professor Ernst Senkowski in Mainz. With a background as a physicist, he had experimented with EVP with positive results since the mid-1970s. In Europe and in the world, he was the researcher with the best overview of the entire field. Senkowski participated in experiments in Luxembourg, compiled and evaluated the respective results. He wrote reports for the members' magazine "CETL Info News" which had started being published in simple form in 1986. In his dense book *Instrumentelle Transkommunikation* he thoroughly describes the whole area.

Towards the end of 1986, information about image transfers was received and it soon happened. The couple H-F were instructed to put a video camera on a tripod in front of a black and white TV that was tuned to a blank channel and not connected to any antenna. Only indistinct images appeared, which gradually became a little sharper—still images of people, animals and landscapes that lasted a few seconds. Later, short moving sequences also appeared. Direct radio voices commented on the pictures, which showed different people and phenomena on the other side. Autumn 1987 was a difficult time for many ITC researchers. George Meek in the United States barely escaped a life-threatening situation. In Sweden, Friedrich Jürgenson died in October of that year. In Luxembourg, the H-Fs felt "burnt out" by all the burdens: allegations of fraud from some quarters in Germany, contacts from many people who wanted messages from their deceased relatives, and the ITC work itself. In the meantime, the H-F couple had acquired a computer. At the end of November 1987, they found a file in their computer under the name Burton. It was a text that they averred nobody could have entered since the computer was not connected to any modem or network. The text was signed Richard Francis Burton, a famous adventurer, explorer, and author, who lived from 1821-90. He was a member of the group Zeitstrom and wanted to resume contacts. The H-F were at first skeptical and unsure whether Burton was genuine, and if so, whether he represented the side of light or of darkness. However, they answered the calls and the contacts were resumed.

Dr Jacobson resumes his reflections on ITC

If we imagine that EVP and ITC really have a "sender" in another world, the question is, which world? Obviously, messages come from different levels: some do not seem to be so elevated. "Test the spirits!" is, after all, a classic call in esoteric literature and it should apply here too. One message will not necessarily be more true or spiritually developed because it comes into a computer.

If ITC as a whole had been created through cheating, then an individual would not be able to cope. The phenomena are so wide-ranging and complicated that an unknown number of participants in an international conspiracy should reasonably be required, which, in that case, would have been going on for almost ten years. They must have also large financial resources and be fluent in half a dozen languages.

The essential result of my own experiences is that I became convinced that EVP exists as a real phenomenon, and that I do not find a normal explanation for the voices. So I consider them paranormal.

The couple H-F continued their research in Luxembourg and received direct radio instructions on when they should make their recordings. They also received long text messages on their computer. Those who made contact, among many others, were Konstantin Raudive, Swejen Salter and Friedrich Jürgenson.

Adolf Homes, who claimed to have received images and written messages from Friedel, was considered one of the most important researchers in the field. A few kilometers from him, in a place called Schweich, lived Friedrich Malkhoff. They got in touch with each other and began to experiment. In 1988, they obtained electro-acoustic voices on tape. Their research and amazing results developed to advanced ITC communication with voices that came up on the phone, answering machine, computer texts and radio connected to a tape recorder.

I assure my readers that what I am reporting here is the voice phenomenon confirmed by intelligent, well-educated people. Cheating to create sensation is virtually excluded.

Ever since 1991, several researchers and groups stated that they received messages from, among others, Friedrich Jürgenson, Konstantin Raudive, Hans Bender and Swejen Salter. The pair H-F in Luxembourg were some of the recipients but also Adolf Homes and Friedrich Malkhoff obtained messages from the same communicators, both on the phone (EVP calls have never been recorded by the telephone companies), voice mail and in writing on the computer. Particularly, Raudive and Bender got in touch through text but also by radio.

Adolf Homes received two pictures of a person on the other side that was described as Friedrich Jürgenson. One picture is difficult to interpret but, in my opinion, the other one is almost certainly a picture of Jürgenson. At the first image transfer, the following happened:

On February 28, 1992, Maggy Harsch-Fischbach in Luxembourg received a telephone call. The caller identified himself as Friedrich Jürgenson and said that the next day he would hold a kind of conference and discuss the technical possibilities and soon try to send over a picture of himself with the three suns of planet Marduk in the background. This caused frantic activity and normal telephone calls occurred between Maggy H-F, Ernst Senkowski, and Adolf Homes. A few months later on June 11, 1992, Adolf Homes' phone rang. His daughter Kerstin answered, and she immediately recognized the EVP voice she had heard on the tape recorder. It was Konstantin Raudive who would repeatedly contact Homes by 'phone.' Raudive announced that they would try to send over a picture of Friedrich Jürgenson the next day. No specific time was mentioned.

At 08:45 the next day, Homes placed his camcorder in front of the TV and set it to an empty channel. He turned on the camcorder and waited. After a while, a picture appeared on the TV screen. It lasted barely a second.

Five minutes later at 08:50, a written message appeared on the computer of the couple H-F, in which Swejen Salter said that the picture showed Friedrich Jürgenson in his current appearance. It had been very difficult to transfer the image. They had intended to send a text at the same time but had not succeeded. Swejen Salter later commented that Jürgenson was in the fifth level and, therefore, that made it very difficult to obtain a sharp picture of him.

In connection with the second image transfer of October 13, 1994, Adolf Homes received the greeting from Friedel that I reproduced in the Introduction. I do not know how thoroughly that picture has been examined. Since credible witnesses averred that Homes, who himself went over to the other side on October 5, 1997, was not a fraud, I am prepared to say that it is Friedel. The instant image that appeared in June 1992, where the three suns are clearer, also has similarities with Friedel if you look at the hairline.

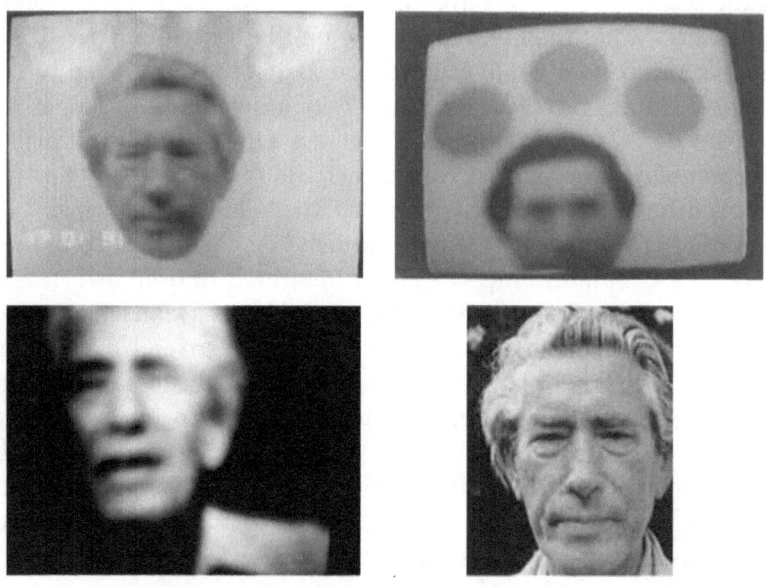

Bottom left: Image appeared on C. Thorlin's TV on the day of Jürgenson's funeral. Bottom right: Jürgenson in life.

Naturally, it feels completely unreal that the image would come from another life dimension, and, like the usual holiday pictures, showing the exact date. But then Friedrich Jürgenson in the 1994 greeting that I transcribed above, wrote that the projection was in the no space-time quanta since 17/01/1991, whatever that may mean. Friedel had often said that there is no concept of time on the other side, so we should not be surprised that it was shown to us three and a half years later in our chronology.

I write "Friedrich Jürgenson" because I do not exactly recognize his way of expressing himself. However, on the other hand, it is very likely that language and expression also change on the other side.

On the issue of the three suns featured in the famous pictures of Jürgenson, Anabela Cardoso informs that during the year 1998, a very interesting voice, shrill as if from an adolescent, chanted via the DRV during one of her ITC experiments, "We live in a very lovely world with three stars!" (Translation from the Portuguese). She says that she does not recall exactly if at the time she knew about the Jürgenson photos with the three suns although she thinks that she did not. She keeps this recording in her files.

2

BEFORE THE VOICES

Friedel was six years old when his father took him to the slaughterhouse in Odessa. There, he heard the death screams of the animals being slaughtered. The incident came to dominate his life and he became a vegetarian. "It is not right for man to eat dead animals," he said. He explained that the animals should not have to suffer so people can eat them up. His ideas about death started here, and they were reinforced when the Russian Revolution broke out and people were shot dead in the streets. He was just 13 years old when he saw a man fall to the ground with a bullet in his head. He refused to believe that this was the end for the man.

Friedel's parents were of Scandinavian origin; both were born in Estonia but his mother, Helene's parents, came from Norway and his father, Reinhold's parents, from Denmark. Reinhold studied to be a doctor; he became widely renowned and made a fortune that gave them the opportunity to buy a manor in Sibbola, in Estonia. The farm was handed over to relatives when Reinhold Jürgenson was offered a post as director of a sanatorium in Odessa, a thriving commercial center in Ukraine, and the gateway between East and West on the shores of the Black Sea. Tsar Nicholas II wanted the renowned and talented physician of Estonia to lead the operations in the newly established sanatorium in Odessa. Friedel was born there on February 8, 1903.

He grew up under prosperous conditions and enjoyed a very good education. He went to the same school as Lev Davidovich Trotsky who gladly spread his Marxist ideas among school friends but never managed to influence Friedel. Trotsky was a companion of Vladimir Lenin, one of the main leaders of the October Revolution of 1917. Friedel said that he looked the Russian Revolution in the face, and the killings, as in the slaughterhouse, had made him renounce all thoughts of violence. During the three years that the Revolution lasted, people lived literally in the dark. There was no electricity, running water was a luxury, dogs and cats and rats had been eaten, and in the winter the temperature was at best a few degrees in the residence.

After the revolution came the plague. The young Friedel felt strongly for the suffering in the old Jewish quarter; he was often at the port and took bags of wheat to the families who endured great distress. But he turned his back on the political struggle that was going on and devoted himself to art. He spent time at the Conservatory of Music to educate his voice, where both he and his teachers realized that this could be his future. In the evenings he went to Art school, where he developed his painting abilities.

Friedel married a Jewish woman, Vera, in Odessa and had a son, Salomon. Together with his family and his parents, he moved to the mansion in Estonia near the capital Tallinn in 1925. Estonia had, in the midst of the October Revolution, proclaimed itself as an independent republic. He told me that it was like coming into a paradise after all the atrocities in Odessa. They had a large garden where they cultivated berries and fruits and Friedel travelled by horse and wagon to the market in the capital. There, he continued his music studies and educated himself in graphic arts and lithography. In the evenings he sang in restaurants and cafes but also sometimes at a movie theatre that showed silent films.

At home they spoke both Russian and German, and when the parents had secrets to tell they spoke Estonian. This was probably when Friedel's talent for languages started: one which came to play a major role when the voices came into his life. The other languages he developed a grasp of were English, Italian, Yiddish and Swedish.

Friedel's singing teacher in Tallinn was impressed by his development and arranged for him to be offered studies in Berlin. It was a time of anguish and anti-Semitism in Germany, and this made Vera refuse to move. She chose to go to Palestine with their son Salomon.

Friedel's teacher in Berlin was a German Jew, and he and his family were subjected to such severe harassment that they too decided to emigrate to Palestine. Since Friedel had his wife and son there, he accompanied them. In July 1932, he reunited with his family. In the capital, Ramallah, ten kilometers from Jerusalem, administered by Great Britain until 1948, Friedel had the opportunity of practicing his two major art interests, singing and painting. He also learned English there. Even though they had a modest and simple life, and even though they constantly had to be on their guard against the terror that developed between Arabs and Jews, he felt that this was perhaps his happiest time. He painted and experimented with large pictures and created figures in papier mâché. He sold some of those and, with what he earned as a singer in restaurants and bars, he could support his family. His education in chant and music were perhaps his most important assets. He was part of a small group led by Professor Rocca. They appeared both in Ramallah and Jerusalem.

Friedel appeared in many roles as an opera singer. Judging by this picture, he seems to have performed the role of Lawrence of Arabia.

Friedel rarely talked about his marriage with Vera, and, during the six years in Palestine, they drifted apart and finally divorced. When Friedel, with the help of Professor Rocca, had the opportunity of moving to Milano to educate himself further under the leadership of Emilio Piccoli, he did not hesitate. Tito Schipa, who had been Piccoli's student, was one of the top tenors in the world at the time. Professor Rocca had great hope that Friedel would become a great bass singer.

He lived on a pension for poor singers and studied with Piccoli for over a year. But he also worked as a portrait painter, both at home in his small studio and on the streets, mainly in the piazza. It provided him with the money to finance his life in Milano. But, when war broke out, most of the places closed down.

While Friedel had plans to return to Estonia, he met Nora. She came sweeping across the Piazza del Duomo in the company of a woman whom Friedel already knew. The rather short woman with soot black hair and blazing, temperamental eyes fell for the tall charmer of slightly Asian look. Friedel asked if he could paint her portrait, and, after some persuasion, Nora promised that she would come to his home along with his friend. The portrait painting led to love. (He did not talk about lightning that struck from a clear sky, but of an intense love). Nora had a Swedish father and an Italian mother that would prove to be of great importance in Friedel's future life.

In a world on fire, they decided to go to Estonia and marry. They arrived there in 1940. Friedel's mother now lived alone with her three-year elder sister Elly since their father's death in 1932, the same year that Friedel moved from Berlin to Palestine. Neither Friedel nor Nora liked life in the mansion, so they moved to the old fortress town of Dorpat (today Tartu).

Friedel was worried about his situation and could no longer carry on with his studies or perform at restaurants and bars. He had no time for painting. To the Germans, he was an enemy, to the Russians a deserter who had fled the Soviet Union. He had thought that the town would be a good place to stay away from the war but it turned out to be the opposite. Dorpat was largely devastated as the Soviets drove back the Germans. Friedel and Nora managed to flee back to Sibolla, where they married.

Changing from the climate in the south to the raw, cold air in Estonia had been devastating for Friedel's voice. He had concerts scheduled and did them, but he exposed his vocal cords to a damage that could not be repaired. It was clear that he could perhaps have been a world star as an opera singer but since then he could not be more than a gifted showman. So he decided to focus completely on painting.

Nora wanted to go to her father's neutral country, Sweden, at all costs. She had relatives there. According to Friedel, she not only charmed the German commandant, but she managed to get out a whole box of booze from Sibbola's storage room and offered it to him for exit permits to Helsinki. And of course they got them!

In 1943, they arrived in neutral Sweden, a country that was not at war. They settled in Stockholm, and Friedel was able at an early stage to establish contacts for portrait painting while Nora was employed at a restaurant.

I must say that this was a dark chapter in Friedel's life, one that he actually tried to hide. Not even when my brother Goesta Elmquist, who for many years was also Friedel's friend, convinced Sweden's most popular TV host, Lars Holmquist, to choose Friedel as the protagonist in his acclaimed TV show *This is Your Life* in 1985, were the secrets of this time in Sweden revealed. Goesta found it impossible to depict this on the TV show because Friedel was reluctant vis-à-vis meetings with a few important people. And two of great importance refused to participate: Nora, his ex-wife and his current wife, Monica.

Friedel in the TV show "This is Your Life," in 1985, together with his grandchild Amit whom he had never met.

But it is still possible to put together some important events in Friedel's life during this period before the voices changed his whole life. He had a dream; to do painting in Pompeii. He told me that Pompeii held a great attraction for him. His thoughts from childhood that death was not the end, projected on the events in Pompeii where about 10 000 people died in a single moment during the eruption of the Vesuvius, on August 24, 79 CE. He wanted to recreate the environment and through this, somehow, bring them to life again. It was a dream, and he knew that with Nora it could materialize.

Nora's uncle held a senior position at the Vatican. Pompeii was in the Vatican's custody and a foreign artist had not yet been allowed to paint there. But Nora's obstinacy and her uncle's contacts, who were close to Pope Pius XII, managed to get the unknown Swedish artist Friedrich Jürgenson permission to paint in Pompeii. However, with a reservation: his work was to be presented to the Vatican for approval.

Ludwig Kaas was a German Catholic priest with a solid education—two doctoral degrees in theology and philosophy—but he was also a scholar and an important politician in the Weimar Republic of the German Empire. When Hitler came to power, Kaas, due to his expertise, was appointed to deal with issues related to the Catholic Church. He became the direct link between Germany and the Vatican. After the war, he was closer to the Vatican and Pope Pius XII named him Monsignor. He was an important personality who paved the way for Friedel.

After a few months in Pompeii, in the summer of 1949, it was time for Friedel's private exhibition at the Vatican. What they saw were paintings "without modernist novelties," as he used to say when he spoke about himself. And added: "See how beautiful the world is!" He considered it a privilege to possess the gift to reproduce it. His paintings were naturalistic but with a personal style and subtle colors.

Ludwig Kaas was impressed by the Swedish artist's work and decided to promote him. The representative of Pope Pius XI had started the archaeological excavations, which took place in St. Peter's Basilica in the 1930s because there was an unanswered central question in the Catholic Church's organization: Is Peter's tomb really the basis of St. Peter's Basilica, there, under the huge papal altar and the huge canopy in bronze? Are his bones there?

History tells us that in this place, in the heart of the Vatican district in Rome, was Emperor Nero's huge circus where the gladiators fought battles against one another and people were thrown to the wild animals. Peter, Jesus' apostle, who came to Rome around the year 60 to preach the teachings of Jesus, was arrested for subversion. He was tortured and crucified upside down along with one of his companions, Marcellinus. A Christian woman brought the disciple of Jesus, who had died a martyr's death, to a burial place outside the stadium and gave him a Christian burial.

In the year 324, Emperor Constantine, the Great, became a Christian and he decided to build a majestic church over St. Peter's tomb. It took over 20 years before it was completed. And in the 1500s it was rebuilt and then changed according to the reigning emperor's wishes until the building took on its present form. The tomb was then more or less immured in the very foundations of St. Peter's Basilica. The location was almost exactly described, under the papal altar and canopy in bronze.

Archaeologists had discovered through a hole in a wall, something that was interpreted as a tomb, and in 1949 Pius XII decided that the archaeological excavations under St. Peter's Basilica would not only continue but that the aim was to confirm that Peter was indeed buried there. And, during the ongoing work, the unknown artist from Sweden came into the picture. The excavations showed that the walls up to the necropolis of the church's foundation were adorned with traces of magnificent works of art. Ludwig Kaas came in with a fantastic offer: he wanted Friedel to attempt to reconstruct them in paintings.

They decided that Friedel would return after the Holy Year, which took place every 25 years. Then the Pope would open the Holy Gate (Porta Santa) in St. Peter's Basilica, which is sealed from the inside. Those who passed through it obtained forgiveness for their sins if they confessed and were pilgrims.

Friedel returned to Rome in 1952 and began his work, which would last for four months. He told me that this affected him very heavily. I cannot quote him because I do not have any notes, but he talked about going into another world: perhaps he interpreted it as another life dimension, something that would become a reality for him later on when his predecessors, the artists on the emperor's behalf more than 1500 years earlier, tried to describe Peter's suffering and death through their art.

Friedel sat in the damp, moisture dripping underground chamber and painted and developed serious pneumonia. Despite the fever, he continued his work and Ludwig Kaas made sure that he had medicine. Not only that, he pointed out to the pope that the Swede who sat down there in the crypt with Peter, had fallen ill because of the raw, damp air, and it threatened his life. As God's representative on the Earth, the pope asked the Lord to heal the sick man and Friedel recovered.

Friedel's artistic work was outstanding, and Pope Pius XII ordered a portrait painting. Friedel painted four portraits. They hang in the museum of the Vatican with Friedel's paintings from Peter's crypt and his portraits of a later pope. They are there next to works by his colleague Michelangelo di Lodovico Buonarroti Simoni! Quite a feat.

Since then, Friedel had complete freedom to paint in Pompeii and remained there on several occasions during the 1950s. The marriage with Nora failed. Nora told my brother Goesta that Friedel lived in a sort of dream world in which painting was the only thing that mattered.

And then he met Monica who would become his third wife. He painted her portrait, and she introduced him to the finest circles in Stockholm. Subsequently, he got a lot of work as a portrait painter. Nora used to say that it was the "fucking dentist" who had ruined her life!

3

THE FIRST SIGNS

Friedel has very carefully described how everything began with a series of strange events and telepathic messages. He said that in 1957 he had the first contact with people on the other side, or the fourth dimension as he called it. It was simply a technical phenomenon, not real voices that hit his tape recorder. He did not understand what happened, but two years later the explanation that this had been an attempt from an unknown world to establish contact via a carrier wave came through.

Monica and Friedel lived at Tyska Brinken in Gamla Stan (the Old Town) in Stockholm. But, as I mentioned above, they had a country house, Nysund, in Mölnbo, a few miles from the royal capital. It became something of a "central" to the unknown voices from space that often used the keyword "Mölnbo."

Friedel bought his first tape recorder in 1957 for two reasons. He was a talented pianist who still had an impressive voice and wanted to record himself on tape. Bird life thrived among the giant trees of the forest and he wanted to capture the different birds' beautiful songs, too.

Friedel and poodle Carino in search of birdsong.

FJ house in Nysund

Friedel in Mölnbo

Friedel's garden at Nysund

FJ

Young Friedel

House of first recording at Nysund

Villa Nysund in Mölnbo

It was when he recorded the chirping of the birds that his mother, dead for five years, came through with a greeting. This made Friedel cancel his amazing artistic career and devote himself entirely to the voice phenomenon.

It was a neighbor in Stockholm who owned a well-known music publishing company, and on occasion listened to Friedel, who suggested that he ought to get a tape recorder and record a couple of songs in Russian. Friedel also chose something from Federico Fellini's film *Nights of Cabiria* and translated the Italian lyrics into Swedish. As always, when Friedel undertook a task, he invested all his energy in it. He transformed "and disfigured," as he said, his painting studio into a soundproof recording studio by dressing the walls with flannel.

He practiced diligently in his studio at Tyska Brinken and made short recordings and he was out often in the garden at Nysund with his best friend, the poodle Carino. The tape recorder worked perfectly normally on the day when he would make his first test recording along with an Italian pianist. And then, strangely, there was no recording!

Friedel auditioned and the pianist did what he could; it was time to check the volume and see how and where the microphone should be located. But after one minute the sound faded away. There was a slight murmur and it slowly disappeared in the distance. They both looked in disbelief at the tape recorder and made new attempts. The phenomenon occurred several times. Friedel's voice fell almost completely silent, and the only sound registered was the noise that increased in intensity until the voice came back to normal.

They both thought that it was certainly a problem with the tape recorder. A representative of the company that had sold it (an expensive US model) did several tests and found no fault. Everything he recorded was on the tape without any interference. Still, the technician replaced all the vacuum tubes and, when Friedel used the tape recorder that night, he did it with a brand new tape.

He sat down at the piano and sang a Russian song, which he later released on a cassette tape along with some other Russian songs, and titled it "Swan Song." But this recording was totally unsuccessful. Suddenly the tone of his voice and the piano floated in rhythmic waves. Just as if repeating the lowering and raising of the volume. Friedel was heartbroken and tried several times with the same bad results. Then suddenly the recorder worked perfectly. No disturbances. The occurrence would be explained a few years later. By then he had become tired of the tape recorder and he let it stand in a corner of the studio. There were no recordings of birdsong until about two years later.

In the meantime Friedel had neglected painting. One day he pulled off the dreadful flannel from the walls and began to paint. He did several designs of Pompeii from photos and memories. However, he felt that he had to return and in 1958 he and Monica travelled there during the summer months.

He painted from early morning to late evening and assembled a comprehensive collection of Pompeii paintings. It impressed the administrators of Pompeii, and he was offered to be the first foreign artist to hold an exhibition in the heart of the ancient city, in the palaestra, at the Forum Baths. Simultaneously, he worked on a painting of a Pompeii motif, which was about 9 meters long. It required lots of space and he could use the so-called "tragic poet's" beautiful house. During his breaks, he wandered around in the narrow alleys and into the excavated houses. He had access to master keys and could move freely. Thus he got a deep knowledge of the partially excavated city and felt as if he knew the people who had died there, in a moment, while at their daily work.

At the official opening of Friedel's exhibition, he received an offer to conduct and document an archaeological excavation. This was the fulfilment of his dream of many years. It was planned to occur the following Spring, but he would have to finance this project. He felt that he was at the summit of his artistic career. Shortly thereafter, however, his whole life changed. On his return home, Friedel was completely immersed in thoughts and in the planning for future excavations in Pompeii. He thought of trying to engage the Swedish Broadcasting Corporation (Sweden Radio and Television, which I will call SBC) in the project. He thought that maybe he would do some radio shows around the excavations and, thus, help with the financing.

Friedel had made several radio programs about the events and people of the Russian Empire's history for the SBC, including the legendary Grigory Rasputin and the Grand Duchess Anastasia. Both their amazing life stories fascinated him, and the famous radio journalist Arne Weise produced Friedel's programs.

Weise had become one of the most renowned television personalities in the SBC and, to a certain extent, had a decisive role in Friedel's credibility when he publicly talked about his recordings with him. They had made those recordings together and they are some of the clearest and best documented in Friedel's voluminous collection.

And then some strange impressions

At a certain point he began receiving bizarre messages. In his slightly complicated way, Friedel described himself as a person whose natural disposition was of a visual type. By that he meant that he entirely, spontaneously, in a visual way, could perceive all processes and changes around him. He writes in the book *The Voices from Space*: "My observation of this Earth derives, so to speak, from a most prosaic way and I have never been surprised or worried about supernatural phenomena."

And perhaps this was an explanation of his receptivity when he began receiving what seemed to be telepathic messages. To understand Friedel's first encounter with something that appeared to be sentient living beings, I reproduce this almost surreal event that provided him with "a clear trail, an inner readiness to be vigilant."

> One Sunday morning I was lying on the couch in my studio listening to a concert on the radio from an adjoining room. I had closed my eyes, was completely relaxed, and enjoyed the music. I was in such a pleasant and liberated state, like when you completely stop listening

and thoughts no longer have much to say. I had lain still for a long time when my attention was diverted to a color process that began to unfold before my closed eyes, that is, in my inner being.

First, I clearly saw a violet background on which clear veils in rhythmic pulsating movement began to pull past. After a while the veils disappeared, and I saw from the depths of the dark violet background a small ruby red spot grow whose color and shape increased until a small but still fairly compact heart floated forward before my eyes and like a light mask performed a semi-circular, soft movement.

Surprised and fascinated, I followed the movements of the ruby red heart that now tried to perform a series of graceful oscillations, all in a half-flying, half-dancing rhythm which seemed to transform into soft bands, semicircles, and other rotating figures. But, at the same time, a soft fan-shaped downy wing emerged from the upper part of the heart, which in pulsating rhythms changed shape and color. It seemed very much alive and revealed a very peculiar, constantly evolving movement, which in some way seemed to be connected with its mother-of-pearl color shifts.

I lay completely still and could clearly hear the radio. It seemed as if my heart was beating to the beat of the music. Nevertheless, I did not dare open my eyes, as I feared that the phenomenon would disappear. Never before had I seen anything like it; I could clearly follow the swinging movements of the heart and its mother-of-pearl feathers and observe every phase of change in the shades of color. It danced only a few centimeters in front of my closed eyes, but still remained constantly in the periphery of my inner field of vision as if it could not exceed an invisible circle.

I cannot say now with certainty how long this spectacle lasted: maybe ten, maybe twenty minutes. In any case, it disappeared when the concert ended. It somehow receded into the velvety depths of the violet background, and when I, for the first time, opened my eyes and then hastily closed them, my heart showed itself once more. It appeared very clearly, entirely alive, but then it suddenly disappeared, or rather it went out like a light bulb usually goes out when you turn off the switch.

This was a strange experience that gripped and captivated me, but far stranger than the phenomenon itself was the clear certainty of a real encounter with something alive, with a concrete reality. And even though I could not understand the meaning of this meeting then, it left a clear mark on me, an inner readiness to be vigilant.

Shortly after this incident, Friedel received his first telepathic message. He lay again on the couch in the studio and fell into a state of inner peace. He described it as if his thoughts were disconnected while he was awake and aware and had not fallen asleep. Suddenly, the words formed in his mind, a kind of internal words in the German language that were constantly repeated as if it was important that he remembered them. After a while he got up, took a pen and paper, and wrote directly from his memory: "The sun is a cold star. Some atmospheric layer that surrounds the Earth gives off heat when the sun's rays penetrate through these layers arched like a lens which also provide light and resemble a mass of water."

This was completely contrary to the astronomical knowledge he had; indeed it was against what he saw as common sense. Yet it was the great contradiction in this peculiar statement that somehow made him ponder that this was not of his own making. And suddenly, he had a feeling that he had received this message from outside, perhaps from some mysterious beings in space.

Just a few days later, on a magazine rack at the big department store PUB in Stockholm, he saw two scientific journals, one English and the other one German; one had a picture of the sun, the other one a cover, also illustrated by the sun and its radiation. He said he had heart palpitations when he read the headlines as both dealt with "the cold sun."

It was the renowned American artist, writer and scientist Walter Bowman Russell (1871-1963) who researched a kind of confirmation of the theory of "the cold sun" as originally introduced by the astronomer William Herschel (1736-1822).

Friedel would experience many strange situations in the times that followed but he told me that seeing the cover pages of the two journals had been one of the most powerful ones. Russell's report had, thus, reached Friedel a few days earlier and was written down by him as a message, as he understood it, from another world, another life dimension. In his own words, it was received, "by an unsuspecting layman who learned to sing and paint but never studied astronomy."

However, Friedel still doubted that he had truly received a telepathic message. But could it really be coincidence that he got the message, which was to be confirmed a few days later? It certainly could or it could be a case of precognition.

And there was another strange occurrence in his life, which in a sense dispelled his doubts and made him understand that something was going on that he simply could not grasp with the help of his senses.

In his youth he used to sketch on a chart, much like an artist shaping thoughts and ideas and improvising a painting. It consisted of a circle divided by a horizontal line in the center. He describes it this way:

> From the center of the circle emanated a spiral or a worm-shaped line like the sun—from left to right—widened in uniform ledges until it finally reached the circumference of the circle just where the horizontal line intersects this. The chart would clarify the interaction between micro and macrocosm; the microcosm representing the center, the periphery the macrocosm, while the two poles symbolized the infinity from which creative life as a spiral in constant evolution manifests.

One day when he was sitting in his studio and found it difficult to concentrate on a new painting from Pompeii, he started a pen sketch on a sheet of paper on his old table. He did not explain why he did it; it was just an impulse, much like when you doodle figures while talking on the phone or are thinking about something else. His sister-in-law Annica 'phoned and she wanted to come on a visit because she had found some books in a bookstore that she thought would interest Friedel. Two of them were in Norwegian but she knew that Friedel had no problem with that language.

They had a few glasses of wine and Friedel mentioned something about telepathic messages without revealing what had happened. When Annica and Monica left him, he leafed through the books quite uninterested, and the breath-taking feeling, as when he had seen the magazines' covers, overcame him again because when he opened the second to last page of the book entitled *Introduction to Theosophy* authored by someone named Djinarajadas and translated into Norwegian, there were his charts! Just with a single deviation, the circle was not closed but open like a seashell.

Amazed, full of conflicting emotions, he felt guided by forces he could not find any reasonable explanation for. He also felt anxiety, doubt, and doubt again. Was there an invisible bystander, a witness to something, someone who followed him?

The content of the book that had been put into his hands by his sister-in-law seemed almost deliberately directed at him: without her knowledge and without his knowledge!

There was a period, before the voices, of maybe one year, during which Friedel claimed to receive telepathic messages. While they filled him with excitement, curiosity, and joy, he was also seized by strong distrust and doubt.

The day after Annica's visit to Friedel, he received a clearly telepathic message. He sat at his worktable fully awake and relaxed. It was as if he suspected that something would happen. He writes in *The Voices from Space:*

> After a short period of nice inner calm, long English sentences formed in my mind which I had not perceived acoustically, but they began to form as long dictation phonetic syllables and, more specifically, I perceived not the words, which usually tend to be in correct English, but I understood them in a distorted way. I heard no voice, no sound, not even a whisper. I understood it all completely without any sound. When, after a while, I used a dictionary and began to translate the message, I discovered to my surprise that some words unknown to me were spelled orthographically, while the other words I knew presented a purely phonetic word formation and for the most were orthographically incorrect.

Friedel did not reproduce the content of this message nor even of the other telepathic messages. After I read the book, I asked him why he had not transcribed them. He said it was impossible. What he wrote down could not be presented in a sensible way so he preferred to make some summaries. He wrote:

> I had received more than strange messages, which at once aroused my admiration, my amazement, my doubts and dismay. Although I was convinced that my telepathic connections were a fact, it seemed difficult for me to believe in the contents of these—to put it mildly—extremely amazing reports. The whole thing was, for me, too new, too impossible to imagine, it exceeded my own dreams; it conflicted with common sense, or, at least, with all that we for centuries have acquired as empirical-scientific experience, and which is the basis of our stable three-dimensional world view.
>
> First, I received messages from a "Central Investigation Station in space," a central research station in space from where they made profound observations of our humanity, an issue which was acceptable. But when it came to the methods they used, my doubts woke up again. Fortunately, I got these messages, so to speak, in small doses which gradually increased as I was able to assimilate their contents

without, thus, awakening in me the resistance which I used to build up against all claims that are contrary to common sense in my own life. The friends talked about some electromagnetic "screens," or radar[9], which constantly, day and night, send out messages by the thousands to our three-dimensional life plan and which had the task to act as mental messengers.

At this point, I should point out that when we talked about this, I insisted that our world was extremely "bugged," not least by the NSA (National Security Agency), America's security service that could eavesdrop on a conversation "in the smallest shithouse" as the CIA chief William Casey put it in an interview. They would not miss a syllable of this if there were some sort of communication as from a radar antenna.

Friedel's answer was quite simple—it concerned mental messages that could not be perceived by some kind of instrument but could be received by the human brain in all life ages, if only it had the proper preparation and, as he now discovered, could be reproduced in electronic instruments.

And a question arose which I put to him: how is it that messages from a fourth life dimension that can be received by objective, electronic instruments here in our third dimension, cannot be obtained by anyone else than the recipient? Or can they? No, said Friedel, and he was very positive about this. It is the inner core in contact with the other side, he averred. The messages sent are directly addressed to the person, or persons, who seek contact and cannot be detected and recorded by others. Besides, it is very important to be prepared to receive them, said Friedel, otherwise they would be lost. And he continued:

> Undoubtedly, these radars could be compared to half-living robots which, although remotely controlled, still had the ability to correctly register and convey all our conscious and unconscious impulses, feelings and thoughts like a hypersensitive TV and radio. But they had far exceeded the capacity of our electron brains, calculators, and translation machines. In addition, these radars spoke with female or male voices and could, under certain circumstances, provide independent answers.

It is absolutely clear to me that I, with this amazing assertion, will not only be seen as having entered the world of science fiction, but, above all, will put the reader's confidence and patience to a hard test.

Nevertheless, I ask the reader to understand the following: also for me, who stood still in the middle of the action, a whole year was necessary before I could make myself familiar with these new thoughts, and closer to these radars' nature and function. It was only after having done this that it became possible for me to record their voices, and a series of sounds associated with their activities, on audio tape.

4

FIRST CONTACT

June 12, 1959 is considered the birthday of EVP. On that day Friedel's deceased mother Helene spoke to him and his life completely changed. Friedel and his wife Monica were at Nysund; it was one of those beautiful summer days and evenings that we rarely see in our latitudes. The farm was secluded with a rather overgrown garden surrounded by a forest with huge trees, and next to the beautiful lake—a perfect setting for bird life.

Ever since Friedel had bought a recorder in 1957, he had planned to record birdsong. It didn't happen initially and instead he devoted himself to recording his own songs. There were the inexplicable problems with the tape recorder. The apparatus was left standing in a corner of the studio, while again he began to paint and dream of an excavation in Pompeii. Finally he dusted it off and decided to record the lively twittering of the birds.

Friedel once told me that somehow birdsong had always fascinated him. The beeping and twittering sounded like voices from another world, a world in which he wanted to take part. He and Monica were sunbathing by the lake, enjoying a fine spring day, but Friedel found it hard to relax. Strange telepathic messages that talked about a different dimension of life continually ran through his mind as if striving to break through and connect with people in our dimension. He knew that there are people who claim that they hear voices and whispers but who simply suffer from schizophrenia, so he experienced some uneasiness about the voices, and, thus, Monica was the only person he discussed it with.

Towards the evening, Friedel decided to record the birdsong. He placed the microphone, connected to the tape recorder on the window frame in the attic, and a finch landed and sang beautifully. He listened to the tape and, once more, he saw how the sound of the device changed. His first thought was that something had gone wrong again, that maybe the vacuum tubes were damaged.

He played back the recording and heard a distant birdsong and, suddenly, a signal like a trumpet blast. Next, he could make out a man's voice speaking Norwegian. The man spoke about "nocturnal birdsong" and the noise increased.

Then, he heard a female voice that seemed to shout from far away. He could not immediately decipher the message but could undoubtedly identify his mother's voice. She shouted in German: "Friedel, Friedel, hoerst du mich? Mamma!"

(Friedrich, Friedrich, do you hear me? Mom!).

Then the noise disappeared and the finch close to the microphone could be heard clearly without interference. It is not possible to describe Friedel's feelings. When five years later he told me about the event that changed his life, he did it objectively and calmly. He played the voice repeatedly and I could hear the female voice, and perhaps slightly influenced by Friedel's interpretation, I could understand it. Of course, I could not say if it was his mother's voice, but both Monica and Friedel's sister Elly confirmed it was.

It would be almost a year before his mother approached him again. It happened the same day that Friedel saw his friend Felix Kersten's obituary and, for the first time, recorded his voice. Until that time he would be tossed between faith and doubt. Daily, and even at night, he made short recordings and listened to them but nothing significant happened. He realized that he might have missed some because he was not proficient in the difficult task of interpreting the voices. He was confused by all the background noise and did not understand how he would overcome the interference. Later, he realized that the difficulties he had in the beginning would hit anyone who tried to do these kinds of recordings.

Personally, I had help from Friedel as he taught me the art of concentrated listening. When you hear whispers and voices that do not fit into the context, you need to try to filter out other sounds. There is the danger, however, that you end up making interpretations, which you, then, cannot get rid of and which may be incorrect as no one else can hear the utterances clearly. As a matter of fact, Friedel pointed out that he had made false interpretations, which he was not able to change afterwards.

Initially it was thought that Friedel's original tapes had been lost. But I discovered that they are at the museum ZKK in Karlsruhe in Germany. There are around 130 tapes consisting of approximately 6000 recordings.

His mother's voice was there; there was evidence that they on the other side had contacted him, that they had established a link between the living and the dead and that life continued after death in a way which is difficult for us to understand. Friedel felt that it was his mission to spread knowledge about this. From this day on he put everything else aside.

He wrote in *Radio and Microphone Contacts with the Dead:*

> When the voices began to appear on the tapes, I interrupted my creative activity at a time when I was standing on the pinnacle of my artistic career. I had, among other things, completed an interesting mission in the Vatican (reconstruction of the paintings in the newly discovered tomb of Peter in St. Peter's Basilica) and painted portraits of Pope Pius XII. Furthermore, I had been promised [the opportunity] to attend and film the archaeological excavations of Pompeii. An artist who stops painting and who also does not exhibit his work not only loses his old customers, but also will be forgotten.
>
> Then I was compelled to acquire the precious tape recorders, and, above all, constantly needed a lot of tapes. I had to realize my paintings! My wife Monica also suffered additional expenses. We formed a joint company, which in any case possessed the advantage of operating without competition. We didn't understand that our quiet home would turn into a busy beehive, or a place that people came to visit immediately after the first press conference. I don't know how many hundreds of articles about the voice phenomena have been published in Sweden and abroad. One thing I do know, however, as long as I live, neither a religion, a sect or ideology will be formed around me.
>
> But a great thing followed after all the publicity. I have known many people who, through the loss of their beloved ones, also lost their joy in living. Even the wisest words I could think of would not be able to deliver peace to these desperate people because words

in such cases are powerless. However, what we jointly recorded on tapes were other words, perhaps words that they could identify, and they changed their earlier perception of death and eased their sorrow burden (Jürgenson, 1968).

Shortly afterwards, Friedel got another strange telepathic message. They asked him to have patience and spoke of "A new path." He wrote down the following:

> We do not want the coming messages, which will be of greater importance, to be misunderstood as a result of any disturbance. We want you to be completely safe and satisfied.
>
> As you can listen to the birds and the wind, in the same way you should also be able to hear us. It need not be long until you can. You must throw out of your consciousness distant streams of impatience and intolerance against yourself. You need to understand the cause of disturbance and remove it. As soon as you become free of it, the new path will open for you. There is something else which will then offer a pleasant feature in your life. For this, you just need to be happy, still, and constantly pay attention to yourself. Outside yourself, the path will be built. Additionally, patience and vigilance become your leaders.

Next, Friedel experienced a turbulent time. He knew that something big was about to happen to him and realized that "a new path"[10] had something to do with the tape recording of his mother's voice. He spent whole days and evenings with the recordings and the listening to check if she would return. But nothing occurred that he could interpret as alien voices, until exactly one month after his mother's voice appeared. Friedel made some cultural commentary on Russian history for the Swedish Broadcasting Corporation, SBC. He was particularly fascinated by the case of Anastasia Romanov. He gave a talk about the murder of the imperial family in Ekaterinburg. He amassed a large amount of material in search for the answer to the question: had Anastasia been rescued? His desk was overloaded with translations, plans, notes, and books.

Late in the evening of July 12, Friedel allowed the tape recorder to run, as usual, in short bursts of recording. He had not yet acquired headphones to amplify tones that the ear normally does not perceive. The tape recorder had a pilot light that flashed when he recorded the sound through the microphone, for example, his own voice or the chirping of birds, but on this occasion, there was complete silence in the room. He felt sleepy and thought of turning off the tape recorder and going to bed. Then, suddenly, the indicator started flashing.

It flickered and flashed and faded out but then went on again. Friedel thought that something must have happened that ought to be heard on the tape. Wide awake, with a pounding heart, he rewound the tape and played it back. He heard a voice very far away in a vibrating noise. He could not decipher what was said but it was clear that it was a voice that tried to break through. Yet he had not perceived it, nor the strong noise in the room.

The next day, he played the tape repeatedly. Friedel had, it would later be proven in tests, extremely good hearing. He tried to shut out the noises and eventually could hear a man's voice speaking English which conveyed a strong emotion, but Friedel could not easily decipher what he uttered. Immediately after a short break, he thought he had heard the name of Churchill and then immediately, another man's voice broke through in German. It was a clear voice speaking German but the grammar was not correct. Friedel interpreted it as saying: "Zarengebiet müssen wir noch Frühlings besprechen" (we still have to discuss the Tsar issue in Spring).

"Zarengebiet." His thoughts went to Anastasia immediately. And right away after this, with a strong and clear emphasis:

"Friedrich, du wirst beobachtet!" (Friedrich, you are being observed!)

And quickly a longer and clearer sentence (translated into English below):

"Friedrich ... even if during the day you translate into German and think—try every night to find the truth about the ship—about the ship in the dark!"

He took what he heard as a rebuff, but one thing was immediately clear to him: the broadcast addressed him personally. Of course he was upset but experienced a fantastic feeling of happiness.

He continued recording in the afternoon after he had finished listening and was then able to listen to a peculiar tone reminiscent of the vibrating whistle of a projectile that was rapidly approaching. And in the midst of the whistling sound a voice was heard:

"Federico!"

It was a name that became a regular call to Friedel. And, subsequently, a vibrating voice uttered:

"In look."

He was overwhelmed. Did the whistling sound come from the ship that was mentioned before? And was it the vibrating voice of someone on board this ship?

Many questions came to his mind. Had he received news from space, from another life plane where his mother was? Had he discovered a connection to that life plane, to the fourth dimension as he called it?

Monica listened to the recordings. Both were shocked but felt enthusiastic. There, in Nysund, something unbelievable had happened: something amazing, an objective reality, and a truth above all subjective errors; something that could be listened to repeatedly. Was this a complicated puzzle game where significant pieces were lost in the noise of the airwaves? Would they regard these disturbances as an interrupted communication; as a prelude to something else much bigger; as fragments that in time would eventually be compiled into one unit?

Friedel did not receive more sound phenomena or voices that day, but, when in the evening he began to doze off, he felt that he had received a mental message once again. He interpreted it as some sort of explanation for the tape recordings and concluded that it concerned a kind of preparatory work, which entailed great difficulties. According to Friedel's note in Swedish, the message finished with (translated into English):

"Tomorrow perhaps the moon could help dispel the obscurity, indeed, only if you are vigilant."

When I got to know Friedel, he often spoke about the mental messages he received. He wrote some down but I never managed to see anything in writing. Maybe they disappeared over the years in the chaos around his materials. I had a hard time absorbing the information he claimed to receive mentally. These messages often referred to the moon. (And the day after the calls on the tape, it was the full moon.)

In the afternoon, Monica's mother came on a visit to the residence Tyska Brinken in Stockholm where he had his studio in the small attic at the top. Friedel started the tape recorder after he helped the old lady up to his studio. The tape recorder was, after all, a novelty and he wanted to play the recording so she could hear her own voice. There was no opportunity to play music for her because, as she said, "she was in a hurry and had no time for such things."

Firstly, Monica's voice can be heard in a normal tone when she said something to her mother. Then the voice fades away and it becomes almost silent. Friedel said he turned up the volume to the maximum and perceived a distant conversation in German. A female voice was heard, as before, from afar:

"Jetzt kannst du radar hören, sehen ... lass mich hören." (now you can hear, see the radar ... let me hear.)

A male voice replied.

"Sie will ja gar nichts sagen!" (She *really* doesn't want to say anything!).

Friedel recognized the voice that had said he was being watched.

A second male voice interrupted with these words: "Monica is homely!"

Suddenly, Friedel heard the voice of Monica's mother and was forced to instantly lower the volume. She asked a question and, after a pause, the response from Monica: "Let's not talk about it."

Then the two became silent. Friedel increased the volume and heard a man's voice utter:

"Das hörte sie!" (She heard that!)

And so in Swedish: "Sa ivrigt hon arbetar! Jag ser henne! Jag hoer direct!" (How eagerly she works! I see her! I hear directly!)

Immediately Friedel turned off the tape recorder. He wrote:

> This was undoubtedly something outstanding. Here was clear evidence in daylight. Our conversation in the attic had been listened to and observed by the radar in space. And at the same time we would also participate in a conversation that took place behind the radar screen and was in direct connection with us.
>
> This irrefutable evidence was a major advance, and I asked myself if this clear recording came about thanks to the full moon's magnetic influence.
>
> All these small unassuming recordings had a core of reality. They were real and felt invigorating. Nevertheless, I still groped in the dark. When I now look back on these events in the summer of 1959, and reflect on my conjectures and conclusions, I can easily understand the detours and misunderstandings, which at that time puzzled me.
>
> Despite all my caution and skepticism, I had not experienced these events entirely without prejudice. I had been influenced by other people's claims and fallen onto a sidetrack that made me lose much time and caused me great discomfort. It would undoubtedly take too long if I would describe the numerous phenomena of that autumn 1959 in detail. The whole thing was, as I said, a modest prelude; a tentative start, which, nevertheless, I misunderstood in many respects and this because of certain beliefs, which did not really correspond to reality.

This eventful year of 1959, we became—Monica and I—convinced that we were connected with some "planetarians," and when our invisible friends preferred to remain anonymous, we could only exchange conjectures.

It would be a noticeable change when the voices not only identified themselves but also Friedel and others who eavesdropped on them, identified the people behind the voices.

From mental messages to radio contact

Later in the autumn of 1959, Friedel suffered a crisis. He had not obtained important recordings despite constant attempts both day and night. He finally put away the tapes and stored the tape recorder far under the desk. He felt disappointed and bitter, but hints that he barely understood urged him to wait. But wait for what? It was extremely stressful for him to make one recording after another and then listen without any result. Moreover, he received no telepathic messages.

Then, something strange happened that had neither to do with the tape recordings nor with telepathic messages. In various sound phenomena he thought he could often hear a whispering female voice, which reminded him of the one he had heard earlier on the tapes. It emerged with short phrases constantly repeated with slight variations. As he sat in his studio and listened to the rain splashing and dripping, he could clearly make out the whispering voice. She spoke alternately in German and Swedish, and, according to Friedel's description, it sounded something like this:

Kontakt halten! Mit dem apparat kontakt halten, bitte hoeren ... tag kontakt med apparaten ... Bitte, bitte hören!

(Keep in touch! With the apparatus keep in touch, please hear ... please contact with the apparatus ... Please, please hear!)

He heard the same voice when the fire crackled and when he crumpled paper. He could clearly hear the female voice. In crisis he fought against this invisible contact. He could not help thinking of schizophrenics who often claim to hear voices and whispers. He felt healthy and normal, yet it gave him a sense of uneasiness. The doubt was there and the suspicion that he was not functioning normally assailed him. He noted that he slept very well, was not troubled by anxiety, neurosis or obsessions, and his powers of concentration worked perfectly, but he still doubted because the whole situation felt weird.

And then the feminine voice, the "she" who had eagerly tried to get Friedel to make contact "mit dem apparat," [with the apparatus,] became his assistant on the other side. He called her Lena and she was very active when he started with the radio recordings. It was she who, with infinite patience, repeatedly urged Friedel to go ahead with the radio. Without Lena's assistance, it would have been difficult for Friedel to find his way in the maze of radio waves, and when after frequent setbacks he lost his courage, Lena showed up with her whispers and urged him to continue. He got the feeling that she observed him via some radar as her comments sometimes alluded to something he had done right then.

Before we go further, we will dwell upon the contact phenomenon that Friedel called Lena, which became highly important for his continued activities with the "Voices from Space," the voices from the other side.

Friedel told me that Lena not only tried to assign him the right frequencies, but she also commented on the situations and could sometimes reveal the names of the people who spoke. But he had difficulty understanding everything. Her whispers came with such speed that he had to play them back at a lower speed almost always. She also used a special sound frequency that resembled chirping. It required a lot of attention and it was Friedel's receptiveness that allowed him to be able to interpret these messages. When he listened to a regular radio broadcast from Radio Sweden, sometimes his own program about Russian history, he understood her quick whispers and calls to seek the contact. He got the idea that she was always there and kept him under observation.

Before we listen to some recordings with Lena's voice, it might be useful to explain how Friedel finally started to use the radio and the tape recorder. It all began with a new phenomenon for him. He placed the microphone always in the same place in the studio. There was no radio there; he had it in the living room. Yet, now and then, when he made microphone recordings, radio broadcasts (mostly from the Swedish Radio) would come through. Sometimes foreign stations broke through with higher volume. He perceived it as some sort of electronic interference, and, once again, he wondered if there was something wrong with the tape recorder.

He had no clear memory of how he got the idea to connect the recorder directly to the radio. He thought that, probably, he was influenced by Lena's whispered messages received directly through sound in the room, as well as in the recordings.

Friedel made careful notes on a notepad, and gradually assembled a huge collection. I own some of them. Here are some direct transcripts of Lena's messages that may have influenced him to start using the radio with the tape recorder. She used the language which he called polyglot—preferably German, Russian, Italian, Yiddish and Swedish—the languages that Friedel mastered.

"Fritz, pa radio budet" (Russian); (Fritz, on the radio will [be]) "Lena kan hjalpa Laurent" (Lena can help Laurent).

She referred to Professor Torbern Laurent at the Technical University in Stockholm.

"Ta kontakt! Wir vantar am abend um neun ... am abend, radio hoeren" (Contact! We are waiting in the evening, nine o'clock).

"Am abend, radio hoeren" (In the evening, listen to radio).

At the beginning, when he connected the recorder to the radio and listened through the headphones, he got overwhelmed by the chaos of noise and radio broadcasts. He searched from one channel to the other without perceiving anything abnormal. But when he played back the tape, in the midst of the muddle of voices, he could hear her whispering voice saying: "Stopp, stopp ... direkt kontakt med Churchill!" (Stop, stop ... direct contact with Churchill!)

The well-known name of Churchill had been mentioned earlier during the microphone recordings and somehow became a code word.

Once again, he connected the radio to the tape recorder and began to search in the medium wave. Then he heard a woman singing with a resonant voice. Although believing that it was a regular radio broadcast, he investigated further. But when he played back the tape, he heard with some disruption, a female voice singing and this time he understood the words:

"Friedel, Friedel."

And it followed in Swedish with disturbances:

"Tala ... pa den sista tiden ... svenska ofta stoerande" (Speak ... in recent times ... Swedish often disturbed).

Unaware of the contact, he searched further and then heard the woman's voice louder than the disturbing sound:

"Bitte, stoere nicht, Federico!" (Please don't disturb, Federico!)

He identified it as Lena's voice and although she spoke in German, he could detect a Slavic accent. Friedel now realized that to search the bandwidth on the radio and to record on the tape recorder was the right way for him to get more and clearer messages than through the microphone.

None of the above recordings are included in the available collection but there are three others with Lena's voice that I want to discuss, although some may be difficult to understand for an untrained listener.

Friedel's notes (A) after the first recorded contact with Lena.

Friedel wrote the following about this first recording:

> Shortly after the connection was established, a melodious female voice began to speak, low but extremely evocative. It was the peculiar intonation of the voice, which immediately captivated me long before I understood the words. This time she spoke in three languages: German, Italian and Swedish. This peculiar language mix sounded completely natural.
>
> The more attentively I listened to the voice, the more I liked it. Nevertheless, it was not the funny language mixture with childish naïvety nor the charm of a beautiful, happy, and eager female voice; it was rather the feeling of direct contact, which flowed out of the vocal vibrations that suddenly made me understand that the planned connecting line had finally reached its goal. Thus, I had after long wanderings arrived at a border area where, like a shimmering rainbow, a bridge stretched over to a life plan that for most of us had been hermetically sealed.

The Recordings[11]

TAKE 1 (LISTEN)[12]

Friedel begins by presenting Lena's voice. After that you can hear the first recording of her voice in Italian and German:

"Bambina, arriva, arriva ... horcht die Radio... noch mer reinkommen wahrscheinlich... ihr habt dovino!" (Child, come, come ... listen to the radio ... even more coming in probably ... you've guessed it!)

In his note (A), above, on the top of the page about this recording, he translates the word *dovino* to the Italian *indovinare* (guess), so it could be:

"You guessed it!"

In the original note, there is another phrase in Swedish and German that is not included in this recording:

"men kommer inte russisk ... mein mann kaput" (but does not [speak] Russian ... my husband kaput).

TAKE 2

Friedel comments Lena's voice also here. This one is a whisper of the type he often got:

"Vi vantar am abend um neun." (We are waiting for the evening at nine o'clock).

TAKE 3

Here Lena mentions her own name in a Russian variant but also the keyword Mölnbo and calls Friedel, Frederick and Fred.
"Frederik senta ... Du wirst sprechen ... lieber Fred ... Mölnbo Lenotschka" (Frederick listen ... you will speak ... dear Fred ... Mölnbo with little Lena).

TAKE 4[13]

Lena sings in Swedish/Russian and next Professor Hans Bender can be heard commenting on Lena's voice.
As I mentioned earlier, in May 1970, Professor Hans Bender visited Friedel several times in Nysund and tested the voices. The experiments demonstrated that the voices actually existed as recognized by Professor Bender and his team of scientists. When he first heard the female voice that Friedel called Lena, he remarked: "I perceive this as a spiritual voice, I have no other explanation. It is a voice you can fall in love with. A beautiful voice."

Back to 1959

At the beginning, besides Lena's whispers, Friedel claimed that he had heard a man's voice, which seemed to be close to him in the room, say clearly:
"Hoer mich an! (listen to me) ... nimm Teil an der Arbeit" (take part in the work!)
Friedel claimed that he got a shock. It was so clear, so compelling, an invitation to continue the work he had started one year before. Thus, he took out the tape recorder and began to make short recordings, which were unsuccessful. Patiently, every day, he recorded without getting any connection. He was close to completely abandoning the mysterious voice phenomena behind and devoting himself to painting and achieving his dream of leading an excavation in Pompei.
The decision was still to come. He had just started the tape recorder when he was visited by an American friend, Freddie T., who knew of

Friedel's attempts to contact with the other side via tape recorder and the radio and was one of many who thought that it was impossible. When Freddie saw the spinning tape recorder, he shook his head and said cheerfully: "I am a Thomas" (alluding to Jesus' disciple, the doubting Thomas). Freddie did not get the opportunity to hear it but when Friedel played back the tape, he could hear Freddie making his comment. Next, Friedel affirmed that he had clearly heard a woman, whom he thought was Lena, and this time she spoke in Swedish:

"Nu skrtyter du! (Now you brag!)"

I have not heard the voice, but when Friedel told me about this episode several years later, he affirmed:

> It was probably one of the most recordings in my life. So short but directly linked to what had happened. I got back my faith, if I shall speak of faith, that I was on the right path. I don't know what would have happened if my friends there, somewhere in space, had let me down. Probably I would have given up this work of tape recording completely.

When whispers from his assistant Lena appeared on the tape, sometimes they came so quickly that he found it difficult to interpret them. Then he tried a new technique. In this type of tape recorder, he normally recorded and listened at the highest rate of 7½ ips, but he tried to decipher the recording in the lower speed of 3¾ ips. It was extremely time-consuming and stressful for him to hear, for example, his own natural voice in a slowed down mode. But sometimes it worked when Lena's whispers were so fast that he could not decipher them. At the lower speed they became clearer. He also did short monologues that included a wish that his friends would send him a message. But the disadvantage of these recordings was the huge loss of time when he played them at the lower speed. If a tape at the speed of 7½ took an hour of time, it became double time at the reduced rate. It required extreme patience when it amounted up to 10-12 hours of his time to listen to a single recording.

Friedel listened with excitement to Lena's whispers, her expressions, and her linguistic techniques. She took advantage of certain frequencies of Friedel's voice, or other sounds, on the tape. She had difficulty in producing longer sentences. He refers to phrases such as this one: "Hilf, nimm kontakt mit Radio (Help, get in touch with Radio) Radio hemma, tag kontakt... Abends Radio helfen, hilf mein Mann (in the evening with the help of radio, help my man)."

Mikrofoninspelningar
från 1959 – 1969

1959

№1. Är Apparaten din Börje!
— (ska) 1,2 manmm så kallt!

№2. F.J. Ja än Tomas — du skriver
F.J. säg någonting för mig — jag Tomas
du skriver

№3. F.J. ... inte tala kanske för högt inte-sand!
K.R. Ni lekhören röstförstärkning.-

№4. (K.R.) Poskala! F.J. nu! hörs nu!

№5. F.J. (många, många.) K.R. lyssna lite
K.R. Tanto partis ! F.J. nej nej!...

№6. Två smällar !

№7. F.J. va? K.R. Tanner! Tanner!
nej nej

№8. K.R. Har du lykat?

№9. A.W. vard är Tanner? x2 — sss i Sverige
A.W. jag Tanner en gång till på bandet...
jag tror inte på du här inte ett dugg!
om det inte finns någonting på bandet när
ni spelar upp det så tror jag inte på...
Vad är det så till kalt nånstans? 2x.

№10. A.W. var är det så kalt nånstans? 2x.
Vi är intresserade att veda vad Ni heder
och varför vi kommer hit, vi är also
inte skepksiska, utan vi är positiva

Friedel's notes (B) number 2.

Even other sounds were converted into voices at the lower speed. One that I have heard but is not included in the collections, is a barking dog that came in when the microphone was standing on the windowsill. The dog was on the other side of the lake, about 200 meters away. One can hear the barking on the tape. When Friedel changed to the lower rate, there was a voice in the barking that spoke German and said: "Mölnbo! Hauptblock, zwoelf Uhr zwoelf!" (Mölnbo! Haupt = head, block = block at twelve o'clock, twelve!)" It sounded like some sort of command.

Similar phenomena, such as when the sound of an electronic instrument is transformed into a voice sometimes with a little unnatural intonation like a robot's voice, have been tested by the experts interested in the voice phenomena. They simply cannot explain what happens but it has been confirmed that the voices are there. Technically it may be possible with the right tools and great skill to create something similar. But there is no doubt that Friedel lacked the prerequisites for that. And, once again: definitely fraud is excluded in regard to him!

Then, one day, something changed in Friedel's way. He was extremely sensitive and this developed without his being aware of it. He writes that in his anguish, he started smoking. On one occasion a strange sound phenomenon occurred, which would later occur frequently. [It was] something that I came to experience in a recording; also when my own voice turned and lowered and somehow seemed to be used by the alien voices.

Coming from his own voice that had dropped down to the bottom, he could hear a clear whisper. It was Lena who had come through with the help of Friedel's voice. She spoke to him again and again with different names and finished with the Swedish word: "Hjalp!" (Help!)

Sometimes he perceived a vague concept and could interpret it as he heard the words in Swedish, German, and Italian. And the names she mentioned would return later in other messages: Uncle Pelle, a name that children who visited him used, Friedel, Frederick, Federico, and Friedibus.

He had a feeling that this way of mentioning him by several names would dispel his doubts since those were the names used by his friends in real life. Perhaps it was one way to show that they knew about his relationships with other people.

In September 1959, friends of Monica and Friedel visited from Germany. They told them, among other things, about Boris Sacharow who had been Friedel's childhood friend. He was considered the foremost yoga teacher in Germany and had written a book, which the reviewers considered the best book on yoga in Europe, *Das grosse Geheimnis* (The Big Secret) published by the Drei Eichen. [the Three Oaks]

Friedel and Boris had grown up together in Odessa because their fathers were doctors and often collaborated. The boys sat in the evenings and tried to solve the mysteries of life. They met for the last time in Berlin, in 1932. Next, Boris ran a yoga school, which was presented as "Indian sports." Then the contact ceased.

His German friends promised to contact the publisher and ask them to send a book and Boris' address. Friedel was happy with the idea of getting in touch with his childhood friend again. But it would all happen in an unexpected and tragic way.

A few days before Christmas, Boris Sacharow's book arrived from the publisher. Along with it was a short letter, which announced that on October 6, Boris Sacharow had died in a traffic accident on the A6 in West Germany. This was shocking news for Friedel. He decided that at every recording session in the near future he would simply call him. A few days later, Friedel got the recording that definitely convinced him that he was in contact with the dead. It was December 25, 1959.

In the afternoon, he was alone in the studio. The tape recorder was on and he went to get the headphones. The moment that he put them on, he heard a loud hissing noise directly from the room that sounded like a forced and long exhalation. It was as if someone emptied the lungs so thoroughly that he could hear how the air squeaked in the bronchi. He realized that this must have been caught on the tape, also, and he played it up excitedly.

I remember when I heard it for the first time. First, a weak roaring sound was heard. Then suddenly, one could hear loud noises that sounded like inhalations and exhalations—with such strength that I actually jumped up. Of all the voices I heard at Friedel's, this was the only one that got spiders crawling on my spine up to the neck. Immediately after the exhalation a voice says very explicitly:

"So kalt! (So cold!)"

TAKE 5
Deep inhalation and exhalation of, according to Friedel, Boris Sacharow who, subsequently, says: "So kalt!"
(See Friedel's note (B) above, number 1.)

I was as excited as Friedel must have been when he first heard it. After he played the recording, he gave me Boris Sacharow's book *Das grosse Geheimnis* with the last page open.

In the picture the author himself sat in one of the yoga practitioners' characteristic lotus pose. He sat upright on the floor. The right leg was bent so that the foot rested on the left groin. The left leg was bent with the left foot over his right thigh. Both foot soles were turned up. Boris sat as if carved in granite. The chest was so deeply shrunk that it seemed to touch the spine.

We were both convinced that it had not been by chance only that Friedel got the book, only days before this recording. There was something predetermined and I could not do anything else but agree with him that it was a message from his dead childhood friend, Boris, who, at different times and in strange circumstances, would later contact him.

Friedel and Anders Leopold studying Boris Sacharow's book.

5

SWEDISH TV PERSONALITY, ARNE WEISE

Friedel had now overcome the high threshold that differentiates between faith and knowledge. For him there was no doubt that he had found a bridge to the other side. The contact with Lena had, in a way, already convinced him. But the ultimate proof for Friedel was when he found out that his dead childhood friend, Boris Sacharow, lived in another life dimension and could orchestrate a breathing exercise just days after he received Boris' book with a picture of his exhalation. Friedel also claimed that he heard a whisper from Boris precisely in connection with the exhalation, in which he uttered: "Am Apparaten, din [dein] Boris!" (On the apparatus, your Boris). Naturally, I didn't hear this but "So kalt!" is undeniable (See Friedel's notes (B) number 1).

After the powerful recording with Boris, Friedel got rid of the last shadow of doubt about the possibility that he suffered from a mental disorder. However, Monica was worried. She told me when we talked about it, long after this initial period, that Friedel seemed completely unrestrained after he had heard Boris' voice. He was one moment inside the studio and would paint. But it didn't last. He went around talking to himself as if in conversations with his new friends. He smoked more than before and he drank a few extra glasses of white wine. She tried to contact him but it was as if he was in another world. What she found strange was that he had not made a single attempt to record.

When I met Friedel for the first time in May 1964, he could not explain his reaction after the contact with Boris. It was a kind of shock effect. And he was convinced that he had had the opportunity of building a bridge between two life dimensions: one before and one after physical death. This was something he already suspected in his childhood, that death is not the end. However, that there would be a possibility of contact between the living and the dead in this objective way was inconceivable for him!

Only Monica, a few relatives and close friends knew what Friedel was doing. But then, he felt the strong wish to share what he had discovered with a wider circle of people. And not only share but, hopefully, get a confirmation of his discovery from a scientist, someone engaged in parapsychological research.

On the morning of December 27, 1959, he appeared completely normal and very controlled, according to Monica. He asked her to find Dr. John Bjoerkhem's telephone number.

In the last few years he had heard and read about John Bjoerkhem (1910-1963). I have already mentioned his breakthrough hypnosis research. But he was also a pioneer in the Swedish parapsychological research. John Bjoerkhem had a thorough education and was both a Doctor of Philosophy, Doctor of Theology and Licentiate of Medicine. He had become known far beyond the borders of Sweden through his hypnosis work. He is reported to have hypnotized some 1,500 people experimentally before his doctorate in psychology in 1942 titled "De hypnotiska hallucinationerna" (The hypnotic hallucinations). Before that, in 1940, he had completed a doctorate in theology with a religious-psychological and religious-historical study of the mystic Antoinette Bourignon (1616-1680). John Bjoerkhem's most famous book is *Det ockulta problemet* (The occult problem), 1939, in which he portrays both hypnosis experiments with remote viewing and clairvoyance.

Thus, Friedel decided to try to get this man involved in his research. But he did not have great hope about John Bjoerkhem's reaction, a 49-year-old brilliant mid-career man who had many assignments both in Sweden and abroad.

But one phone call was enough. Bjoerkhem was immediately interested. He would go away days before the New Year and was ready to visit him on Storkyrkobrinken the next day.

Naturally, Friedel was excited. But he also felt unsure regarding the meeting with a man of this caliber and telling him about a matter so sensitive and personal. He wanted to have support, so he called his friend Arne Weise of the SBC. Weise was then a well-known radio journalist who had made several high-profile programs. He is still known in Sweden 30 years later as the TV host on Christmas Eve and of many other popular TV shows.

Weise told me long after the shocking events at Friedel's home, on Christmas 1959:

> When Friedel phoned me, I was naturally skeptical at the beginning of our conversation. He was very upset and sounded a little frightened when he first talked about the fact that he had recorded voices in the garden and heard his mother's voice and how she came with a greeting directly to him. I knew Friedel well and knew that I had every reason to take him seriously. Then, to my amazement, I heard that he had been in contact with John Bjoerkhem and the next day he would come to visit Friedel and listen to the voices and participate in recordings. That settled it. I decided to join in and took a couple of virgin tapes from SBC so that, in any case, there would not be any talk of groomed tapes.

As mentioned previously, Weise knew Bjoerkhem well and had taken part in his hypnosis experiments as a student.

In the evening of December 28, they met Monica and Friedel in their apartment in Stockholm. Besides Monica and Friedel, Bjoerkhem, Weise and his wife Else-Marie, Friedel's sister Elly and his sister-in-law Annica also participated.

The discussions at the dinner table, and later on in the living room, became something of a review of what had happened to Friedel. His conclusion that he was in contact with living beings in another life dimension was by now unshakable.

So, Friedel played up Lena's voice. They heard her whispering directly through the microphone and then her melodious voice in "Bambina, Arriva, arriva." (Take 1).

Both Weise and Bjoerkhem agreed that they really heard her voice but they were still reserved about Friedel's eager presentation of what the voice said before he played it up. The risk of suggestion was obvious.

Friedel went on to describe the decisive manifestation of Boris Sacharow when he made his yoga breathing exercise, which ended with the words "So kalt!" and displayed the image in the book. Arne Weise declared: "In this situation, I was actually very nervous; by the way, I think everyone in the room was nervous. Meanwhile, impatient to do some recordings, too."

Friedel wrote:

> Despite the happy mood, I could detect that there began to be some tension in the room. Personally, I felt a little unsure. I found myself somehow in the painful position of a theatre director who doesn't have a clue if his cast will appear for the scheduled performance or not. I moved as far as possible from the microphone and sat most of the time next to Doctor Bjoerkhem.

John Bjoerkhem was known to speak very carefully about his research. Friedel did not expect any critical comment from him. And the worst situation would be if the voices did not come through. He even thought that perhaps he should simply dismiss the whole thing.

At 7:30pm it was time for the first recording. This was done through a single microphone placed approximately in the middle of the group. Friedel wanted them to continue the ongoing conversation, but they should be alert and aware of any unusual noise or strange voice in the room. He also asked them to think about what they would say and try to commit to it by heart. So, the conversation continued and Friedel could see that the needle on the tape recorder was moving. "Nu hoers det!" (Now hear this!), he exclaimed as a sign that the recording had started.

Elly said right after this: "Friedel, har du satt pa nu?" (Friedel, have you turned it on now?). Friedel replied: "Ja, ja ... va.?" (Yes, yes ... huh?)

The recording lasted five minutes. Before he played it up, he wanted to know if anyone had heard anything unusual in the room. They agreed that such a thing had not happened. He was very excited but expected nothing at all.

When he played the first session, everybody heard very clearly a distinct, strange, powerful voice that uttered: "Poskola!" (possibly Paskala). The voice pronounces the word directly in the snap while the tape recorder is turned on.

Everybody agreed that this voice had not been heard in the room. The voice was played several times and there was some disagreement if it said "poskola" or "paskala." Friedel believed it was "paskalla." For some incomprehensible reason, he got the idea that the word referred to the Swedish resort Paskallavik on the Swedish east coast. I pointed out, when I heard the voice a few years later, that in this case it ought to have uttered the whole name "Paskallavik." But Friedel argued that just the fact that the voice had forcefully entered the tape without anyone hearing it in the room was a convincing proof that the phenomenon existed, and in this case the interpretation of the meaning of the word was not so important. I agreed with him and so did John Bjoerkhem and Arne Weise. Besides, the fact that the strange voice was there on the tape affected them profoundly and increased the tension in the room.

Before listening to this recording, I must tell my readers that it would take exactly nine years before Friedel got an explanation about the meaning of the word. At that time, after two international press conferences and after having written two books, one of which was translated into German, he was well known in many parts of the world. And so, people in grief after the loss of a loved one or of a friend, contacted him and in some cases also visited him.

On December 28, 1968, a Finnish woman, resident in Sweden, Anne M. Hansson, came to pay a visit. Her fiancé had died in a car accident. The next day, Friedel phoned me and told me excitedly, as usual, what had happened. He wanted me to take my photographer and come to photograph a picture that he had borrowed from the Finnish woman who had visited him, and write about it in my newspaper, *Aftonbladet*. We also had the possibility to interview her because she lived in the City Hotel in Eskilstuna.

When the woman heard the voice clearly pronounce the word "poskola", she became very upset and took a photo out of her purse. It was a picture of her and her fiancé leaning against each other, cheek to cheek. Then she explained that "poskola" in a Finnish dialect that she spoke, meant "cheek to cheek."

This was an example of what came to be known as "precognition" or foreknowledge: something that in later recordings, mainly via radio, would be more understandable when the messages became a little longer. Here is the recording of the voice that takes over in the snap from the recorder's start and comes directly into Friedel's voice: "Nu hoers det!" (Now hear this!).

TAKE 6 (LISTEN)[14]

"Poskola!"

They continued listening to the first recording. Shortly after Friedel found that the call is heard on the tape recorder following his sister's question: "Friedel, have you turned it on now?" and he replied, "Yes, yes ... huh?"

And then a very clear alien voice says a little rushed:

"Tanner ... Tanner!"

It is a female voice with a Finnish accent. None of those present had heard the voice in the room, otherwise they would have immediately reacted. But the reaction was strong when they played back the tape.

TAKE 7 (LISTEN)[15]

"Tanner ... Tanner!"

A couple of alien voices had been registered. Friedel felt that these voices and others in these recordings were the best he had received. And the great thing was that it all happened when John Bjoerkhem and Arne Weise were present. He could not have had better witnesses, and the voices were there on Weise's new tapes from the SBC. Friedel was obviously very happy and enthusiastic but the same cannot be said of Arne Weise.

I will give you the explanation for the name Tanner. For this was another case of precognition, according to Friedel.

In the spring of 1963, he was visited by a young, desperate woman whose fiancé had committed suicide. She listened to part of Friedel's recordings and they also made a few unsuccessful attempts to record. A short time after the visit, she sent Friedel a book written by an English scientist named L. Johnson. It was translated into Swedish and was entitled "Det stora problemet" (The big problem). She urged him to read the passage she had underlined. It was a "message from the other side":

> Studera alla slags tradloesa meddelanden. Vi (de doeda) hoppas snart kunna fa fram moejlighet till foerbindelse mellan oss och er. Det hela ar en fraga om vaglangder. (Study all kinds of wireless communications. We [the dead] hope to be able soon to attain the possibility of connection between us and you. It is all a matter of wavelengths).

He found the book interesting and read on. Suddenly, on one side, he saw the name of an English medium, previously unknown to him. His name was Tanner.

When I wrote this book, I was careful to try to verify the information that Friedel gave me verbally but especially in his books. I have not been able to find any Dr L. Johnson or find the book he mentions. There may be several reasons for this, but, once again, what the voices say in their messages is, perhaps, the most important thing. The fact that they are there on the tape in a completely inexplicable way is crucial.

According to Friedel, John Bjoerkhem was very moved by what he heard. He nodded in the affirmative when Friedel asked him if he had heard the voices and what they said. But Arne Weise was very upset and could not sit still. He jumped up and down and made various comments and his wife tried to calm him.

He suddenly got up, placed himself in front of the microphone and loudly ordered the invisible guests to leave the house.

Friedel recorded the incident in his book:

> I tried to deflect this embarrassing incident with a little humor explaining with a smile that we had all gathered here precisely for the purpose of listening to these voices. I jokingly remarked that we should be polite towards our unknown visitors. Inside, however, I was shocked for I feared that Arne had driven my "cast" away. As the tape recorder was switched on to "record" again, I asked aloud the question, if there was anything we could do for our unseen friends and if anything was actually expected of us.
>
> Annica suggested a short, silent pause, after which we sat for a few minutes without making a sound, and then I replayed this part of the tape.
>
> There, from the quiet of the room, sounded that tireless woman's voice whispering in German with deep emphasis:
>
> "Ihr seit doch Menschen!" (You are only human!)
>
> The voice is weak and is not included in this collection. But in the noise one can hear a voice that says something in German. That was enough for Weise.

The following recording contains multiple voice phenomena, and some are included in my material. So I split it to make it easier. Weise comments without having heard what had been received. His comments were recorded on the tape, and I heard his familiar voice several times. He described to me how upset he was and that he simply wanted to come to some sort of judgment; he would ask questions and wanted to get answers to them.

(See Friedel's notes (B) number 4, 7, 9, 10.)

Arne Weise grabbed the microphone again and added almost aggressively: "Where is Tanner?" he asked a few times in his clear strong voice. And got a quiet whispering answer: "I Sverige!" (In Sweden).

TAKE 8

"Vad är Tanner? Säg Tanner en gång till på bandet!" (What is Tanner? Say Tanner once again on the tape!)

"sss, I Sverige!" (sss, In Sweden).

The recording continued and obviously Weise had not yet heard that he had received an answer so he insisted.

Arne Weise: "I do not believe in this, not a bit. Can you now answer, if there can be any answer at all. If there is nothing on the tape when we play it, I do not believe in it!"

Previously, in the evening, he had been listening to Boris Sacharow's greeting to Friedel with the yoga breathing and then the utterance: "So cold!"

Weise: "Var ar det sa kallt nagonstans? Var ar det sa kallt nagonstans?" (Where is it so cold somewhere? Where is it so cold somewhere?)

Later in the evening Arne Weise would get a shocking answer.

Weise:

> Vi ar intresserade av att få veta vad ni heter och varfoer ni kommer hit. Vi ar alltsa inte skeptiska utan vi ar positiva och vill veta varfoer ni kommer hit. Ja ... Jag kan inte komma pa nagot mer att saga ... stang av far vi hoera. (We are interested to know what your name is and why you come here. So we are not skeptical but we are positive and want to know why you come here. Yes, I cannot think of anything else, turn off and we'll see).

But Friedel let the tape recorder run for a while. He said to me: "No doubt, most of us were ill at ease. The uncertainty or, better said, the fear of the unknown, made itself felt in the room. One could clearly sense that the mood grew tense."

When he finally turned off the tape recorder and everybody had calmed down and were full of expectations, he played the tape back. They listened to Arne's outraged voice when he finished with a call for Friedel to switch off the recording, and they heard a very clear voice utter a single word:

"Grecola!" (Graecola!)

Arne and Else-Marie had their son sleeping in the kitchen and she wanted to go out there and check on him. But she was upset and afraid, and said immediately following Arne's silence:

"Were I not afraid I'd go into the kitchen. Monica, do you want to come with me?"

Friedel said: "They [the voices] don't want to do anything [bad] to you."

Else-Marie Weise: "But I'm afraid to go out into the kitchen."

Friedel spoke again: "They have no reason to do anything wrong, they cannot hurt, they want to be with us and have some fun."

The voice that uttered "Grecola" is very clear and appears one second before Else-Marie Weise asked Monica to follow her into the kitchen. It is yet another strong example of precognition if one manages to understand its meaning. It happened in 1963 when the renowned philosophy Professor Alf Ahlberg visited Friedel. He commented that it was an expression used in ancient Rome when speaking of "a frightened Greek." "Graecola" translates as "scaredy-cat."

Thus, those who pronounced the word knew about Else-Marie's fear before she expressed it, something that opens a breathtaking perspective. We can also ponder that it was pronounced in Latin in the knowledge that its meaning would be revealed in the future.

TAKE 9 (LISTEN)[16]

"Grekola" (Graecola)!

Shortly thereafter, Friedel turned off the tape recorder. When everyone calmed down and were enthused by the expectation, he played back the tape. Needless to say that the voices heard in these recordings caused quite a stir in the group.

John Bjoerkhem and Friedel's sister Annica left after that. Bjoerkhem wanted to come back and listen a little more closely to what had come through that evening and in previous recordings, also.

Arne Weise wanted to make more recordings, so they took the tape recorder up to the studio. They closed the door and Weise paced restlessly back and forth in the room.

When the tape recorder was turned on, he said: "Eftersom man maste prata ... man kan ga." (Because you have to talk ... you can give).

Alien voice: "Fie wie cold!" (Could be translated as: Oh, how cold!)

Weise continues: "... a andra sidan maste de val vila nogon gong." (On the other hand, they have to rest sometime)

The sound changed and a weak voice:

"Nein, am apparaten halten wir pa morgon till." (No, on the apparatus we hold on until tomorrow to.)

Here the sentence is disturbed by Weise who says: "ahh" and Friedel who says: "Tonight."

This is perhaps the most impressive recording in Friedel's collection because of being directly linked to the situation and Arne Weise's question. As there is an interval of several minutes since Arne Weise asked his question and got the answer, a cut was done to his own voice.

TAKE 10 (LISTEN)[17]

Arne Weise asked again: "Var ar det sa kallt nagonstans?" (Where is it so cold, somewhere?)

"So kalt ist in dir!" (So cold is in you!), replied the voice.

Friedel continued before they listened to the recordings:

"You understand ... I have to say that we humans ... as long as the realization has not been achieved that there is another world, nothing helps ... a certain maturity—"

Here Weise interrupts: "Men Friedel ... jag tror ju på det här!" (But Friedel, I believe in this!)

Very quickly a voice comes in with a question:

TAKE 11

"Goer ni?" (Do you?).

The tests done on this very clear and important recording concerning the voices' credibility, have demonstrated that the alien voice enters Friedel's voice right in the break, "you understand ..." and uses, therefore, his voice as a carrier.

Bjoerkhem died in 1963, so I never had the opportunity of talking with him about this recording. He was also, as I pointed out, very sparse in comments about his research. Friedel told me later that John Bjoerkhem had become completely convinced of the voices' existence. He was also convinced of the soul's survival and belonged to the leading researchers on reincarnation. He pondered that this was a discovery of great importance for further parapsychological research.

In his book *Radio and microphone contacts with the dead*, Friedel cites a comment by John Bjoerkhem: "It is enough if only one word is taken up on the tape in a quiet room. Several empirical pieces of

Friedel's notes (C) number 11, 12, 13.

evidence are not necessary because in such tape recordings there are not subjective elements."

The recordings with Weise and Bjoerkhem were very important for the scientific tests carried out at the Max Planck Institute in Munich, University of Freiburg, Institute of Physics in Göttingen, and the Para-Psychological Association in the United States.

I close this chapter with the transcript of an interview I did with Arne Weise in the mid-1960s and a response letter from him. I have no exact date for the interview. But it was probably after the press conference in 1964. I also talked with him on a couple of recent occasions and did an interview with him after the broadcasting of the Swedish much acclaimed entertainer Lars Holmquist's popular TV show "Here is Your Life," in which Friedel was the protagonist.

As of this writing in May 2013, Arne Weise replied to a letter I sent him about the book I was working on and wanted to know if he had pondered the matter over the years. I transcribe his reply:

> Friedel, I have not given it a thought for a long time, but your letter naturally aroused memories. I remember very well how it all began, the seánce at Friedel's and Monica's home, the voice that answered my question "Where is it so cold somewhere?" saying: "So kalt ist in dir! (So cold is in you!). It was frightening, not least because this happened before Friedel began using radio waves. I remember Monica and her loving faith in everything Friedel came up with, and I remember, unfortunately, more of those nasty comments on the tabloids, and that Friedel hoped for an international breakthrough that never came.

Here is a summary of the conversations I had with Arne Weise over time:

> Friedel is an extremely complex and versatile person whom you do not always know where to place. He has been through so much, it's amazing, from Odessa and ahead in life—his experience of life is different from other persons'.
> This and to be an artist and a singer and to have a son in Israel whom he does not see [he was reunited with his son Solomon after 18 years on the TV-show "Here is Your Life"] and not being at home anywhere, has created an incredibly interesting and exciting person who is used to fighting for survival.

When we first met, he told me that he was reunited with Pope Pius XII and had painted him and Peter's grave in the Vatican crypt, and all that. I was completely fascinated by him and we developed a friendship that lasted for about twenty years. He is so special and I love original people.

And since I am baptized and confirmed in Swedenborg's teachings [Emanuel Swedenborg, Swedish scientist who had a spiritual awakening and claimed he could speak to angels, spirits, and deceased persons], I asked myself why I, of all people, happened to meet him and had this strange experience with the voices. It is strange and it happened several times.

He has a lot to talk about, not only about voices, but what is difficult for me is that in Swedenborg's teachings it says clearly that it is here on the Earth that we shall live and be happy. We should not keep on trying to get in touch with the other side. What Friedel's spirits are talking about has very little to do with Swedenborg's teachings in any way.

I find it strange that over the years [five years since the recordings with Weise and Bjoerkhem], the messages have not become much better and easier to understand. When I point this out, he becomes very blunt and says that the voices will come on video also and that I would like to see and hear them. Then I am sad when he does not make any demonstration.

When I was in Höör before Christmas [Friedel moved to Höör in Skane, southern Sweden, in July 1977], it was basically the same voices that I had heard earlier. It is so important that the voices would say something more than these short messages.

Friedel is an unusual person who has experienced a lot of things in his life and has a message that complies with mine, that there is life after this existence. But there are things that I very much doubt and I would hope that there will be good scientific evidence for this. Perhaps we should not ask for more, but he takes a tremendous responsibility towards all the people who miss their deceased friends and relatives. He has to be careful about that. And there are risks. He must stay away from people who try to make money on him and his message.

"So kalt ist in dir" [so cold is in you] is the best of everything and it is strange that it would happen to me. But from there to doing the research myself, no, I'm too busy with other things.

I am absolutely convinced that he is not a scam. I am absolutely convinced that he believes in this and I would not even rule out that there is something behind this, otherwise, I should not even be able to keep my own faith.

The problem is that the world Friedel believes in does not match what I think of when it comes to the afterlife.

6

RECORDINGS ON NEW YEAR'S EVE

After the successful recordings with John Bjoerkhem and Arne Weise, Friedel was full of confidence and made frequent tape recordings and spent much time capturing the anomalous voices. He obtained several contacts but of poor quality. When, after meeting Friedel in 1964, I listened to many of these later recordings, it was often difficult for me to make any interpretation unless Friedel himself repeatedly hammered the message into my brain. I cannot deny that it could have been some form of suggestion. Therefore, I choose to primarily rely on recordings of such quality that even you, dear reader, whom I hope will wear good headphones, should be able to hear the voices without other influence, other than the one you get through my text.

On New Year's Eve of 1959, Friedel could not refrain from sending a New Year's greeting to his friends on the other side. He had placed the tape recorder in the studio and pulled a cord to the microphone positioned about three meters from the radio in the living room. In Radio Sweden they broadcasted a New Year program that would run over midnight. At the end of that year, Radio Sweden did not broadcast the usual poem "Nyarsklockan." The tradition ended in 1956 when the Swedish actor Anders de Wahl passed away and was not taken up again until the Swedish Television started a new tradition in 1977.

Friedel's New Year celebration was attended by several friends and some of Monica's relatives. Friedel set the tape recorder so that it would be running during the twelfth stroke of midnight. He had very quietly asked the friends on the other side to get in touch. Due to the festivities, Friedel did not listen to the recording until the next day.

Immediately after the connection someone announced a name: "Bismarck!"

Then we can hear a feeble melodic female voice singing in the same mode as the radio music, which had no soloist:

"Nur Deutsche," (Only Germans) "frid på jorden" (peace on Earth), "Hallelujah!"

Friedel believed that he heard his name mentioned several times, including from his deceased friend in Pompeii, Pasquale. I did not hear it, but then a voice came through with a direct greeting to him. A woman, not unlike Lena's voice, uttered: "Federico war so süss!" (Federico was so sweet!)

Possibly one can also hear the word "freund" (friend) before the name (see Friedel's notes D, 17). And immediately thereafter, Friedel lifts a glass of champagne towards the radio and says: "Skal!" (Cheers!)

TAKE 12

"Federico war so süss!"

Before the end of the tape, a German radio voice is heard and in it an alien male voice says:
"Der Tod ist gut!" (Death is good!).

TAKE 13

"Der Tod ist gut."

In the early hours of the New Year, Friedel made another recording, despite the annoying chatter from the party. When he listened to the recording the next day, in the middle of the buzz made by the others in the room, he heard a broken, dull, and hoarse sounding voice. In the monotonous tone of the masculine voice we can sense a certain resignation and sadness. It speaks as if in a half-asleep state:

"Wir Leben in der tiefsten Wirrnis ... die Menschen herunterdrücken und knechten ... die anderen entzogen sich, ich nicht ... Darum bin

N°17 (Kv.röst) Freund Federico var så söt!
F.J. skål!

N°18 (K.röst) Hail (heil)... das war Hitler
en skamt ... nicht!
                                                     sich
N°19 (KT.röst) das war Hitler en siekt endl
A.d.f. 1960

N°20 (Un. sk.) till sveriges Radio sender vi en hjärt-
erg Nyårshälsningen... (Kv.) von den Toten!

N°21 P.C. skål Hugo!
H.Fahlkrans: Slå högre! M.J. näs var...

N°22 N.a. 1962 / Hugo Fahlkrans / Nej allo!
F.J. de fruxt M.J. spumante...

N°23 E.H. F.J. St. Söd.
F.J. alt möglt - E.H. - ja kenventioner..
H.Fahlkrans gla
F.J. - ja vist... H.Fahlkrans: glaub't fest!

N°24 Alf Ahlberg - vi har hört så mycket kan
jag tro att lilla Ruth jo och jag i varje
fall - jag är övertygad att de är någonting så sällsamt som är vi för lära
oss att om livet och döden...
de markeras bättre om det är
ett blandat språk tyska eller engelska
... så det skulle vara en fördel för oss.
(A.D.) en gumba! ...F.J. gudet tycker jag
också...

Friedel's notes (D) number 17.

ich." (We live in the deepest confusion ... to oppress and enslave the people ... the others withdrew ... I didn't ... That's why I am).

The voice would come back several times and Friedel finally decided that it belonged to Adolf Hitler.

Friedel made the mistake, at this early stage, of inviting people—some scientists and a few technicians—and allow them to take part in the remarkable voice phenomena. He had too little knowledge of what was really going on and was too eager to have people with expertise to confirm his discovery. Those who came to visit him were expecting to hear voices when he made the tape recordings. If the former did not materialize, they had all sorts of theories about the origin of the voice phenomena. On one occasion, the secretary of the Parapsychological Society in Stockholm, Eva Hellstroem, arranged for Friedel to get in contact with two audio experts at Stockholm University. They participated in a few unsuccessful recordings during an entire evening and were very skeptical about the whole thing. When Friedel played the recording from the New Year's Eve, they could certainly hear the voice that came out of the tape before he exclaimed, "Skal!" (Cheers!) But one of them suggested that it was a radio ham who played a trick on him. Friedel answered:

> Yes, perhaps; it is not inconceivable. If it's just a radio ham, in this case he must have been clairvoyant; how else would he be able to wait for the right moment, just when I was about to start my tape recorder.
>
> The benefit of this evening was that I finally realized how senseless these kinds of public demonstrations were. Why would I ask strangers about a matter of which they had not the slightest idea, because they had never dealt with such things? After all, I still fumbled in the dark, and even if I began to get a glimpse of the unknown here and there, it was, in any case, too early to try to demonstrate my results to others.

Remarkable contacts with his deceased friend Felix Kersten

A childhood friend, Felix Kersten, was another of his contacts. Their parents owned estates in Estonia that bordered on each other, so the boys were often together. In 1943, they had both come to Sweden and re-established contact with each other. Kersten was renowned for his efforts during the Second World War when he helped hundreds of Jews to escape the concentration camps; that was achieved thanks to his strong influence on one of Hitler's closest men, Reichfürer-SS commandant für Schutzstaffel (SS), Heinrich Himmler.

Himmler suffered from a stomach illness that afflicted him tremendously and the only relief he could get was Kersten's special massage. Kersten was not a Nazi sympathizer but he won Himmler's confidence and was able, through him, to intervene on behalf of old friends and patients in the death camps. In World War II, he arranged a meeting between Himmler and Norbert Masur, the leader of the World Jewish Congress. This led to the release of 7000 female prisoners in the concentration camp Ravensbrück. He also played a crucial role in enabling Folke Bernadotte to start the operation with the so-called white buses that transported thousands of prisoners to Sweden.

Kersten was a highly appreciated and skilled masseur during his time in Belgium but was ordered to go to Berlin in 1939 to become Himmler's personal masseur.

Kersten and his wife Irmgard settled in Sweden but it was hard for Kersten to liberate himself from the accusations that he had sympathized with the Nazis. In 1953 he received full redress and Swedish citizenship. Felix Kersten came to play a big role in Friedel's contact with the other side. Not least in connection with historical figures like Hitler, Churchill, van Gogh, and others. It was a controversial chapter in Friedel's attempt to convince the world that he had found a bridge to a fourth dimension of life where these people lived. It led to some sensational articles in the world press but also ironic, somehow depreciating stories about the artist who sat with his tape recorder and had direct contact with Hitler fourteen years after his death.

Personally I can say that I could not understand Hitler's monologue from the other side that Friedel caught via radio. Of course, this was of great interest to the researchers at the Max Planck Institute who obviously took it very seriously. They did not go further, after testing the approximately ten-minute recording, than declaring that the voice print, to some extent, matched Hitler's voice. But due to the dictator's different voice levels and the disturbances in the recording, it was impossible to confirm that it was the same voice. They listened to it but did not want to comment on the content: perhaps for obvious reasons.

Friedel now took up most of the recordings directly on the radio, a technique which obviously meant that the voices could express themselves in longer sentences, sometimes in monologues, although at times almost incomprehensible to someone who could not count on Friedel's guidance, but still audible. A few days before Easter 1960, Friedel visited Felix Kersten in his home in Stockholm.

Friedel wrote:

> He suffered from kidney stones but attended our conversations despite being in pain. He seemed tired and overworked but nevertheless had to go to Germany the following day where many patients waited anxiously for his treatments. It is the old story of a doctor who is not allowed to be sick because he does not have time for that.
>
> It was late. We talked about my space contacts, about the bridge I wanted to build, and about the unknown life. Felix gave me his book *Conversations with Himmler* and wrote some lines in it. We talked about the South, dreamed of a villa on the Mediterranean surrounded by pine trees, boxwood hedges and cypresses.
>
> I had the privilege of enjoying Felix's friendship for many years. I knew his boyish temperament and good nature; I knew what this corpulent man with his little, soft, smooth hands had done in this world of misery: all this—and much, much more. And someone who gets to know Felix intimately will always love him.
>
> When, late in the evening, we took leave of each other, none of us suspected that it would be the last time.

Felix Kersten died on Easter Eve and Friedel was informed of his death a few days later.

Friedel told me that he took Kersten's death harder than the loss of friends who had died earlier, and he worked almost day and night to try to get in touch with him by radio. It took him only two weeks before he succeeded. It came in a radio broadcast with strong interference. I have heard this first communication and can say that I perceived the most important thing, namely Kersten's name.

"Kersten ... Kersten ... hier Kersten ... Vorsicht, Aufpassen" (Kersten ... Kersten ... here Kersten ... Caution, listen carefully). His voice broke through with more messages.

Before we listen to the powerful and most sensational recording with Felix Kersten, I will reproduce below some of Friedel's thoughts about death.

> So here was a man who had died in a hospital two weeks ago. The haunting phantom of our humanity, a blood clot, had burst the blood

vessels of the heart. The dead body was cremated; a small pile of ashes was all that was left of him.

The man Felix Kersten, husband, father, doctor, and friend had died, perished into nothing. Death is a reality, an inflexible, brutal fact—the only certainty—the one that never fails.

This is the wonderful thing about death. I remember how my nanny, when I was little, took me for a walk to the city cemetery in Odessa. Even at that time, I felt a clear certainty about the resting place of the dead. Without having to dress the feeling in my mind, I knew that there was a screaming contradiction that came out of all these graves, crosses, marble tiles and tombs.

I knew instinctively that here everything was somehow sham, villain and fraud. Yes, even more, it all seemed false, artificial, and theatrical. It looked like a false backdrop. In contrast, light, warmth, and movement radiated from the clear sky, from every blade of grass, every bird, every tree and flower.

I was to learn about death from a different perspective when, years later, the terror of the civil war came crashing down over Odessa like waves gone wild. At that time, starvation, typhus, and cholera existed in the city, and one could helplessly witness the daily death of many people in the streets.

It was especially bad on the streets after bloody hand-to-hand combat facilitated the "liberation" of the city by some power-hungry people. I remember when, one day, I had a glimpse of the municipal mortuary where hundreds of bloody corpses were laid out to be seen by the public. It was a cloudless beautiful spring sky. In the streets, the acacias were in full bloom, and their magic scent filled the whole city.

But my mood was miserable, and an icy cramp tightened my diaphragm. The contrast was too stark. Here, life and renewal flourished; there, meaningless murder and annihilation. Despite the anxiety and nausea, I did not avoid death. I wanted to find out its secret and get the big contradiction on track, and I still remember that when I was again confronted with death, I felt a growing calm, reminiscent of the confidence I felt in the cemetery as a little boy.

Felix Kersten contacted Friedel several times during his perhaps most active period in the 1960s. He presented several of these recordings in his book *The Voices from Space.*

Once again, I must say that it would be unfair to Friedel, in a story about his life's work of trying to build a bridge between the living and the

Kersten with Himmler

Felix Kersten receives medal from the
Dutch government for saving people during WWII.

Kersten with Himmler

dead, not to reproduce some of the surrealistic recordings he got from radio where a number of historical figures were mentioned and sometimes got through: Hitler and Goering, Van Gogh, contact name Churchill and others. But also people who were close to him, such as Boris Sacharow and Felix Kersten. In addition, less famous people and a variety of unidentified voices broke through in radio broadcasts with keywords such as Mölnbo, Malarhoejden and a number of the names Friedel was known for.

At the end of November 1963, when the remarkable recordings with Felix Kersten were achieved, there was real turbulence around "the man with the spirit voices." As I told in the Introduction, in June Friedel arranged for his first press conference and invited the world press. He drew attention abroad while Swedish newspapers including the *Aftonbladet*, behaved quite aloofly. I did not come into the picture until the spring of 1964 in connection with the second press conference. Only then did the Swedish media begin to take a serious interest in the startling voice phenomena.

Note: Friedel's childhood intimate friend, Dr Felix Kersten, is a European figure who is well-known not only for his position as Himmler's private doctor but also, and mostly, for his humanitarian action in favor of the many thousands of Jews that he saved from a horrible life and death during WWII.

In recognition for his extraordinary deeds, General Charles de Gaulle awarded him, posthumously, the Legion of Honour, the highest French decoration. He died suddenly of a heart attack in 1960, in Germany, on his way to France to receive the honour. Kersten was endorsed for the Nobel prize on several occasions.

The Swedish Broadcasting Corporation top experts test the voices—a technically impossible recording.

In November 1963, the SBC contacted Friedel. Arne Weise had put forward a proposal for a radio or TV program about the voices. He was prepared to unconditionally play the voices he had heard and comment on the matter. But it was understood from the beginning that this was a very sensitive thing that could be uncomfortable for some people.

It was decided that the SBC's foremost expert in radio and television technology, studio engineer Kjell Stensson, would visit Friedel in Mölnbo with a team to try to make his own recordings.

Kjell Stensson (1917-1990) deserves a special mention. He appeared frequently on radio and television in both entertainment and technical development programs. He was also a respected crime novel critic.

Kjell Stensson.

But he was best known to the Swedish people when, on April 1, 1962, he launched color TV. He described how, with the help of a nylon stocking, one could get color on the TV screen—cutting it apart and slipping it over the TV. It is said that several old nylon stockings were torn down after his April Fool's joke.

But more serious things were going on. Together with engineer Robert Koistinen and journalist Daisy Karlberg from the morning newspaper *Stockholms-Tidningen*, he arrived with his own tape recorder and sealed tapes from the SBC. First, they had to listen to Arne Weise's recordings and Stensson admitted that he heard voices but was restrained in his comments. The most important thing for him was to succeed with his own recordings. It was late at night before they got started and the short recordings they made yielded no results. But what they heard was enough to make new attempts and it was agreed that they would return in a week.

SBC's interest was there and Friedel had several requirements. He wanted several programs on parapsychology in which both Swedish and foreign experts would be introduced. He also wanted Arne Weise to be the host, and that the tapes recorded in 1959 would be broadcast. He also requested that John Bjoerkhem attend. He believed that they could make some live recordings if it was clearly indicated that the possibilities to succeed under such circumstances were very small.

In the days before Stensson's return with his team, Friedel made frequent recordings in the hope that something extraordinary would happen, now that there was an opportunity to spread knowledge widely about the bridge to the other side. He was clearly worried and anxious. What if his friends didn't show up when they were most needed? Monica reassured him and said she was convinced that they would not disappoint him.

One evening when he was sitting with headphones on, and as usual, turned the tuning knob from left to right on the medium wave, he suddenly heard a whispering from Lena:

"hålla, hålla direkt kontakt!" (Keep, keep direct contact!)

The tape rolled on and he listened to a male singer and perceived, to his delight, both German, Italian and Russian words. There was no doubt about the familiar polyglot language that he could hear directly through his headphones: a great proof that he had recovered the contact with his friends. His name also appeared in the song on two occasions. Both uncle Pelle, as the kids called him, and the surname Jürgenson.

Friedel thought that the recording was a hit. The singer mentioned his name on two occasions and Friedel immediately identified the person communicating as his old friend Arne Falck who had died in 1962.

Friedel's notes number 90 E.

I reproduce a part of the recording even if it is of poor quality and because it is an example of the many messages that came to Friedel via songs, in which the former text was manipulated. This encouraged him before Kjell Stensson's second visit.

TAKE 14

Falck sings and gets in the background accompanied by some male voices:

"Jag vet ... no stars ... att jag mar kein sterb ... jag kan tala med Pelle ... jag Jürgenson pa band ... har bor Falck ... och don't ... tra-la-la ..."

(I know ... no stars ... that I feel no death (not mortal) ... I can talk with Pelle ... I ... Jürgenson on tape ... here lives Falck ... and don't ... tra-la-la ...)

The discussions with the SBC led to the conclusion that they wanted to make a TV documentary about Friedel and his voices. Friedel and Arne Weise met several times and Weise was prepared to stand as the host.

Friedel was keen to participate in the arrangement of the program and was determined to refrain from broadcasting if the subject was presented in an incorrect light. He had heard that they wanted to offer a "natural" explanation for the voice phenomena. But by then it was clear that there was no natural explanation for these recordings, and Friedel began to suspect that probably the Swedish Radio (SR) experts would not dare say that the voices came from the dead. He realized that Kjell Stensson would have the last word.

Stensson was very busy but they had lunch together a few times before his second visit to Mölnbo, and a friendly relationship between the two men developed. That did not stop Stensson from revealing that he wanted a "harmless" explanation for the phenomenon. Friedel said it needed no explanation: the listeners could make their own opinion about the voices. Stensson believed that the type of program Friedel wanted to do would cause a huge shock in the world.

"And the Church?" Stensson asked.

"It will recover quickly from the shock," Friedel said. "After all, I think the Church believes in the existence of the soul after death."

Thus, Kjell Stensson came with his team, which, in addition to Robert Koistinen and journalist Daisy Karlberg, consisted of a few other technicians from the SBC. Even this time Stensson brought his own tape recorder, radio and sealed tapes.

They started with several microphone recordings on Stensson's apparatus. He said he had never heard that alien voices had been registered during control recordings at an insulated studio. When the tape was played, they heard a male voice whispering:

"Nonsense!" (Poppycock!)

They all agreed that they had really heard the voice and the tension rose in the group. The tape recorder was turned on again. Friedel said that he was happy that they understood the short and quick whisper "nonsense" which was heard in the general conversation.

Friedel reported on the occurrence in his attic in September 1959, when Carino was left alone in the room while he was on the telephone with his wife in the apartment below. When Friedel returned, after the telephone conversation with Monica, and played back the tape, the silence was broken by a male voice uttering:

"Carino kanner du mig?" (Carino, do you know me?)

Directly after this, we can hear how Carino jumped up on the chair next to the table with the tape recorder. The dog was panting noticeably, and, in the sound of this, a man's voice formed which said: "Carino ... har ar apparaten... kanner du mig?" (Carino ... here is the apparatus ... do you know me?

I have not heard this recording but I have heard what follows. The tape recorder was turned on and Koistinen said that he was interested in listening to the recording with the dog at a later time. Friedel continued his story briefly before the recorder was turned off. When the recording was played, a violent bang like someone hitting their hands hard, close to the microphone, could be heard. The blast had not been heard in the room, so it came as a complete surprise and they suspected that the speaker of the tape recorder might have been damaged.

According to Friedel, Stensson became noticeably upset and had no straightforward explanation for what happened. Maybe [it was] some kind of failure in the tape recorder, was his dubious comment. He thought that the bang, which had not been perceived in the room, was more remarkable than the voice proper which said "Nonsense! (Poppycock!)"

Later the blast was tested at the Max Planck Institute and played at different speeds. They considered the possibility that it was a kind of compressed communication, which, at the right speed, would disclose a message—a technology that was actually used during the Second World War when the so-called audio items contained encrypted messages. But that could not be disclosed. And they found no explanation for the sound.

At half past nine in the evening, they took a break. Friedel and Koistinen connected the radio and the tape recorder to make radio

Friedel's notes (F), number 27 and 28, and Professor Torbern Laurent's comment 29 and 30.

recordings. The others gathered downstairs for coffee. Koistinen hung up a room antenna and grounded the radio to the radiator.

Friedel put on headphones and started to gently turn the tuning knob. Koistinen sat with his finger on the tape recorder start button.

According to Friedel, he thought that he could hear Lena's signals on almost every frequency. He got a very strong feeling that his friends on the other side would do everything to help him.

They made short recordings to test and Koistinen turned on the tape recorder each time Friedel gave him notice with one hand. They listened attentively and, in the middle of radio interference, Friedel thought that he heard a man's voice say in Swedish: "Skrapledning!" (Debris line!)

The radio and the tape were running when he heard an opera singer singing the Tatjana aria from the opera "Eugene Onegin." Friedel reacted frantically and gestured toward Koistinen to start the tape recorder. Friedel was highly disturbed because during his time as an opera singer, he had repeatedly sung Onegin's role and the text both in German and in Russian.

It is a far too short recording, but Friedel suspected that there was something in it aimed directly at him. The singer sings in German and, when she is at the middle of the aria, a disturbance occurs and Friedel interpreted the utterances as:

"Friedrich, die Tote sieht allein!" (Friedrich, the dead see by themselves!)

Meanwhile, Friedel heard Lena's voice and excitedly whispered that he must continue recording. He became more and more nervous and they switched on and off.

Then, perhaps one of the most amazing recordings in Friedel's collection happened; one that is impossible to explain technically. It begins with a male voice that shouts:

"Contact!"

What happened next is almost incomprehensible. The piece of music that was being recorded plummeted down and subsided and at that very moment the same voice continued admonishing: "Friedel hoer mich... Friedel drehe unten!" (Friedel hear me ... Friedel turn /rotate/ under/below!)

For Friedel there was no doubt, "It's Felix Kersten!" he exclaimed.

Koistinen also heard the voice, called Friedel and reacted strongly. He ran upstairs and shouted at Stensson and the others:

"Come on up, Kersten is talking on the radio!"

Friedel had previously told them about Felix Kersten and that he had contact with him. They were all upset because nobody besides Friedel could identify Felix Kersten's voice. But everyone heard the recorded voice and what it said and they talked about it to each other.

But before you listen to the recording, I will tell you what happened with Kersten's wife Irmgard and their son Arno. Friedel wanted to find someone who really knew Felix Kersten's voice and could confirm that it was he on the tape. So he and Monica invited his wife to Nysund. It had been three years since Felix's death in 1960, and they had had no contact since then.

I met Irmgard Kersten at Friedel's home a few weeks before the second press conference on June 12, 1964. Later, I did an interview with her in German for the documentary *Last gate to eternity* by Rolf Olsen, one of Germany's top documentary filmmakers, with whom I worked for some time on Friedrich Jürgenson's story.

She told me that she suspected what had happened when Friedel and Monica invited her to Nysund, for the first time after her husband's death. Furthermore, she said that when Friedel seemed very disturbed during the lunch and asked if he could play a special recording for her, she understood that he had had contact with her husband.

He played up the first greeting from Kersten:
"Kersten ... Kersten ... hier Kersten ... Vorsicht, Aufpassen" (Kersten ...Kersten ... here Kersten ... Be careful, watch out!)

They heard the voice but wondered if he had really shouted "Kersten." So Friedel got the copy of the SBC tape and played it up:
"Friedel hoer mich ... Friedel drehe unten!" (Friedel hear me ... Friedel turn down!)

In my interview, Irmgard Kersten said that Arno jumped up and shouted: "Das ist Pappy's Stimme!" (That is daddy's voice!) And confessed that she had heart palpitations, also. There was no doubt; it was Felix's voice. She could even identify his Baltic accent.

It was such a powerful experience for her that she volunteered to participate in the upcoming press conference: something that made Friedel extremely happy.

TAKE 15 (LISTEN)[18]

Firstly, you will hear a short section of my interview with Irmgard Kersten. She told me that they had repeatedly visited Friedel and that Felix Kersten was very interested in the voice phenomena. She identified the voice and stated emphatically that she recognized his Baltic accent.

She also said that her son Arno jumped up from his chair and shouted, "Das ist Pappy's stimme!" You will hear the sound from the movie when she listened to the tape together with Friedel and commented on it. Then follows the recording of Kersten's voice:

"Friedel hoer mich ... Friedel drehe unten!" (Friedel hear me ... Friedel turn (rotate) under!).

According to Friedel, Kjell Stensson was obviously affected. His reaction reminded him of Arne Weise's. He could not sit still. He went around and repeated several times: "Strange, strange, I do not understand anything!"

Friedel was now convinced that Stensson had received the proof that the voices existed. But would it be enough for a radio or TV program? Very tense, they continued with a few more recordings.

Suddenly, they received a man's voice singing the famous Jewish song "Hava Nagila." Friedel was shaken. He even recognized that voice. He said it belonged to a friend named Gleb Bojevski who had died in 1945. Friedel declared that Bojevski identified himself and also mentioned the name Jürgenson in the Jewish text. He sang, according to Friedel, about the dead with completely different words, and in a segment you can hear the password, Mölnbo:

TAKE 16

"Bojevski ... Mölnboes spuck"

It was impossible for the people present to interpret the text but they could hear the singing and, with Friedel's assistance, maybe also the names. I suggest that you listen to these recordings through your headphones. Otherwise, it is difficult to interpret what is being said. In this case, it is a song and it is difficult to determine how much Bojevski's words differ from the original text but I admit that I can hear him sing: "Bojevski ... Mölnbos spuck."

The meeting ended late at night, and a gloomy and pensive Kjell Stensson took the tapes to test the recordings using the SBC's advanced technical equipment.

Then something happened that neither techniques nor sound experts in the world could offer any explanation for. Kjell Stensson found that it was a technical impossibility. A sound engineer pondered what the words "drehe unten!" (rotate under/below) could mean. In an impulse he played back the tape in the reverse mode.

You can clearly hear how the tones are distorted and the sound that was lowered is now rushing upwards. And there shouts the same voice, in Swedish and German, identified as Felix Kersten's voice:

TAKE 17 (LISTEN)[19]

The tape reel is turned and the music is played backwards (in reverse).
"Problem! Hoert ihr verkligen?" (Problem! Hear you really?)
For Friedel this was great progress for the confirmation of the voices' anomaly and how his friends on the other side could explore the technology.
During the spring and summer of 1964, negotiations were still ongoing between Friedel and the SBC. After the second press conference in Mölnbo, when Friedel, among other things, revealed before the world press that the voice phenomena would be presented on the Swedish Television, I made contact with the head of the SBC (Swedish Radio and Television at the time), Nils-Erik Baehrendtz. In my article in the *Aftonbladet* on June 7, I wrote:

> The selected tapes will be tested firstly at the Max-Planck Institute and their opinion will be decisive.
> "We will certainly agree on the forms of a transmission," said Baehrendtz. "This issue is very sensitive and we have carefully considered this. I have visited Jürgenson in the past but in the summer I will listen through selected parts of his material."

Kjell Stensson was a counselor, and his attitude to Friedel and the voices was of paramount importance. I published the text below in the *Aftonbladet* after my interview with Kjell Stensson and the uprising from the second press conference:

> Kjell Stensson: I cannot explain how the tracks on the tapes have occurred. I've investigated the matter very thoroughly and I am pleased that the Max Planck Institute will also address the problem. In my opinion, it is very possible that in the future Jürgenson will be regarded as a pioneer in a whole new field. But I cannot currently accept his own explanation for the phenomenon. I do not believe that the dead speak to us. But that's what I think. However, it does not make it any less important and interesting.

Kjell Stensson alleged, instead, that there is a large amount of undiscovered energy resources that we cannot detect with our five senses, even with far more sensitive scientific instruments. It is perfectly logical to think that a large number of discoveries remain to be made. A certain type of electrical impulses in the brain can be revealed in an encephalogram but there might exist another brain energy that is not recorded that way.

> Kjell Stensson: For my part, I am completely convinced that all the utterances and other strange sounds on the tapes come from Jürgenson himself, not from his conscious "I" but from his subconscious. They reflect his own worries, his desires, his repressed memories. And he himself honestly believes in his hypothesis.

More than 20 years later, Stensson was present in the audience when Lars Holmquist had Friedel as a guest at his television show, "This Is Your Life." Then, said Stensson:

> He is not very technical; thus, it can be taken out of the question that he is cheating. I cannot explain it. There's something on the tapes that should not be there. Intelligibility is not so good. I think we disagree about what we heard on the tape: it was a question of how to interpret what was said. What hit me most powerfully was that we sat in the room and talked and took long breaks but when we played back the tape, there was a bang, like when you slam a door. It could not have happened in the room because we would have jumped high. This bang is for me a concrete proof that something exists on the tape that should not be there. I cannot explain how it got there.

However, it was now decided that the TV project would be cancelled. Torbern Laurent, senior Professor at the High School of Technology in Stockholm, as I mentioned earlier, was now engaged. He had come to Nysund several times and became very interested in the voice phenomena. He told Friedel that he found it so exciting that after his upcoming retirement, he would devote himself to the voices' research.

But Friedel told me that Laurent had very poor hearing. Moreover, he had trouble staying awake when listening to the recordings.

One of the radio recordings in particular convinced Laurent that there were indeed strange voices on the tapes and that the individuals who spoke had insight into our human life.

Suddenly, a tenor sang in Swedish: "Farbror Churchill kontaktar Ove, tackar Ove ... " (Uncle Churchill contacts Ove, thanks Ove).

Friedel asked Laurent if he was also called Ove or if it alluded to something else. Laurent replied:

"It is very strange. In the college, we constructed two electric language devices, which, through electrical impulses, could induce human voices on tape. A little playfully, we called them Ove one and Ove two."

Laurent wanted to take a copy of the recording with him to test it at the High School. But the only way to copy it over to his tape recorder was to take it through the microphone. It was of poor quality and he could not hear the recording or Lena's whispering voice. When it became known that he was engaged in plans to broadcast voices on television, he declared in an interview that he was very disappointed, and that it must all have been suggestion.

But his interest was still there. This thing about "Ove" had shocked him. He suggested a testing of Friedel's tapes before the students. With great hesitation Friedel accepted because he felt it was important to show that this was not a question of suggestion. He invited two witnesses, the author Sture Loennerstrand and Ivan Troeng, technically very literate and with extensive knowledge of parapsychology.

Although they were at the High School of Technology, it happened that the tape recorder Laurent used was of very poor quality and the recordings could not be understood by those present. Therefore, the recording with "Ove" was played on Friedel's tape recorder and then an audio amplifier was also connected and it played so clearly that everyone could hear it! An upset conversation started in the audience, and Sture Loennerstrand turned spontaneously to Laurent and asked loudly: "Professor Laurent, do you still think that one can speak of suggestion?"

Laurent replied, troubled: "No, no, not in this case."

Finally, there were no 'shock' programs on radio or television. I never found out what the reason was. But probably, it was Stensson's idea about the origin of the voices that decided the matter.

7

THE WORLD PRESS PUT IN THEIR PLACE

After four years of research on the voice phenomena, Friedel decided to make his discovery public and on June 15, 1963, he called an international press conference as we saw above. The invitation went out through the news agencies and the effect was unexpected as an impressive crowd of journalists and photographers attended. Besides some Swedish magazines and newspapers, representatives from the news agencies, Reuters, UPI, Norsk Telegrambyra, and known magazines such as *Life, Times, Der Stern,* as well as the radio stations RIA (Italian radio), BBC (English radio), NBC (American radio) also attended.

Most of the journalists and correspondents had their own tape recorders of varying size, ranging from small notebooks to large professional appliances.

Swedish Television "Here is your life" 1980s

Swedish Television "Here is your life" 1980s

Press 1963

The world press stood up and spread the news of the Swedish artist who claimed to be able to record the voices of the dead on tape.

Friedel's book *The Voices from Space* had been approved for publication by Saxon and Lindstroem's but would not come out until the following year. He told me later that he was too impatient. He should have waited until the book was published and to use it when he presented his discovery. Moreover, he was completely alone.

At a second press conference in June 1964, he had two witnesses who had both recorded voices independently of his own, and who had heard relatives seeking contact. Also, Irmgard Kersten was there and shared her experience when she heard her dead husband, Felix Kersten, on Friedel's tape.

I was not present at the first press conference and therefore cannot comment on it. Hence, I have chosen to reproduce three articles that give an interesting picture of how the journalists perceived Friedel and his message.

They were written by Anne-Marie Ehrenkrona, one of Sweden's most famous writers who wrote an objective article published in the weekly magazine *Veckojournalen*; she was later my colleague at the *Aftonbladet*. Ivan Bratt, the local newspaper *Folket's* representative in the region and a strong doubter; a colleague of mine when I began my journalistic career at the newspaper, and Rune Moberg of the magazine Se (*Se & Hör*), one of the foremost chroniclers of the Swedish press who, with a few well-chosen words, could lift or sink celebrities.

By Anne-Marie Ehrenkrona

The world press is currently reporting on "space voices" in Mölnbo. It is said that voices from the four-dimensional world made themselves known through the radio and tape recorder. The human recipient is a cosmopolitan artist, Friedrich Jürgenson, who for four years has registered those voices on 80 tapes.

The techniques rule out forgery, but one still stands puzzled. The public shows great interest. Lots of young people find this phenomenon completely natural. Why should not someone in Mölnbo, a small community south of Stockholm, be able to get in contact with the invisible world with the help of technology, when Marconi, Einstein and Edison had already had evidence that it worked? Edison actually managed to record space voices on tape, but unfortunately only on wax rolls, which could not preserve the sound.

If the experiments in Mölnbo can continue in a scientifically satisfactory way, we would be facing, perhaps, the most epoch-making discovery. The timing is logical—cosmonauts have discovered space. The next stage is contact with the living creatures that are likely to be found outside the Earth. Maybe this will help us solve "the mystery of the human being." After the meteoric development of technology—150 years between the steam engine and the atomic bomb—it is time for the human being to come to the forefront and get a deeper explanation. What are these voices? What have they to say and how do they make themselves heard?

Jürgenson talks about spirits and assumes that the dead want to communicate with us. He has recognized voices that belong to deceased relatives, he says. But does it not give us a greater perspective to talk about Space Voices? The concept of spirits implies a taint of mediums and seánces, which is certainly not the case here. The recorded Mölnbo tapes have nothing whatsoever to do with the occult.

Jürgenson is a man with his feet on the ground and has not come to this conviction effortlessly. Even for a trained musical ear, the sounds are difficult to hear, so every radio message must be carefully checked after being registered on the tape recorder. The voices intervene in the regular programs—in opera arias, popular songs, speeches or messages—by changing the text, simply flushing over the real program. Some passwords indicate when the "four-dimensional" transmission begins. But the posts are usually so short and nicely adapted that they must be listened to over and over again in order not to be distorted.

To break away from the ordinary speech more easily, the voices use a mixed language and ungrammatical forms—German articles, for example, do not matter. "Vi är döda" can be called "wir är Toda" All seven languages that Jürgenson masters, happen in the registers.

The voices intervene as "pops"—intruders, and "copyists"—imitators. The former change music, songs, often choirs, and may even get instruments to sound like voices. The copyists change a number of regular programs so that a lecture in Hebrew suddenly changes to a personalized polyglot message to Friedrich Jürgenson.

It was these personal messages in the middle of the regular programs, which from the beginning got Friedrich Jürgenson interested in the voices' origin. Direct calls went to him, to the rest of the family and to their home, for the last four years. He even got messages of such a nature that they could not possibly be broadcast by living people.

It all started with "voices" heard through the microphone directly on the tape recorder. They only used radio later. Each message was recorded.

The fact that Jürgenson was selected lies on an unusually trained hearing—he is an opera singer—language, mind, interest, patience and a tolerant attitude toward life. He gave up a great job to devote himself entirely to the voice listening work in 1959, and the results are reported in a book, [*The Voices from Space*] which comes out this autumn.

But then, why do not the voices sound more official? Why is Friedrich Jürgenson in Mölnbo privileged? His own view is that we should all be able to hear them later, but the start must take place in silence and under objective control. No matter how convincingly the voices behaved, no one would take them seriously if they appeared on the Swedish Radio. We would immediately talk about pirate transmitters or political disturbances—blame the Russians and the Americans. Before space voices can be heard on a larger scale, people must become aware of their existence.

The contact is made possible by the radio waves, which they, the communicators, thanks to a higher frequency, amplify or throw away. Or more transcendently put: the radio waves pave the way for vibrations from a higher plane. In fact, the initiates are already talking about a newly opened bridge between two worlds: the invisible one and ours. And we expect a lot more sound-sensitive tapes for our tape recorders. Philosophy and Doctor of Theology John Bjoerkhem, ahead of his time when it came to parapsychology, was one of Jürgenson's encouraging contributors. He listened with interest to some "space recordings" just before his death this spring. He found the development completely natural and expected that this phenomenon would also be accepted as obviously as other technical phenomena, which we associate with on a daily basis.

If we presently hold to these new experiences, the world would be in a new era, which would once again change the scientific worldview. The consequences are dizzying. There is also talk of a new solar energy and magnetic energy, which surrounds the Earth, that may facilitate space transmissions of this kind.

Jürgenson's "space" theory is that the voices want to make our lives more pleasant by eliminating the fear of death, our great anxiety, and to teach us to live harmoniously in the present. Man, thus, continues to live without his body of matter. Real freedom comes only when you have death behind you. True socialism exists, according to the voices, first in the four-dimensional world, where no one condemns, threatens or preaches. The new worldview puts an end to hypocrisy and priestly anointing. Belief in hell and the punishing god is shattered forever—the individual finally discovers the god within himself.

According to Jürgenson, these spiritual intelligences present a new "doctrine of atonement," which frees people from all prejudiced "isms."

When we in these space broadcasts recognize the former famous Nazi and the Jew and hear them both coexist in all conviviality, then we have an example, which can finally bear fruit, he says.

Another prejudice, which we must let go of, is that man does not have the right to discover the invisible world, as Jürgenson puts it.

Anne-Marie Ehrenkrona, with good journalistic stringency, has understood Friedel's "space" theory, as she calls it. In addition, I think she also understands his philosophical reasoning.

When Friedel and I sat on one of our late nights with white wine in our glasses and could not be bothered to listen to more—at least not me—we found our souls on the same platform for a new-old philosophical thinking, which Ehrenkrona joined in her article also—the voices' existence is proof that there is neither heaven nor hell and that the devil, or the punishing God, do not exist other than in the imagination of the human being. Whereupon I formulated it in a short thesis that occasionally appeared in my philosophical reasoning with close friends, and repeated in what I wrote over the years: "God did not create man—man created the gods."

Next, I will offer you an article by Ivan Bratt, which I think is representative of most of the articles that were written after the press conference.

By Ivan Bratt

It is extremely rare that a Swedish private individual is visited by representatives and journalists from the world press as was the case on Friday at Nysund, in Mölnbo. The 60-year-old artist and opera singer Friedrich Jürgenson was interviewed about his astounding theories on life and death. Journalists and radio anchors listened with understandable skepticism to Mr. Jürgenson's statement and even if one cannot simply dismiss it as nonsense, one can probably without exaggeration say that he could not dispel the doubts of the visitors.

Mr. Jürgenson's statements that the dead are alive and that he can prove this by the tapes he recorded with voices from the dead now sent out into the world, were put forward.

What a few days ago was an unknown small Swedish country village, became the subject of an entire world wonder and debate. Undoubtedly, the crowd of skeptics will be the dominant one, at least in the current state of affairs, but still, if one looks soberly and realistically at the matter, one must wait to take a stand for or against. After this press conference, however, it should be inevitable that Mr. Jürgenson's theories and his tape recordings are subjected to both scientific and technical testing.

Another side of the matter is the purely philosophical one, which, however, should stand back until the mentioned tests have been done.

Jürgenson reported with passionate insight about his contacts with friends from the other side of the grave. His eagerness to convince his audience could not be mistaken, nor his absolute conviction that he is right. He accompanies his story about the messages and communications with the other side with lively gestures and there is something suggestive in the way in which he reports. He stated emphatically before the press that he had in his possession tape recordings that gave irrefutable proof of his theories.

There were, among others, a 15 minute speech by Adolf Hitler, recorded almost 20 years after his death, but, despite repeated calls, he refused to play this or other equally amazing tapes. The timing for this was not yet ripe, he said, but the visitors had to make do with other recordings, which in themselves are astonishing but not so interesting as Hitler's or Caryl Chessman's messages.

He said, however, that soon he would be ready to reveal all of his discoveries. He was hoping that the book he wrote on the subject would come out in a few months in Swedish, German, Italian and English, and then there would be nothing to prevent him from revealing the names of those who spoke to him or what they talked about.

He would certainly not disclose this to the press people, but emphasized that nothing prevented them from visiting him and listening to the "secret" recordings more privately.

A few days ago my newspaper *Folket* published a report on Mr. Jürgenson's dealings with the dead so there is no reason to go into that. Some new information in connection with Friday's press reception should be noted. The language the dead use in their messages is a kind of polyglot speech in which most European languages are represented.

On Christmas Day 1959, he heard for the first time a real message, which he was able to record on tape. It was, incidentally, a deceased friend, and after that he did not understand what was going on for a long time. But Mr. Jürgenson now clarifies that the dead have appointed him as a link to other living people.

The dead have 'radar' and can use it to see us walking around on the Earth. They can also see and hear what we think and feel. With this radar, they send their messages carried through radio waves to Jürgenson's radio. The dead are in the fourth dimension and want to have contact with us but we cannot reach them from the third dimension in which we live.

In simplified form, the problem may be represented by the metaphor of a movie screen. We see and hear those involved in the film but cannot reach them. Now, the dead have built a kind of "bridgehead" between the third and the fourth dimensions with messages to us. Mr. Jürgenson stated, on a direct question, that he feels authorized to forward the message from the dead to us, the living.

On the other hand, all the physical, material and ethical concepts have ceased and all have the same starting point. No sorrow and no pain, no worries but only joy and mirth, this is life in the fourth dimension. Through Mr. Jürgenson and his "bridgehead," the dead want to tell us, the living, how things really are regarding life and death, and that we have nothing to fear but can wait in happy anticipation.

They want to teach us what they are after death: something that should definitely give us a much happier world to live in. We are trapped in time, which causes misconceptions. We see everything against a tight background and this means that we cannot see the truth as it really is and as it is perceived in the fourth dimension.

An account of the dead's ability to move puts our own world speed records in deep shadow. According to Jürgenson, movements in the fourth dimension take place in a kind of death ship or teleship. The dead can move in the frequencies with incredible speed. He himself had heard their call when they were over Strängnäs (ten kilometers south of Stockholm) and two minutes and forty-one seconds later they were already over Jokkmokk in the north of Sweden, a distance of 800 km.

The fourth dimension is the prototype of everything, and all that we have here in the third dimension is only the echo from the fourth. This applies to music, art, technology and generally to everything except war, enmity, hatred, and the like that we in the third dimension create for ourselves. The fourth dimension is, in other words, the reward we get subsequently to our probation in the third. This is what the dead tell us through their bridge, which they otherwise call Portanova, and which Mr. Jürgenson claims to have been appointed to convey to us.

Thus, the information provided at the famous press conference was rather hard to digest and as previously mentioned, it was received with obvious skepticism. The impression remains that there must be something there, but the big question is what is it? Maybe we will eventually get the answer, maybe not.

In any case, none of the participants at Friday's press meeting received an answer, but the fact that they do not know what to believe may be confirmed by the fact that most representatives of the major foreign radio and newspaper companies will return to Mr. Jürgenson's home in a few days to further research the matter. A tape recorded during this conference will then be played to hear if some message came through during the press visit.

Ivan Bratt clearly expresses his doubts, but he still reproduced Friedel's thoughts and ideas about life in the fourth dimension in a respectful manner. Nevertheless, I thought that Friedel's attempts to make us, living people, believe that life after death in the fourth dimension is joy and merriment was a downright dangerous message. Both Arne Weise and I pointed out to Friedel that he took on himself a great responsibility when he talked about this. Because if a man living in difficult circumstances believes in this bright picture of life after death, suicide is very close at hand. Friedel's explanation was not exactly convincing, but he said that if he interpreted his friends on the other side correctly, those who deprived themselves of life would not have the opportunity of any soul migration, rebirth, according to the rules that apply to reincarnation. And that might be a little daunting.

Rune Moberg (1912-1999), of the newspaper '*Se*,' chose, as always, a bantering tone when he wrote about his experience at Friedel's in Mölnbo.

Rune Moberg visiting Friedel's home. The title of the article is "A nervous, frantic female voice singing a gruesome melody."

By Rune Moberg

The house is ghostly, there hidden in the forest, with a little lake that no one has heard of, except residents of Mölnbo who have it near their building plot. A shaggy poodle runs to meet us and we understand that we have the honor of being escorted by Carino who sees spirits where the master only hears voices.

Dad himself is a tanned handsome man in his sixties, though he looks younger, who speaks with many lively accents. He was born in Odessa in Russia and has gone far and wide before he had a sanctuary in Sormland, a county which lies south of the capital Stockholm where he started a family with a Swedish dentist.

If I were a talkative spirit, I would with small happy screams throw me over this environment and this exuberant and nervy man named Friedrich Jürgenson who is a mixture of Russian and Swedish, and German, of liveliness, charm, openness and gambling imagination.

It started when he heard voices in the room. They called on him from a very definite corner of the room. There was nobody. But the poodle Carino stood in front of "none" and wagged his tail, just like he always does with all visitors.

It continued that Friedrich Jürgenson took up these voices on tape. The room where he receives spirits and journalists, is cluttered with four tape recorders—one being worn-out—two radios, one the size of a bureau, a microphone on a stand and tapes, tapes, tapes stacked in piles along the walls. Then there is a number of paintings, almost all with antique motifs. Friedrich Jürgenson is namely a painter and he has painted much of Pompeii before the spirits came and laid hands on him so the excavated Italian antiquity lost a conscientious, gifted but a little color pale, portrayer.

Tensions rise while Friedrich Jürgenson talks. I look longingly at the tape, which he has already placed on a tape recorder. The tape has captured the voices that arose directly in the room, not in the radio. On this tape, says Mr. Jürgenson, a dead friend comes speaking. He came forward a day after he died. He was a specialist in yoga. He has written a worn German book on yoga exercises that I turn in my hand. And Mr. Jürgenson starts the tape.

First we heard two deep breaths. Then, clearly, pronounced by a deep male voice:

"Sa kalt!" (So cold!)

So we hear on the tape how Jürgenson is sitting and talking with some friends. It sounds quite natural and it is, too. But suddenly a woman's voice breaks in and says:

"Tanner! Tanner!"

The voice has a clear Finish-Swedish accent. No one in the room had mentioned Tanner. A little further on a man's voice says:

"Tanto partis!"

There were several futile words from the spirit world on the tape. Then Mr. Jürgenson apparently played back the tape for the people present. And after that interruption, it continued to run and one of the guests stood in front of the microphone and asked: "Who is Tanner?"

"Vem ar Tanner? Var ar det sa kallt nagonstans?" (Who is Tanner? Where is it so cold?)

He repeated the questions several times and eventually his voice got an impatient tone:

"I don't believe in this! If I don't hear anything on the tape from you now, I consider it to be phoney."

So much, he said.

The tape was played. And the lady who had said Tanner kept quiet. But when the questioner for the fifth or sixth time asked: "Var ar det sa kallt nagonstans?" (Where is it so cold?) the deep male voice came back and said in German:

"So kalt ist in dir." (So cold is in you.)

The skeptical inquirer who got this astonishing reply was the well-known radioman Arne Weise. He went plodding from the place.

The tape recorder kept spinning, and spirit voices filled the room: enigmatic, elusive and sometimes stupid, like when his son Peter came out of the toilet. They had guests and the tape had clearly registered the conversation of the people in the room. Then a strange voice broke into:

"Pillemansen har kackat" (Pillemansen has defecated).

I heard it clearly.

Firstly, Jürgenson said, what adult would want to embarrass a boy that way? Secondly, we have not called Peter, Pillemånsen, for several years, because he hated the nickname.

So far, we had only listened to tapes that had picked up other voices directly from the room.

And this is just the beginning, said Mr. Jürgenson, who stated: "Wait until you hear the radio recordings. When I spent some time with the tape recordings directly from the room, the voices started saying: "Take the radio!" Eventually, I figured I would set up the radio and connect the tape recorder. And then it began in earnest. Choirs sang directly to me: opera arias that I have known for a long time, since I was an opera singer, and suddenly the text changed with a message to me. The spirits went into the regular program, took it over and sang their own text. It is fantastic. And that's the proof that I'm not bluffing. Who am I? How can I get orchestras and choirs across Europe to sing special lyrics to me? You can listen for yourself. You will also listen to a ten-minute speech by Adolf Hitler and a song that I think Eva Braun, Hitler's wife, is singing."

By that time, I had heard so many voices that I just nodded and said thank you very much. Hitler or yoga enthusiasts, arias or Pillemansen—everything was just amazing. But I realized that when I got to hear a great opera chorus sing directly to Mr. Jürgenson, my lingering skepticism faded.

God help me, I began to believe. And it felt good. Imagine that you do not die when you die. And the spirits seem to be well wherever they are staying. They sing and joke.

I prepared myself for the decisive evidence: tape recordings from the radio.

I have an assistant on the other side, said Mr. Jürgenson while he prepared the tape. Her name is Lena. She whispers to me when and how to tune the radio. Now you will hear something miraculous. A saxophone, or whatever it is, suddenly starts talking to me, he added.

The first radio recorded tape starts to spin. It beeps and whines like when you set up a radio anywhere on the scale, without tuning in any station, and the reception conditions are good and all European stations broadcast in full. You hear several stations at once. Sometimes one penetrates up into the foreground; sometimes another one. And all the while, a merciless interference tone sounds like a kind of dental drill into the ear that one must try to endure.

Somewhere in the jumble I hear a jazz band. And an alto sax (I guess) frees itself and does a solo figure.

"Did you hear what it said? Mr. Jürgenson is eager: "Jag kan tala med Pelle hos Jürgenson på band" (I can talk with Pelle at Jürgenson on tape). It's clear, is it not true?"

Let me hear it again, I said.

I was positive. I WANTED the saxophone to talk. But for me it just played. May I hear the chorus again? I said. Yes, but first we shall hear Hitler, said Mr. Jürgenson.

A dark male voice, which resembled Hitler as he would have spoken if he had been older and calmer, fought about the sound with a piano concerto by Mozart and strong interference.

Hitler began like this (translated from German): "If you do not want to stink on the Earth and often stand in the middle of time and swear reparation, then the one who takes on all the guilt is the father of his time."

This is what Mr. Jürgenson had listened to and what I also thought I heard. We also thought that Hitler said: "What does the state need? Malenkov." And suddenly: "Beware of Myrdal!"

I was crawling into the device to get some sense out of it. I tried to listen through the interferences. I tried to figure out what it could be if it were not the dead Hitler. A Russian propaganda broadcast in German? Why is he talking so meaninglessly? I asked Mr. Jürgenson. Whatever one may say about Hitler, he could express himself.

The dead, explained Jürgenson, have not the same kind of consciousness as we do, and not the same conceptual realm. What we think is pointless can have a deep meaning for them.

I do not know what to believe. However, I know what I should not believe. I do not think Friedrich Jürgenson is a deliberate hoax. Would he, if so, wait nearly four years to tell the world what he has heard?

And who dares to say that I heard correctly and he heard wrongly? His ear has more practice than mine, which suffered badly from the interferences. On the other hand, there is a dangerous source of error when you sit and listen to such a mixed noise. Just as it is, the soundscapes sound together into a phrase that no one has said, it just happens to be a fusion of sounds. You may have experienced it yourself. You hear a singer sing in a language that you do not know. Suddenly, you think he is saying something in pure Swedish. You get impulses of what he really sings and the rest is filled by your own sense of listening.

Such things can happen to anyone. And for someone like Jürgenson, who somehow masters eight languages and thinks that the spirits speak a mixture of these languages, the risks are great. He with his open mind and his general attitude might think that he hears phrases that are addressed to him. If you sit and WANT to hear "Mälarhöjden" or "Mölnbo" from a spawn of voices and songs and disturbances, probably it does not have to be long before the expected calls arrive.

In this way, Mr. Jürgenson has been unlucky. The clear voices, the ones about which there is no doubt, are on tapes recorded in the room. They are just voices and since it would not be a difficult art to prepare a tape that way, these simple other voices that address the people in speech have far less scientific evidential value than a single tape, where a large foreign choir undeniably sings a message to Jürgenson.

I did not manage to hear any such message. Others with more trained ears may succeed. Jürgenson is convinced. He now knows that the dead are alive. He knows that Hitler socializes with Jews and Stalin has retained his sense of macabre joke. Hitler makes himself constantly reminded.

The spirits fly in formations, says Mr. Jürgenson. They get special assignments after death. Those who have behaved badly in life on the Earth may get the worst jobs. The hardest thing is to take care of people who died very suddenly: for example, in a car accident. Hitler must take care of such cases.

Imagine waking up when you are being taken away in a car accident, open the dead eyes and the first thing you see bending over is …

Strangely enough, there is a lot of banal old spiritualist stuff in Mr. Jürgenson's new faith. But here we have heard something new and strange, we understand that. We have heard about Hitler's new job. In addition, we have heard the strongest argument for driving carefully.

Yes, Rune Moberg stated that what was recorded in the room with a microphone produced clear voices, about which, in his opinion, there was no doubt. But he thought that it might be possible to tamper with the recordings. At the same time, he took position and averred that he did not think that Friedel was a scam. So who would have tampered with them? But what eliminates his reflection on the possibility that the tapes could have been prepared, is the fact that the best recordings were made on sealed tapes from the Swedish Radio, both in the case of Arne Weise and Kjell Stensson. Thus, we can completely exclude the possibility that the tapes had been tampered with.

The second press conference

I visited Friedel for the first time in May 1964, when the book *The Voices from Space* was released. I did not return to Mölnbo before the second press conference on June 12. The invitation had gone out in good time and the journalists who met up seemed well informed. The book had created a lot of interest but Friedel was not happy with it. He thought that it had been a kind of rush job and he was forced to accept that the publishing house had made some changes, which he felt were unnecessary. He had already begun writing a new book.

We were a group of perhaps 40 expectant journalists and photographers. At the first press conference, Friedel had just spoken about the remarkable recordings: among others, the ones with Hitler who appeared in a long monologue. Friedel had promised to come back and even invite journalists to personal visits to hear this and a whole lot more.

The big attraction were the messages from Felix Kersten that would be played while his wife Irmgard and son Arno participated and could testify to the authenticity of the voice. Friedel had received assistance, regarding the technicalities, of a good friend who linked a sensitive filter to the recording equipment.

Besides Irmgard Kersten and her son, Elna Falck was also present. She had been married to Arne Falck, who sang "that he was with Jürgenson on tape" two years after his death. And then a third person, photographer Claude Thorlin who became a good friend of Friedel and me and made his own recordings, which in some cases were better than many of Friedel's. It was Claude Thorlin who took the single picture on a flickering TV screen with a Polaroid camera, which captured Friedel's face while he was being buried in Höör, October 19, 1987. In 1969, his psychic wife Ellen had succeeded in capturing the spirit girl Caimy's face floating above the tape recorder when he and his wife were making a recording.

The image was so sensational that Sweden's world famous photographer Lennart Nilsson, who, among other things, photographed fetus development in a human uterus, examined the picture. He could not point to any kind of falsification and could not provide an explanation for the photo.

Claude Thorlin got a prominent role in Friedel's press conference. For here was a man who, irrespective of Friedel's, made recordings in which the messages of the voices could still be linked to Friedel.

As I can vouch for Friedel's credibility, I can do the same regarding Claude. We knew each other before Friedel's time when he, as my photographer, took part in some jobs, both for the local newspaper *Folket* and later the *Aftonbladet*.

Friedel started the press conference by telling a little about his background and then he went over to the demonstration of recordings that he had made with famous people and scientists. The sound system worked well and through it came the clearest voices I heard from the recordings with Arne Weise. And there was no doubt that my colleagues heard how Arne Weise, the famous Swedish radio and television journalist, got an answer to his question.

When I made the first report in Mölnbo and made contact with Arne Weise, I thought that it would have been a big shot if he had participated. I do not know the reason why he did not. Maybe Friedel never asked him.

Next, it was time for Felix Kersten. Friedel briefly described him and their friendship from younger years. He presented Irmgard and Arno and one could almost touch the tense atmosphere that prevailed when everyone started their tape recorders to catch the dead Kersten's voice and his living wife's confirmation that it was he who spoke, or rather, shouted. Even at this demonstration, everybody must have been aware of the inexplicable technical phenomenon when the tape was reversed, and although it was the same voice, the message content was completely different, albeit logical and complementary to the initial message.

In a congregation of about forty heated journalists who generously shared their views, both in English, German and Italian, it became a little chaotic in the room. I noticed that Friedel looked quite pleased. He had accomplished what he was looking for; interest, curiosity, commitment and utter shock!

In the midst of this, requests were made to Friedel to make a recording under controlled conditions: something that he expressed doubts about. In any case, he wanted to continue the presentation, and then it was time for Claude Thorlin.

Claude explained how his wife Ellen after the press conference at Friedel's in 1963, had read in the local newspaper about a man from Soermland who recorded mysterious voices. The headline was: "The dead contact me by radio." And they referred to famous people in SBC who had visited him and stated that there was no natural explanation for the phenomenon.

Ellen had often affirmed that she had had psychic experiences since childhood and believed in life after death; therefore she was very interested in visiting this man and in listening to the recordings. As a result Claude contacted Friedel and then they were invited to Mölnbo.

During the evening they listened to various recordings and became immediately convinced that Friedel had undoubtedly discovered a revolutionary opportunity for communicating with, as Claude put it, an "extraterrestrial" living area. He said that Friedel with his audio tapes "struck a chord in the compact wall of negative skepticism and spiritual complacency. A new path had been opened and many would surely follow it."

Fortunately, Claude's speech did not reach the point where the congregation lost interest. And when he prepared his tape recorder after informing that he and his wife had already received alien voices on their new tape recorder in the first few days, the tension rose. I had not heard his recordings before, so I too was excited about what was to come.

Claude said that the first really clear recording occurred after a few days when they visited a good friend in Värmland and took the tape recorder with them. They sat and talked about the voices. Good friend Joel wondered if the distance from a (normal) voice source to the microphone had any major impact on the sound quality. Claude answered that indeed it had and explained that the farther away you go and even if you shout, the weaker your voice is heard on the recording. When they played back the band, a clear male voice was heard during a pause in the conversation and it interjected: "Hunden ... den kan ju se."

TAKE 18 (LISTEN)[20]

"Hunden ... den kan ju se." (The dog ... it can see)

I heard the voice, and certainly most of the correspondents in the room, also. It all seemed a little incomprehensible but Claude tried with an interpretation:

> We had discussed the "sound phenomena" and talked about how well we can "hear." The voice, which seemed to break in Danish, apparently wanted to convey that some animals, perhaps especially the dog, have an ability to perceive the "invisible" which far exceeds the human ability ... that dogs see deeper into the hidden.

Eventually, Claude tried radio recordings and gave an example of how not only a voice was heard but that there was a direct connection to Friedel and Mölnbo, too. In addition, we could hear a chorus and it was most likely a radio broadcast but the text had been changed, another phenomenon that Friedel talked about which recurs often. The choir's song was the carrier itself and it was heard very clearly. This was a recording without any involvement from Friedel himself.

TAKE 19

You can hear the keywords, Mölnbo and Friedel.

"Vi gar pa vandringsvag till Mölnbo ... dar Friedel bor" (We go on the trail to Mölnbo, where Friedel lives).

Thorlin also played several short recordings:

TAKE 20 (LISTEN)

"Waren die Tote!" (It was the dead!)

There were also short direct calls from the other side: (It was/is the dead)

Claude Thorlin's appearance had had from Friedel's point of view, a clearly positive effect on the press assembly. And again, there were requests for a direct recording by Friedel. He felt that if he did not accept, the press conference would probably fail. An Italian and a Swedish journalist were the most insistent.

Friedel pointed out that with so many people present, it would be difficult to objectively verify which ones were alien voices and what had been said in the room. Against a promise to have some silence and that those present would not talk to each other but produce only natural sounds like throat clearing, clicks from the tape recorders start, the scraping of the feet and so on, they would attempt a recording. These were sounds that, according to his concept, could be used as carrier waves and induce voices on the tape recorder.

He made an approximately three minutes long recording during which it was guaranteed that no one said anything. And undoubtedly everyone present swore on that.

Those who had their own tape recorder, turned it on at the same time as Friedel. And when Friedel played the recording, after a minute of little rustling and other sounds, a voice speaking in Swedish came through and said: "Elna ... arbetet!" (Elna ... the work!)

Mrs. Falck spoke up. She was agitated and had tears in her eyes. "That was Arne, my late husband, my name is Elna!"

Indeed something very interesting had occurred. Was there the same voice on the other tape recorders that had started simultaneously with Friedel? As a matter of fact, I did not get a clear idea of what had happened because then they spoke all together. The conclusion I drew was that the voice was heard on Friedel's tape recorder only. I cannot guess what the meaning of the voice was but probably it was something on the lesser side.

There were several short recordings via microphone. Suddenly a female voice uttered in German what Friedel with his perfect hearing could hear and told us:

"Listen, contact!"

Maybe a little bit of suggestion, but he played it several times and it was easy to hear exactly what he claimed.

The atmosphere in the room was highly intense and there was also great interest. But Friedel realized, once again, that the recording via microphone was difficult with so many people present; thus, he suggested that they could try to record something via a connection to the radio. Of course, they were all interested in the opportunity!

There were two recordings and I must say that, for me, what was said was not clear until Friedel gave his version of it. Unfortunately, I think that my colleagues reacted the same way because the disturbances were strong and maybe it takes a trained ear like Friedel's to interpret what was said: and good headphones.

Friedel repeated several times what the voices had said before he played back the tape, and perhaps a little bit of suggestion might have taken place. I will quote Friedel's interpretation from his book *Voice Transmissions with the Deceased*:

> A loud babble of voices arose and I suggested turning the radio on. Under these circumstances, the audience could not cause acoustical interference on the recordings.
>
> In short; we obtained two recordings that could be heard by practically everyone present. The first was an older male voice that said in somewhat subdued tones and monotonously:
>
> "Listen to the dead at the press conference ... we are contacting Mölnbo."
>
> Afterwards, a clear female voice sang. We first thought that we were listening to a radio broadcast, but when we listened more carefully, we could hear the following German and Swedish text:
>
> "Little Claude, Freddie ... listen to Ra-di-Le-na!"
>
> The word radio and Lena were fused; I have often received such "synchronized" abbreviations, i.e. "apparadio", a contraction of an apparatus and a radio, or Moelnbro, instead of Mölnbo and bro (bridge).

The press conference ended around midnight and probably I was one of the journalists who went home with curiosity about what this could really mean but I was also skeptical.

Unfortunately, I have no newspaper clippings from my article after this press conference but I remember that I wrote that I had a strong feeling that the man deserved full credibility and that he was convinced of what he was talking about—that he was going to build a bridge from us to another dimension of life, thus, to the dead. For several reasons, the whole thing had so strongly caught my interest that I decided to accompany him not only journalistically but also personally on the trek across the bridge.

There is no doubt that Friedel got huge publicity. Nowadays, when I read some of what was written, I discover that some journalists wanted to appear as doubters to their readers. But at the same time, they could not hide from the inexplicable experience at Friedel's house along with a group of colleagues and witnesses who claimed to hear voices from close relatives, dead for several years.

8

THE SCIENTIFIC TESTS

After the second press conference, people from both Sweden and other European countries phoned and wanted to come and visit him for different reasons. Some were serious researchers while others were people who had lost a close relative. They wanted his help to seek contact, and there were also journalists from near and far.

Friedel received messages on his tape recorder almost daily. He often phoned me to say that they had broken through, and I had to come and listen. And I did. Many times I also left Mölnbo with a slight sense of disappointment because of the bad sound quality of the messages rather than my interaction with Friedel.

He was always in good shape when I went to the studio and there was the smell of his pine aftershave, which was kept in a small green bottle with a cork in the shape of a cone. He wanted me to smell as good as he but I never use aftershave. So, one day when he came back from Pompeii after one of his many visits, he brought me a bottle and I rubbed my face with it before a party. In the house the scent of pine needles and Gordon's gin spread everywhere and it remained for several weeks. My dear wife Mona threatened to move out to the stables if I continued with this facial. She was with me many times at Mölnbo and became Monica and Friedel's dear friend. But when we got inside the door, she winked at me and frowned at the scent of Friedel's aftershave.

Sometime after the press conference, Friedel and Monica fled away to Italy and Pompeii. There, he had a shock. The ancient city, perhaps one of Italy's main cultural monuments, was growing again. A third of the old city was about to turn into a jungle. The devastating weed invasion threatened to destroy a part of the numerous paintings and mosaic floors.

Friedel took advantage of all their contacts, including those in the Vatican and asked, or rather threatened, to do a documentary film about "Pompeii's second downfall," as he called it. At the Italian Ministry of Culture, that was responsible for this cultural treasure, he was obviously speaking to deaf ears but the Vatican stood up again for the Swedish artist who had done such an excellent job during the excavation of the tomb of the Apostle Peter and had painted several portraits of Pope Pius XII. The Vatican fully supported him but the condition was that he himself had to finance the film.

It is unknown whether the new Pope Paul VI (1897-1978) had anything to do with this attitude because on June 21, 1963, there was a change in the Vatican. Pope Paul stepped down from the throne to show his human face and granted the Swedish artist advantage by giving him permission to make several spectacular movies. Maybe Paul also glanced at his predecessor Pius XII's portraits and thought that he could probably ask the Swedish artist to paint his portrait too, which indeed happened.

What surprised us most was that this artist known in the world, not least in Italy, for alleged contacts with the dead, had become convinced through the latter that neither heaven nor hell exists and nevertheless, was so well received by the Catholic Church.

In 1970, I followed Friedel to Rome. By then he had been negotiating with Swedish Television about documenting the excavation of Pompeii, which would have begun in 1966. His good relationship with the TV boss Nils-Erik Baehrendtz, who had met Friedel several times but never managed to implement a television program about the voices, got the SBC to fund the project.

During this wonderful visit to Pompeii, Friedel had access to a radio. One night when he was recording on his portable tape recorder, all other sounds seemed to disappear and a female voice shouted loud and clear, that she came from the realm of the dead: "Here is the realm of the dead ... Monica, Friedrich is strongly decided ... first dispute between the dead." Clear but nevertheless, hard to understand. This is a common feature of voices of which we ignore the antecedents. The voice sounds very anxious about the contact.

This recording became a small trump card for Friedel when he traveled to Northeim in West Germany a few weeks later. He had agreed to meet with Hans Bender at the Deutschen Institut für Feldphysik where they would go through a large number of Friedel's recordings.

Next, you can hear the recording from Pompeii, which was probably of crucial importance for Hans Bender's continued interest. It is also important to point out that he was not alone in judging Friedel's recordings; he was surrounded by a group consisting of, among others, Doctor in Physics Burkhard Heim and sound engineer W. Schott, PhD student G. Vilhjalmsson, and observer Dr. F Karger from Munich.

TAKE 21

Here Friedel participates and explains what he hears. The voice shouts:

"Hier ist der Reich der Toten ... Monica, Freddie ist kraftig beslut ... erster Disput der Toten." (Here is the realm of the dead ... Monica, Freddie is strongly decided ... first dispute of the dead.)

The voice is very clear and we understand what she shouts: (Here is the land of the dead, Monica, Friedrich is strong decided ... first dispute of the dead.)

Hans Bender was very impressed with the recording precisely because Friedel was now in a completely different environment, far from the "epicenter" Mölnbo. Friedel was very pleased with the visit and the reception he got or, better said, the voices got. Then, Bender paid several visits to Mölnbo and the fact that his interest was great was confirmed when he returned with his big team in May 1970. One of the recordings they made was regarded by Bender as the main event in parapsychology.

Bender decided that there would be controls at the Max Planck Institute in Munich. There, the originals of the choral songs containing a message directly addressed to Friedel would be subjected to careful review. Among others, Arne Falck's song and the song from Friedel's friend Gleb Bojevski. Some of these choral songs contain several keywords such as Mölnbo, Lena and radio. And Friedel interpreted that it was his assistant Lena who sang with the choir.

Here are some of the recordings that Hans Bender and his research team listened to. I listened to them on several occasions at Friedel's house, and they ranked high on the scale. This song is difficult to follow if you do not have Friedel's text, i.e., interpretation, in front of you.

But one thing is clear, the choir uses a Swedish closing word: "Farväl" (Farewell!).

TAKE 22

A choir sings in Swedish, German and Italian:

"Bambino på bandet, hor, da kommen andre bande ... Apparaten sitz ... Ah! Ho! Mölnbo!" (A rooster's crow is heard). Alter Hahn ... Igrajem mit pa bandet pa radio. Oh, da sitz ein duktig pojke, han duktig. Oh, dann sint (or singen) wir ja mit Lena ... Dann ist man immer gut! Farväl!"
(Children of the band, listen, other bands will ... the unit is—aah! Hoe! No! Mölnbo ... (a rooster crows) Old Rooster! ... Play on tape and radio. Oh, there is a good boy, he good. Oh, then we are (possibly: we sing) with Lena ... which is always good! Farewell!).

According to Friedel, this was another greeting from his childhood friend, yoga teacher Boris Sacharow. They tested this voice against the voice, which after inhaling says "So kalt!" (So cold!). Bender noted that there were similarities, but the conditions were such that it could not be fully established that it was the same voice.

TAKE 23

The voice speaks in German/Swedish and we can clearly hear him say his name at the end:

"Gruss, spielt tennis ... fastar ni nok/nog?" Boris Sacharow (Greetings, play tennis ... are you fasting enough? Boris Sacharow).
This message was for Friedel yet another proof that he had contact with his dead friend Boris Sacharow and other people who were on the other side. Friedel and Monica were vegetarians and occasionally went through a brief period of fasting. One of those was taking place when Boris Sacharow made contact. Hans Bender took this very seriously.
During the same recording session, Boris' name is mentioned in another context.

TAKE 24

In the midst of the radio interference, a rising voice says:

"Hoert pa band hopsi ... voice hört Boris, Freidel (?) heute abend på b-a-a-n-d" (Listen to band hopsi ... voice listen to Boris, Freidel (?) tonight on t-a-a-p-e!).

Of course, Bender and his team tested the clear recordings with Arne Weise and it was agreed that the voices were there and that they said what Friedel claimed they said.

More on Bender's scientific tests

When some of Friedel's recordings of August 1964 were tested at the Freiburg Institute, a part of which is reported above, a recording was made at Friedel's rooms at the Hotel Sonne. He was interviewed by Hans Bender. The interview was recorded on two Uher Report recorders.

Although only two words came from an alien voice, Bender thought that this was an extremely impressive example of the existence of the voices and of their strange awareness of what was going on, in addition to the fact that he himself was present and had control over what was being done.

Besides Bender, two other scientists participated in the interview, G Vilhjalmsson from Iceland and the observer from the Max Planck Institute in Munich, Dr Friedehart Karger.

Friedel informed that he had copied a few tapes on SBC's behalf and that during the copying an unfamiliar voice appeared while the voice on the tape became weaker. Hans Bender remarked that it was noticeable that when an unfamiliar voice occurred, it lowered the volume of other sounds.

Bender: "Yeah, now we have also noticed that the sound quality of the tapes."

FJ: "Yes."

Bender: " ... has changed. It was also highly surprising for Heim and Schott that an audio tape, uh ... can so strongly lose in intensity."

Karger: "You know; it cannot be explained."

Bender: "Was it the first time?"

FJ: "Yes, the first time."

Bender: "When copying audio tapes which words have changed?"

FJ: "I asked Kjell Stensson if he had experienced anything like this before, and he said that it was technically impossible for voices to get into already recorded voices."

Foreign male voice: "VON WO?" (may be translated as "Where from?")

The voice was on both machines, which reinforced the phenomenon, but in no way gave any explanation for its emergence.

The recording was analyzed at the Max Planck Institute and a speech spectrogram was prepared which showed that the voice was there and that it did not come from any of the people present.

There was no doubt that interest in the voice phenomena among scientists continued. Different groups visited Friedel to listen and make their own recordings. He was not always fond of visitors' experimentation. At one point he protested when a recording from the radio was made directly with the microphone placed in front of the radio's speaker. A technique Friedel's followers came to use when sound from both the radio and the room seemed to make it easier for the voices to penetrate into a carrier wave.

The recording was made on October 31, 1965, in Nysund.

Present: Friedel, Monica, Buckard Heim from Freiburg Institute and his wife Gerda and Dr W. Schott.

Heim: "Silence! Recording 12." This recording is done late in the evening of October 31, 1965, at the same house with the same people present. This recording is taken up by Schott via microphone while Jürgenson and Heim record from the radio.

"Attention!"

Jürgenson: "What do you hear [from] here?"

Haben Mer kommerzband" (get more commercial tapes. "Mer" [Swedish] more).

Jürgenson: "That's not good ... the sound becomes distorted."

Schott: "I just want to pick it up from the radio."

Jürgenson: "Ahh, it gets a bad record ... you hear ... hear you ... It damages the whole thing. Do not do this."

Alien female voice, this time in a whisper: "Wie werden noch mehr banden" (We will get even more tapes).

Jürgenson: "certainly not ... ah, ah ... I do not go on" (He switches off the tape recorder).

Hans Bender FJ 1973

Hans Bender FJ Nysund

Hans Bender, Gisela Beckedorf and FJ 1973

Six years after the preparatory studies of Friedel's tapes in Freiburg in 1964, and after a few short visits to Mölnbo, the great experiment was carried out. It made Hans Bender state frankly when I interviewed him that "This was the biggest thing that had happened so far in parapsychology."

In January 1971, he outlined the experiment in the scientific journal *Zeitschrift für Parapsychologie Grenzgebiete und der Psychologie* of which he was the chief editor. As a scientist, he was somewhat more restrained in his statement. But the existence of the voices could no longer be doubted. Under the heading "Zur Analyse aussergewöhnlicher Stimmphänomene auf Tonband" (Analysis of extraordinary voice phenomena on audiotape), Bender summarized:

> Since 1959, the Swedish painter and film director Friedrich Jürgenson has reported extraordinary voice phenomena on tape. He was the first to report such findings. He interprets these voices as "messages from the dead." As a first preliminary study in 1964, we conducted in the "Deutschen Institut für Feldphysik," in Freiburg, experiments to try to determine if the voice phenomena could have a natural explanation or if they had a paranormal origin. A second study with better technical

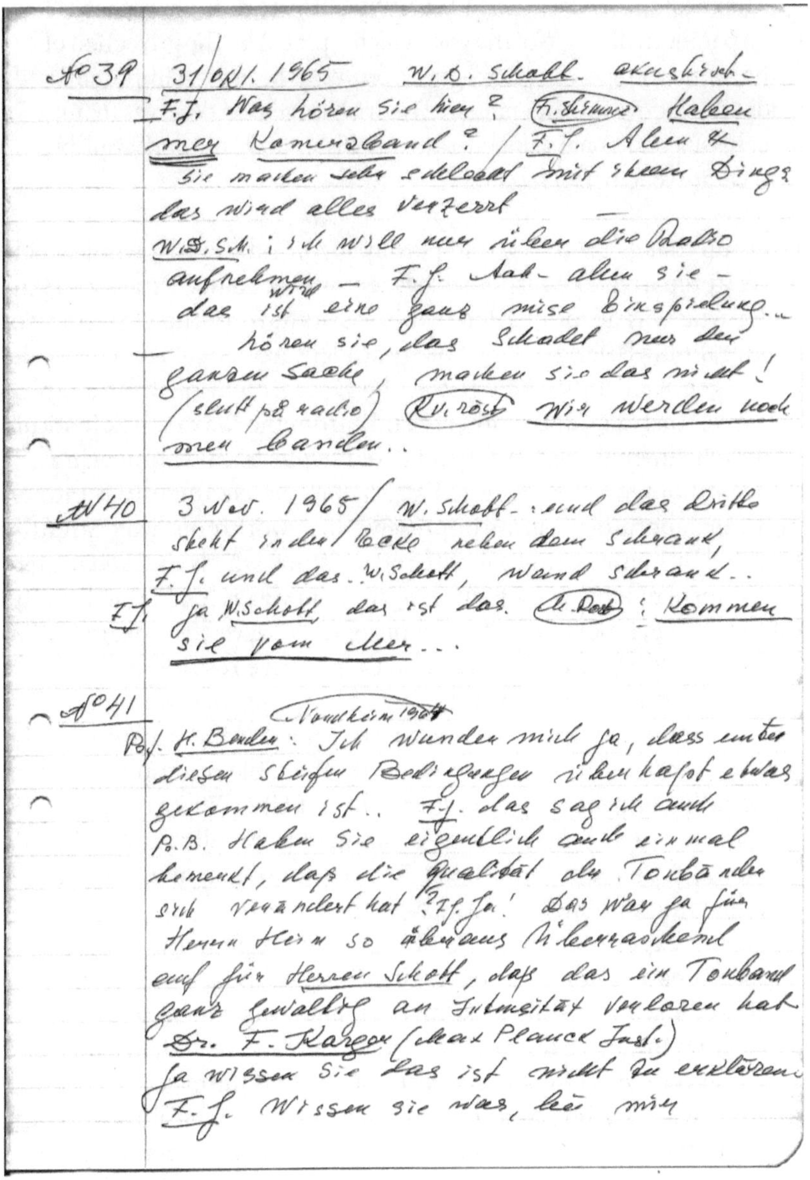

[Handwritten notebook page - transcription of German shorthand notes]

№ 39 31/Okt. 1965   W. o. Schall - akustisch -
F.J. Was hören sie hier? F. Jürgens Haben
mer Kamerband? / F.J. Aber &
sie machen sehr schlecht mit diesem Dinge
das wird alles verzerrt —
W.S.Sch.: ich will nur über die Radio
aufnehmen — F.J. Ach- aber sie -
das ist eine ganz miese Einsprechung..
hören sie, das schadet nur der
ganzen Sache, machen sie das nicht!
(schutzt per radio) Kurios. Wir werden noch
mer banden..

№ 40 3. Nov. 1965 / W. Schall - und das Dritte
steht in der Ecke neben dem Schrank,
F.J. und das W.Schall, Wand schrank..
F.J. Ja W.Schott, das ist das A. Rest; Kommen
sie vom Meer ...

№ 41   (Tonschirm 1964)
Prof. H. Bender: Ich wundere mich ja, dass unter
diesen steifen Bedingungen überhaupt etwas
gekommen ist.. F.J. das sage ich auch
P.B. Haben sie eigentlich auch einmal
bemerkt, dass die Qualität der Tonbänder
sich verändert hat? F.J. Ja! Das war ja für
Herrn Kern so überaus überraschend
auch für Herren Schott, dass das ein Tonband
ganz Gewaltig an Intensität verloren hat.
Dr. F. Karger (Max Planck Inst.)
Ja wissen sie das ist nicht zu erklären..
F.J. Wissen sie was, bei mir

The text is from Friedel's notes taken directly from the tape. It is spoken in German. I have heard this recording on several occasions. Friedel had both versions; the recording by radio and microphone was clearer than the one he had directly linked to the radio. It was surprising but it did not make Friedel carry on recording from the radio via the microphone.

equipment was undertaken in May 1970, which made the hypothesis of the paranormal origin of the voices highly probable. The projection of the sounds on speech spectrograms proved to be of great importance for an objective documentation. Friedrich Jürgenson deserves thanks for his unconditional willingness to unselfishly make his work available to parapsychological research.

The group that came to Nysund in May 1970, and stayed a whole week, was very prepared. The responsible leader was of course Professor Hans Bender who was accompanied by his assistant from the University of Freiburg, Louis Bélanger, Psychology student from Quebec in Canada, PhD Jürgen Kiel, a psychologist at the Department of Psychology in Tasmania, Australia, and Norbert Lemke from the Max Planck Institute in Munich, an engineer who specialized in electrical engineering.

The equipment they installed at Friedel's house turning it into an electronic laboratory was as impressive. The workroom was carefully examined by Lemke using a ferrite rod antenna, which checked if there was any form of long or medium-length radio waves "embedded" in the walls or ceiling, for example: fragments of radio waves. The examination was repeated several times and it gave a negative result.

A directional microphone of very high quality was placed in front of each participant; and a 30 cm long cardboard tube in the form of a funnel could be attached to it. The table microphones were individually connected to two channels in a Uher Report 4004 and a Uher Variocord 263. Friedel was positioned at Bender's side with his own audio tape recorder, a Uher Report 4000, also connected to a "universal microphone" hanging over the table.

In some experiments a type of throat microphone was used that eliminated natural gasps or other breathing sounds.

An oscilloscope visible to all participants was placed on the table. To explain it in simple terms, one can see a green line moving sideways across the screen. The line reacts at voltage and jumps up and down. Readers have probably seen some film sequence at a hospital and how the green dot flattens out when someone dies on the operating table.

Actually, this was not expected to be so dramatic; but it was dramatic enough. A video camera connected to a video recorder to record movements on the oscilloscope screen was placed in front of the oscilloscope. It also had its own microphone and was connected to the signal antenna so that any alien signal which came from outside would be recorded on the screen.

THE SCIENTIFIC TESTS

All the tapes that were used had been played over on metal reels because the plastic reels could produce static effects.

In addition to time-consuming listening and testing of the best of Friedel's previous recordings, twenty-five experiments with a talk time of between four and ten minutes were performed during the six days. These recordings also required patient and time-consuming listening.

The recordings mentioned next are not in my collections, although Hans Bender and I have heard some of them several times. But perhaps more impressive than a recording on tape with interferences, when hearing is the only sense that can perceive what is said, are the speech spectrograms obtained at the Max Planck Institute in Munich. Those make the voice visible and directly confirm its existence and what is said.

There were several unsuccessful recordings on the first day when everything was rigged and ready. Friedel said he was impressed by the participants' patience.

Norbert Lemke was an angler and likened this hunt for alien voices to being out fishing and throwing out and then waiting for a pacifier. And the concession happened late in the evening on May 3, just when the tired participants were about to stop. They had a relaxed conversation and the tape recorders were running but they did not use the tubes for the microphones. The oscillograph was not running either. The funny thing was that Lemke had asked Friedel if there was fish in the small lake. Friedel answered in the affirmative but pointed out that he had never gone fishing there.

Hans Bender writes:

> In the middle of a short pause, a clear voice, which did not belong to any of us, and nor had it been intercepted in the room, is heard saying, "Aber süss!" (But sweet!)
>
> And a minute later in the same recording, the same voice returns, a rough male voice that laughs:
> "Ha ha ha!"

The voice was on all the recorders but slightly weaker on Friedel's Uher Report 4000, which was linked to the microphone that hung in the middle of the room.

They listened to the recording several times and all agreed that the voice said something reminiscent of "Aber süss" but could not draw any conclusions from this. It was understood that the voice went into Friedel's pause before he stated that he had never gone fishing there.

Bender thought that the subsequent laughter was a sign that the voice responded something funny because Friedel had said that he had never gone fishing there. And in that case, he remarked, this was most significant because the being behind the voice must have known what they were talking about. But that was nothing compared to what happened the day after, personally linked to Bender.

May 4, 1970. Encouraged by the result of the day before, better preparations were made. The paper tubes were put on the microphones and oscilloscope and camcorder were prepared to start in connection with future recordings.

Before they took over, Friedel described in detail how he got in touch with his assistant, Lena, and what role she played in continued connections. They had already listened to the recordings with her in Freiburg, but everything was repeated again including the recordings presented in Chapter 4.

When it was time to comment on the recordings, they started tape recorders, oscilloscope and camcorder.

I interviewed Bender before the group left Jürgenson and Mölnbo, and of course taped the interview with ulterior motives. But no voices other than mine and Bender's came in here. I'm relatively poor in German but Bender spoke fluent English so this is an edited translation from my recording in English.

> Bender: Unfortunately, I got a throat inflammation what meant that I occasionally coughed and cleared my throat. But we were all well aware of this, and Jürgenson said that on such occasions, a voice could appear that used those noises as the carrier wave.
>
> AL (Anders Leopold): You guys are scientists, but do you think you were prone to suggestion when Jürgenson talked about his assistant and played up her voice?
>
> Bender: I cannot judge how much we were subjected to suggestion. We all admitted that we heard the voice, as I previously noted in the first tests. But the interpretation of her whispers and vocals was a different matter. The messages from her were there and I was impressed by the soft voice. It was very reminiscent of the voice of one of my female colleagues at the university. She was called Rasmus for some reason. But I did not mention this. However, the name Rasmus was in my mind.
>
> I said, "I hear this as a spiritual voice, I have no other explanation. It is a voice you can fall in love with: a beautiful voice. I want to ask you—" Here I coughed and in the middle of this coughing, a loud

whisper is heard "RASMUS" — if you always have to have contact with Lena when you search on the radio."

When the tape was played everybody reacted to the whisper. I quickly perceived the name "Rasmus." It felt a little upsetting. The voice was on all recorders. Strongest on Jürgenson's and he definitely did not know the name Rasmus, so he could not have whispered into the pipe to the directional microphone, and if he had done so, his voice would not come on the other recorders.

AL: Did the oscilloscope react?

Bender: Because I coughed, it was difficult to discern whether the whisper had been registered on the oscilloscope. None of the participants had heard the name Rasmus. Jürgenson could distinguish 'a" and "mus" and noted that it was a single word like "amus." Jürgen Kiel thought he had heard something like "von uns" but refrained when he heard the recording on track 1 on Variocorden where the "a" was clearly heard.

I told them that I heard the name Rasmus and explained who she was and that shortly before the whisper I was thinking of her name. Since I reported on this and we listened several times, all agreed that the voice had very probably said "Rasmus." But in this situation, I was also aware that I might, somehow, have affected both myself and the others through suggestion.

This was a powerful experience for Bender. It wasn't until August 1971 that I discovered his conclusions of the recordings. Friedel showed me a copy of the journal *Zeitschrift für Parapsychologie Grenzgebiete und der Psychologie* that Bender had sent him as a gift of thanks for the last visit. There was a speech spectrogram of the recording, as I will explain below, which was considered to be the definitive proof of the existence of the voice phenomena. But not only that, linked to Bender's article was another speech spectrogram on Rasmus. Bender wrote: "Given the personal experience, this recording cannot be explained in another way other than having paranormal origin."

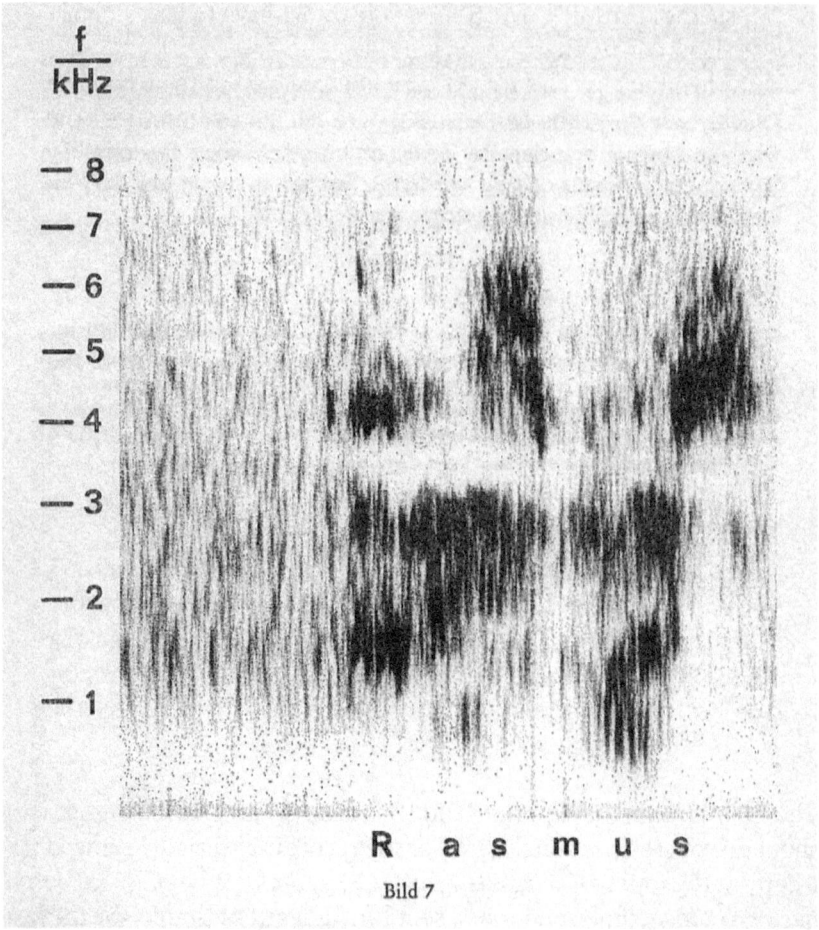

Here is the proof that the voice said RASMUS.

Later that day, Bender had the idea of making a recording in absolute silence. He was disappointed that he had coughed just when the voice uttered Rasmus, and that it could not be detected on the oscilloscope. He had made a similar attempt with a long, silent pause during a previous visit to Friedel but there had been no positive result. After the voice said Rasmus, Bender was very excited and curious about what would happen in the future.

It would all be done under a strict protocol. The participants had to avoid the directional microphones and simply bite their hands to avoid saying something.

THE SCIENTIFIC TESTS

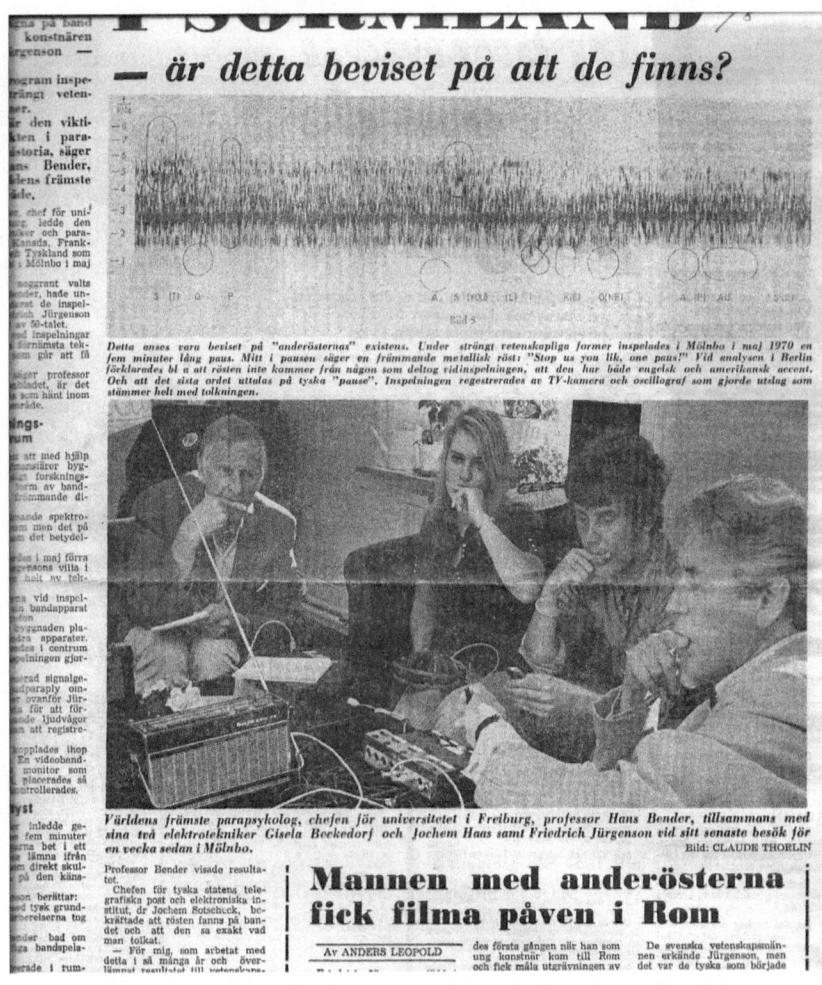

My previous article about one of Bender's visits to Friedel.

Bender had problems with his throat, and was prepared to make several attempts, of which at least one could be performed without him having to clear his throat. But the first attempt was enough. The tape recorders were started as well as the oscilloscope and the camcorder. All conversations before the recording were conducted in German. On the tape you can hear Bender say: "And now we take one minute pause!"

All participants focused their attention on the oscilloscope. If anything during this break came through it would be registered. And it did.

The green beam ran without movement on the oscilloscope screen for 22 seconds. It then made a couple of quick jerks and returned to the same straight line. When I interviewed Bender about this recording, he declared that this was "the major event in parapsychology."

There was obviously a tense atmosphere when one of the tape recorders was played back and "pause" was heard. Both Friedel and Bender found it hard to describe the feelings that overwhelmed them.

We could hear the natural hum from the speakers and 22 seconds later, the silence was broken by a clear, metallic male voice with a light echo that said the following in English:

"Stop as you like ... one a pause!"

All calls had been in German. It was surprising that the alien voice spoke in English.

Friedel said that Lemke rushed around the room with his ferrite rod antenna. But he found no sign of any form of fragments from a radio signal.

Bender stated in my interview with him:

> What was said was directly addressed to us. It was absolutely unbelievable and unreal. The voice did not sound natural; it was more like a robot's voice. The fact that it spoke in English made it all even more enigmatic. And there is no doubt that the voice came through because we had decided, as I said, that we were going to take a break. It was truly a great recording and I am looking forward to having it documented on speech spectrograms.

And here is the proof that the voice phenomenon is real.

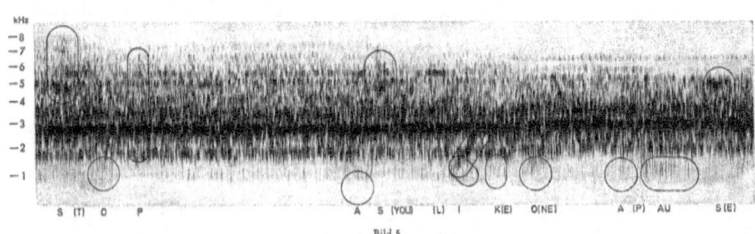

Bild 5

The recording was found to have the same strength in all the tapes and the camcorder recounted the reaction of the oscilloscope.

I wrote about Bender's visit in May 1970 but my article did not attract much attention. It was only when we were able to copy and publish the speech spectrogram and ask the question: "Is this proof that the spirit voices exist?" that Bender's experiment became known in the Swedish parapsychological world.

I heard this recording several times at Friedel's. Here was a voice speaking without any disturbance. It was completely unreal, like Bender had called it—a robot's voice. I copied it on my own tape but, unfortunately, I no longer have that tape.

Bender posted some interesting observations in his article. The word "stop" admittedly contained an "o" but was pronounced almost like an "a" which he felt was an American accent. The end was also difficult to determine exactly. The last word "pause" can be derived from the German "pause" without pronouncing the "e." But at the same time there is an "a" here before the word "pause" and "e" is barely audible. Then the end can be a mixture of English and Italian: "one/un a pausa." But the meaning will be the same. The polyglot language may also serve as proof that this did not come from any radio broadcast. A group that listens simultaneously can easily talk to each other about a certain wording and we should be aware of the fact that suggestion may play a role.

Therefore, several tests were made of Jürgenson's recordings. Jochem Sotscheck, leader of the research group *Akustik des Fernmeldetechnischen Zentralamtes* in Berlin, selected five recordings which were played for two groups: seven members of Sotscheck's research group and six randomly selected people with limited language skills. Under good acoustic conditions, everyone was allowed to listen to each recording twenty times. The recordings tested were: "Tanner, Tanner, Rasmus, von wo, aber süss" and "Stop as you like, one pause!"

Firstly, they had to make a free interpretation and then choose from nine options that were phonetically very similar. One of the nine options was officially correct.

The free interpretation did not yield enough consensus. "Tanner" and "Rasmus" were mentioned by some while "stop" "like" and "pause" were perceived in different combinations.

The nine options, however, gave better results. Custom names "Tanner" and "Rasmus" were now taken by all. Seven answered correctly "von wo," eight "Stop as you like—one pause" and four passed the "aber süss."

Therefore, this shows how extremely difficult it is to interpret the voices. With a written response or someone like Friedel who first says what he thinks he heard, everything becomes much easier. The one who scores the first interpretation of a recording often gets stuck in it and finds it difficult to change.

However, there are certain rules to follow when recording and listening to a recording, as we will discuss.

9

FRIEDEL ANSWERS QUESTIONS

At this point in our story about Friedrich Jürgenson and the voice phenomena, many questions need to be answered: questions which correspond to the questions he received from various sources. Therefore, in this chapter I have edited the questions and answers from his book *Radio and Microphone Contacts with the Dead*.

Before I talk in greater detail about the communications of those who have passed on, I consider it important to clarify a few basic concepts. I believe that the questions which will surface in each reader can best be answered if I consider all of the frequently asked questions as if they had been put by readers of this book and if I answer them one after the other. After all, most of these questions cover the same ground.

Question 1
Has it not already been proven by science that after physical death, which is to say after the disintegration of the body, all consciousness ceases and that life without a body can be absolutely excluded?
Answer:
This purely materialistic view of human life has lost much of its authority in the age of nuclear research, electronic brains and computers. On the other hand, an entirely new branch of science known as parapsychology, has been developed. Even in Soviet

Russia there exist no fewer than eight parapsychological research institutions.

I just want to mention a few internationally known researchers: C. G. Jung, Sir Oliver Lodge, Prof. Rhine, Prof. Broad, Prof. Mattiesen and Prof. Hans Driesch, whose revolutionary research not only demonstrated the existence of a sphere of life and consciousness outside of time and space but also proved that the human being has the capability to greatly transcend the limitation of his physical body and the five senses.

Today there are parapsychological faculties at several universities and special sections of the American and Soviet armed forces are studying telepathy, clairvoyance, hypnosis, telekinesis and other extrasensory perceptions, which can be considered as recognized by science. Besides, the exploration of the subconscious, mainly to the credit of C. G. Jung, has opened entirely new areas to psychology and psychiatry that unavoidably lead to parapsychology.

Among others, the research conducted by the Swedish Physician Dr. Bjoerkhem has placed the problem of reincarnation (the repeated sequential Earthly lives of human souls) in an entirely new light.

These millennial teachings that have been forgotten or denied for centuries in Europe because of church doctrines and materialism, can no longer be ignored since scientifically proven cases of reincarnation exist. In this context, let me mention the case of Shanti Deva whose memories of previous lives have been demonstrated as absolutely accurate.

The results obtained by C. G. Jung, Dr. Bjoerkhem, Oliver Lodge and many other researchers in parapsychology have the same great and revolutionary significance for the exploration of the human soul as the results in physics obtained previously by Einstein and Max Planck.

Question 2
Is it not possible that the voices, which can be heard on your tapes, are the product of your imagination that you unconsciously transfer to them by suggestion?
Answer:
Of course, it could be imagination or suggestion if this would only involve very weak and unclear words or shouts. It happened to me on numerous occasions with my 140 tapes that contain five to six thousand recordings, in which I misinterpreted one or another communication because of strong interference or faulty reception.

Such mistakes are unavoidable in all research activity. But even if I reduce the number of my recordings to one third by eliminating all those that are doubtful, there still remain approximately two thousand recordings characterized by clear text and unmistakable communications that can be understood without any doubt by all who possess normal hearing.

I have tested a large number of recordings with different groups of listeners without revealing the text beforehand. It became evident that 80% of the listeners could immediately understand the text while the remaining 20% did not completely understand all the words, especially foreign words unknown to them.

We should not ignore the fact that the art of concentrated listening is a relatively rare gift. It is one that can be learned under certain conditions with much patience. Basically we are dealing with an introspective concentration capability to focus exclusively on the sounds or frequencies that need to be researched without allowing oneself to be distracted and mistaken by simultaneous interference.

In conclusion, I would like to add that I possess a few tape segments that can be understood 100% by everyone immediately and correctly. They belong to my most excellent recordings and they suffice to render any suspicion of suggestion absolutely absurd.

Question 3

If we are not dealing here with the power of suggestion or the transmissions of a secret radio station, the possibility still exists that you, Mr. Jürgenson, are able to project these sound and voice phenomena in a completely unconscious manner onto a tape through the power of your subconscious. Perhaps you are a kind of medium with the peculiar gift, possibly for the first time in the history of psychical research, to produce electromagnetic impulses and to send these into the ether. What would be your answer to this?

Answer:
I should feel extremely flattered by such a supposition if vanity had been my strong suit. But if we want to get to the bottom of the issue of a possible mediumistic capability on my part in a rational way, we will first have to clarify the physical origin of the voice and sound phenomena.

We know today that all sounds, whether generated by the larynx or mechanical instruments, not only produce sound waves that travel through the air but consist of electromagnetic oscillations that spread through the ether depending on their power source either as radio waves or as sound waves. Since our phenomena cannot be sound waves—otherwise everyone in the room would hear the voices—they must consist of electromagnetic frequencies sent into the ether by some kind of power source.

Now if we want to suppose that my subconscious represents such a power center, I would have the honor of being the greatest genius in the world capable of subconsciously producing the entire dynamics of a radio station including antenna, studio, technical personnel, musical instruments, choirs, soloists and commentators of all kind.

Besides, I would need to possess the magical gift of imitating perfectly the voices of dead people of every gender and age in the most varied languages including voices never previously known or heard by me. But that's not all.

The most absurd "miracle" would consist of my ability to overpower willy nilly any radio wave oscillating in the ether: namely, to alter any current radio transmission totally or partially, such as the British BBC or the West German Radio Network, using the "program" of my own "subconscious transmitter." Not even the most powerful Russian jamming station would be capable of such an achievement.

Such a heroic act would not only exceed the achievements of good old Baron von Muenchhausen but would allow me to claim godlike capabilities. A man with such capabilities would be employed right away by the secret services of the major powers with a fantastic salary and retirement benefits.

Humor aside, question 3 conceals a mental attitude on the part of the questioner that is far from humorous. In fact, it is a doomed mentality that fights desperately for its survival.

Without a doubt, the number of leading researchers that have succeeded in eliminating the underpinnings of scientific materialism in the varied branches of knowledge keeps increasing.

But since we humans are ourselves the sources of all hypotheses, dogmas and ideologies and human nature resists—be it from ignorance, cowardice or to save face—to freely admit errors and failures, the defenders of the materialistic world view have to use all means to protect their threatened dogma against revolutionaries from within and without.

It is a fact that there still exist researchers in our day and age who would rather credit my subconscious with the most absurd magic tricks than to admit honestly and courageously the proven fact that the human personality survives after death in another dimension. If these researchers had only paid attention to other possible insights rather than to the excessive cultivation of their own intellect, they would gain the courage and discernment necessary to revise their obsolete views of the world and mankind. How much damage has already been wrought in our world by ideologies built on cold intellect alone!

Question 4

Why do the dead make use of a so-called polyglot or mix of languages? Why can they not talk like normal people in a single language?

Answer:

Since the dead are completely knowledgeable regarding our ignorance when it comes to "death" and the "beyond" and are also aware of our skepticism and our suspicions, they decided to establish a link that could not be mistaken for any kind of radio transmission.

For instance, if, in the course of microphone recordings, the dead would only use the respective national language, suspicion could arise on listening to the tape recording that the words were spoken by one of those present.

But if suddenly Russian, Hebrew, Greek or Italian words with a strange intonation are heard in the middle of a conversation conducted in German or Swedish, none of those present could be suspected of having spoken them, irrespective of the fact that none of those present even heard them.

Concerning recordings from the radio, we have to take the following facts into consideration: the circumstance alone that the dead appear on radio transmissions with the same characteristic multilingual voices indicates a goal-oriented consistent intent.

Since there is no radio network in the world that would transmit choirs, ensembles, soloists, announcers or commentators using such a curious mix of languages, we have evidence that the source of these voices cannot be found in the radio stations of the different countries.

However, if the dead had spoken to me in a "normal" language, how could anyone be convinced that these transmissions originated in a different four-dimensional sphere? I assure the reader that I would have been called an idiot or a clumsy swindler if I had tried to present such transmissions as "voices from the beyond." The attempts of the dead to link up with us would, thus, have been condemned to failure from the very beginning.

However, this does not by any means resolve the questions posed by this bizarre multilingualism. One has also to consider the possibility that the way the dead express themselves has been altered by the change in their spheres of existence.

Since the beyond (or the fourth dimension) is the sphere of the subconscious freed from the brain, it is entirely conceivable that strict language limitations and grammatical rules are loosened in the sense that henceforth expressions are based on unfettered psychic impulses.

One could describe the language of the subconscious as an unvarnished pictorial and symbolic language as experienced by the living in certain dreams; that is to say, a language that originates in an archaic world of ideas and that is not bound by mundane language limitations.

Friedel with the tapes in his recording studio.

Question 5
Why do the dead prefer to speak on the radio? Could they not reach us exclusively via the microphone, which has less interference?

Answer:
The old principle of "twice sewn lasts longer" seems to apply here as well. In what concerns the recordings via the microphone, it has been demonstrated that this method is limited at present by technical difficulties that are as yet not clearly understood. Even though this method evidently results only in the formulation of short sentences, single shouts or soft whispers, their purpose is usually achieved. These transmissions via the microphone not only have a drastic effect; they also somehow speak directly to the listener. Dr. Bjoerkhem said: "It suffices to hear and record a single word of an unseen being in a quiet room. Stronger proof is not needed because a tape recording excludes ascribing these phenomena to subjective experience."

Links established via the radio appear to offer much greater and better possibilities. I have recordings that last more than half an hour and whose decibel level, content and purely personal character is so totally convincing that even the smallest doubt is excluded from the very beginning.

Question 6
Why did the dead opt for such a technically prosaic method as the tape recorder? Would not a living medium be more impressive, as has been the case until now?

Answer:
No matter how prosaic and sober a mechanical tape recorder may seem, its construction excludes the possibility that it is subject to any personal errors, imaginings, wishes and desires.

A tape recorder will function a hundred percent objectively; it registers in a purely automatic fashion those electromagnetic impulses that come its way, either via the microphone or via a radio receiver connected directly to the tape recorder. However, in the case of microphone recordings, other reception possibilities also seem to exist, namely under certain conditions that have not yet been entirely determined, there are other parts of the tape recorder that can be used as access channels. Perhaps the communicators and singers on the other side can also make use of other parts of the instrument instead of just the microphone. As already mentioned, there is the justifiable hope that this problem can be solved soon with the assistance of scientists.

There is no doubt that a mechanical tape recorder cannot be compared to any psychic medium because of its absolute objectivity. We know, besides, that genuine and dependable spiritist mediums are extremely rare; certainly this is the case in Europe. No matter how talented and basically honest a medium might be, he or she cannot completely eliminate subjectivity. Thus, for instance, no medium can differentiate with absolute certainty whether the impulses arriving from its subconscious originate from the dead or from those present, because the borders in this case are fluid.

I also consider it a disadvantage when participants in spirit-séances unavoidably become, to a certain extent, dependent on the medium. Such a dependence relationship can easily paralyze personal initiative and independent research.

Question 7
Mr. Jürgenson, can you give a rational explanation to why precisely you have been selected for this path-breaking work and what were the reasons that motivated you to suddenly give up your artistic career?
Answer:
First of all, I would like to counter this question with one of my own: a question that I have already asked hundreds of my visitors, and that I now direct to readers of this book.

Would you be willing to give up your profession and leave your comfortable home in the city to bury yourself in isolation in the countryside, to devote all your resources, strength and time to a really dubious kind of research that consists of getting to the bottom of some mystical and initially barely audible voices that appeared seemingly by accident on an audio tape?

As you already know, this is exactly what I did out of a clear, inner conviction. The fact that I was willing to reorganize my life completely, both externally and internally, was of great but not decisive significance. Much more was required—an entire series of inbred and acquired capabilities that motivated the dead to entrust this difficult task to no one but me.

My endowment, by nature, with a very sensitive ear and good musical talent along with the fact that I spoke five languages relatively fluently and had a working knowledge of three others was an essential precondition, otherwise, I could not have understood the multilingual shouts and communications of the dead. I also have the gift of concentration and psychic relaxation (meditation).

I have occupied my entire life with the problem of death. In my youth I thoroughly studied religion and philosophy for five years. I did not fail to become closely acquainted with theosophy, the cabbala, yoga and anthroposophist teachings. I did this in a country in which all religious movements were persecuted ruthlessly, and I risked losing my freedom because of my secret studies as I had formed a small esoteric group. At the same time, I could not avoid becoming acquainted with the basic theses of the Marxist dialectic.

I owe it on the one hand, to my insatiable desire for knowledge, but on the other hand also to those chaotic external conditions that thickened the atmosphere, which made it possible for me to analyze the different ideologies thoroughly, and to free my mind from all of the single-track doctrines and dogmas.

As a result of these studies, as a witness and victim of two world wars and of a destructive revolution, I discovered the source of the failures and sufferings of humanity. I started to look at life candidly and without prejudice and was pained deeply by the suffering of humankind. Most of all, I recognized that all our anxieties and miseries could not be eliminated until we had incontestably solved the problem of death. All this might have contributed to the reasons why it was me who was chosen to build the bridge between our world and the beyond.

Question 8

Did not the publicity that has surrounded you and your work result in many advantages, much income and benefits for you?

Answer:

I understand that this question might be justified under certain circumstances. For instance, if I had been a poor and unknown artist, motivated and ambitious to make a name for myself at any price, or if I had been seized by some fixed ideas and decided to create a sect or movement around myself. But, as already mentioned, I was at that time at the peak of my artistic career. I had been charged with an extremely interesting task at the Vatican, had painted several portraits of Pope Pius XII and had just been planning to take part in an archaeological mission in Pompeii when the voices spoke to me.

An artist who stops painting and does not exhibit his work not only loses his customary clients; he is also soon forgotten. As concerns me personally, I was suddenly required to sell the rest of my paintings, which is practically impossible to manage from a little bungalow far out in the countryside.

Since I also had to acquire expensive tape recorders and large quantities of recording tape on a continuing basis, my wife Monica was financially affected, too. Together, we formed a very successful deficit enterprise that had also the advantage of operating without competition.

At that time, we had no inkling that our quiet house would be turned into a kind of beehive, or more accurately visitor center, after our first international press conference. Today, I don't remember any longer how many hundreds of press articles were published about myself, and the voice phenomena in Sweden and abroad.

But of one thing I am certain, namely that as long as I live, there won't be any sect or movement, ideology or school that will form around me. Also, I have always received and will continue to receive all my visitors without any charge. I was not only born in a country where hospitality is a matter of course, but I would become disloyal to my own principles and lose the confidence of my friends on the other side if I were to turn their bridge, built with such hard work and selfless dedication, into an income source.

Of course the publicity I receive has also had some positive effects. I got to know many people who had lost their joy and courage of living through the death of their loved ones. Even the wisest counsel and solace would not have lightened the burden of these grief-stricken people because words are powerless in these cases.

However, that which I recorded on my tapes and what I played for them and what we sometimes recorded together, changed the situation altogether. I have rarely seen people laugh and cry so happily. And I don't want to give up these "advantages" in the future, either.

10

SURREAL MESSAGES: FRIEDEL'S INTERPRETATION OF THE "HITLER" MONOLOGUE

I repeat what I wrote before: it would be unfair to Friedel not to reproduce the elements of his recordings that he appreciated most, while other people who do not have Friedel's language skills and refined hearing, and depend on his interpretations are of course, skeptical. I would probably say that I, at least in the beginning of our relationship, belonged to the latter group.

Most astonishing, thus, is Adolf Hitler's monologue that lasted for about ten minutes and was entirely interpreted by Friedel. There is so much substantial and credible material in Friedel's account of the voice phenomena that, actually, I could have excluded this chapter. But because he drew so much heed to these surreal and difficult to interpret recordings, I will not put them aside. They were important to him, and I respect Friedel's conviction that he was building a bridge to the other side in which everything is possible.

I have heard this voice several times and have not been able to make a comparison with Hitler's voice because I have heard him only as a madman screaming. Maybe I can agree with Rune Moberg's findings proposing that if one imagines Hitler as a calm and level-headed person, it could be him. But who can do that?

Of course the voice was tested very carefully by Hans Bender and the researchers at the Max Planck Institute. Speech spectrograms were performed to compare the anomalous voice with the original but it was almost fruitless because of the radio interference and because they could not find some sufficiently long comment by a calm and sensible Hitler to perform the comparison, which was not a surprise.

As Bender said: "You cannot rule out that it is really Hitler's voice but it is also not (possible) to say that it is not Hitler's voice." However, he admitted that the voice was there and what was said and interpreted had a content, which definitely could not have been transmitted in a radio program. They got the exact time for Friedel's recording but could not trace any broadcast from any country airwaves reminiscent of this voice and what it uttered.

For my readers' elucidation, I will explain which kind of messages Friedel claimed to have received containing known names of people who had left life on the Earth, particularly during Friedel's intensive period in the 1960s. I listened to a large number of such recordings, some perhaps half an hour long, and warned Friedel about their use during his demonstrations for visitors. They were so difficult to interpret by normal hearing people that he ran the risk of being discredited.

Purportedly, Caryl Chessman often came through in contacts with Friedel. Chessman sat for twelve years in the death row in the United States, before he was gassed to death in 1960—a case that upset the whole world. Friedel said that he got in touch with him two days after the execution.

It took several weeks before Friedel put this recording in order. In addition to Chessman, the mysterious Churchill is present plus three male voices, one of which, according to Friedel, probably belongs to Hitler. He also stated that those present in certain "remote calls" were in contact with other people.

Friedel wrote the following about this surreal contact with the world on the other side:

> He talks lively. Chessman is talking with cheerful voice. He raises questions and receives answers, which, strangely enough, are in German. Most questions are about some aircraft. I share this conversation in translation:
> "Is it possible?" asks Chessman. I can only perceive a part of the answer which, incidentally, is in English, German and Swedish.

"By ... an opportunity (for meeting) with Dr. Kersten! ... The power—friends' ... frequency standard ... aircraft (craft) speed ... Certainly! Forgot ... now ... ... occult script of contact ... everyone has to ..."

Here is probably Hitler's voice through the remote call and he speaks German:

"Do not walk, do not see, do not hear."

"It's hopeless," adds one.

"What is it?" asks Chessman.

"Robots ... in case they are many."

A new male voice suddenly starts speaking English and German. I can clearly recognize a typical Jewish accent. It is an older man's voice.

"Stockholm, Maelarhoejden." he begins, energetic and eager.

"From Maelar, Maelarhoejden, lake, lake, where the transmitter is."

"Aha! Maelaroden," Chessman repeats.

"MAELARHOEJDEN!" the voice with the Jewish accent corrects him.

"... to Maelarhoejden, Maelarhoejden apparatus."

"Why?" asks Chessman.

The answer is drowned by the noise but Chessman is laughing out loud:

"Mr. Churchill, can you believe it?" asks Chessman and now he speaks English and Swedish. A voice says in German: "Freddie, we have no land." and adds in English: "you suffer when you are passionate."

"Karl Johansson," says Hitler! "adds one."

"He's dead," Hitler responds softly.

Despite the broken phrases, it is clear that the call is being made on a flying vessel and that Chessman's questions concern this.

Chessman has not said a word about his execution or touched his painful problems. His new situation seemed to completely capture his interest. It seems that he feels great relief when his voice betrays a hint of joy: yes, it sometimes sounds almost overconfident and you can see that he has difficulty mastering his mirth.

I find it remarkable that the name Maelarhoejden is insistently repeated several times. Apparently, they want to learn a foreign and important name that is difficult to pronounce. "From Maelar, Maelarhoejden, lake, lake, where the transmitter is."

In the beginning I did not understand. I found the words two years later, and only after they provided a supplementary statement and an indication of the importance of the keyword Lake Maelaren.

THE MIND AT LARGE

Friedel's interpretation of these talks and Hitler's "monologue" is not only just surreal but in some pieces also poetic. But the amazing thing is that he actually had those conversations on tape (although some words are difficult to interpret without Friedel's help) and that no one could explain where they came from—certainly not from some radio programs. So, dear reader, join in a strange document.

Friedel wrote:

> Towards the end of May (1960) I received a transmission that now, almost three years later, I consider to be one of the most evocative and interesting I have recorded and one that deserves a detailed description.
>
> As usual, Lena referred the wavelength to me but, when I misunderstood her, the first signal was initially lost for me. Then I set the radio to the correct wavelength. I regulated only the volume and let the recording run its course.

In this regard, I wish to interpose that Friedel's way of reproducing the monologue in the book is rather unclear. Because you may get the impression that he could immediately understand what was said through the headphones, which did not correspond to reality.

Of course, initially he had no idea that it was Hitler who spoke. He had difficulty to interpret what was said. At the beginning, perhaps he thought that it was a regular radio broadcast but since Lena had indicated the wavelength to him, he suspected that there was a message in what was said and that the voice might speak directly to him. Later, he became convinced that it was Hitler who had spoken and he wrote:

> The broadcast and the recording lasts nine minutes and ten seconds. It runs parallel to the Norwegian short wave, which at the same time performed Mozart's Piano Concerto in D Major. Although nearby stations are noticeably disturbed, the clarity and volume of the broadcast can be compared with a regular radio broadcast.
>
> What makes the strongest impression on me are the varied movements of the senses that can clearly be read from the speaker's voice. This is how people usually speak in their sleep or under anesthesia when the boundaries of day consciousness have dissolved. There can be no doubt: this man speaks from the depths of his whole consciousness and one could take his opinion for a monologue if he was not interrupted by other voices. When this happens, lively, sometimes

violent exchanges of words occur in which many listeners are drawn in and which are not carried out without humor.

This transmission could be regarded as an incomparable historical document for it is, in my interpretation, Adolf Hitler who speaks with a voice that cannot be mistaken.

Apparently, the message is conveyed over a 'radar' that is directly connected to my radio and respective tape recorder. Hitler sometimes presents himself clearly and distinctly. He also seems to be fully aware that his words are being recorded on my tape.

I have heard this monologue several times. The voice mentions the name Hitler but not in the first person, at least to my hearing and understanding although, as I said, I have not Friedel's hearing capacity. That the message is directly connected to Friedel's devices is consistent with his explanation that all messages, all the voices we receive, are personally targeted and cannot be intercepted by anyone else.

Friedel continues:

> Goering's, Keitel's and Felix Kersten's names are mentioned but one cannot reliably recognize their voices as they often sound distorted and sound as if coming from far away.
>
> Hitler speaks mainly German. But this does not prevent him from occasionally combining it with Swedish, English, Russian, and even Hebrew words. As most of the dead, Hitler also distorts the verb, occasionally makes grotesque combinations of words and does not seem to use the article carefully. Apparently, the grammatical rules have lost their significance on the other side.
>
> Hitler begins his message with a low voice that sounds somewhat older and dejected. As long as he speaks quietly and calmly, one can distinguish every syllable. But as soon as he gets into a rage or violently upset, his old voice relapses. The voice becomes shrill and the diction unclear. Surprisingly, such a sudden outburst of emotions passes quickly. It disappears as suddenly as it has come without leaving any trace of emotion in his voice. These violent emotional discharges fill his talk with heightened intensity. One gets the impression of taking part in an upset retrospective, or self-analysis, implemented ruthlessly against himself.
>
> Thus, I stick solely to the clear words that I reproduce here—the transmission in abbreviated form: a disadvantage, which unfortunately is inevitable.

Despite his concentrated monologue, Hitler must have been aware of the piano concerto, and also because he speaks twice about the music, he is silent in certain pauses and stops his message at the last chords.

Already after the second set, he gets suddenly upset and says softly:

"If you do not want to stink on the ground ... stand often in the middle of your time and vow to make amends! Führer! Zuhör!" (listen!)

Here, the voice changes and Hitler continues calmly:

"When the characters are no longer sufficient ... then someone takes all the blame on himself, a father for his contemporaries ... Does it not come to each one what belonged to him?"

After this issue there are some vague rebuttals and someone says: "Friedel hear!"

The names Keitel and Hess are also mentioned.

"Pariah ... bring your dignity with Gaut" (?) In time... denounce the thief!" recites Hitler emphatically. Once more the mood switches and Hitler speaks suddenly in a completely confidential tone.

"I'm Hatsch (?) ... The air stinks from the head. No one cares about it ... Maybe now? What does the state need? Malenkoff. Have you forgotten!"

From the distance a voice can be heard which clearly says:

"Contact with Göring two periods. Mrs. Jürgenson may want to ..."

"Go your way Gerlitz" solemnly interrupts Hitler but then adds: "Where?"

An indistinct exchange of words follows and then, suddenly, Hitler's upset shout can be heard:

"There the wealthy Jerntmann! Driver! Führer!"

"Bite Flemmer! If someone falls in the distance."

"Well, we'll see—genuine!" states Hitler. After a while you hear him say:

"And then you climb the Atlantic?"

It sounds like a question that he poses to himself. For a long time, only the sound from the piano concerto can be heard. Then disturbances appear and somewhat later muffled sounds reminiscent of steps approaching can be heard.

"Contact person, there comes Bacchus!" Hitler exclaims suddenly with zeal.

It is wonderful. My father was jokingly called Bacchus by his friends. It was a pun on his name, Backelin. Would Hitler actually have met him?

"Voul schpagetti" (not spaghetti)? asks Hitler and adds something that sounds like:

"Fruit dinner with potatoes."

"Thank You, maybe!" answers someone from afar.

I do not recognize this man's voice.

"Now dawajte" (Russian: now they go). "Goering ... two guilders!" said Hitler chuckling. It is the first time I hear Hitler convey a cheerful tone.

Again the music prevails on the radio for a long time; it's beautiful, clear tones that roll up like pearls.

"Beautiful ... thanks!" Hitler remarks.

"Nice name!" someone agrees.

But what happened then is the strangest thing, to suddenly hear Hitler walk a few steps, namely six distinct steps. Then he sighs and clears his throat discreetly. I must unwittingly think of the ingrained notion, which in most people is connected with the bodily nature of the dead. But in this case one could not speak of any "floating" and "weightless" spirits. On the contrary, the voice, the steps, and the sighs are highly prosaic, normal and concrete. Here, too, we are stuck in notions that in no way correspond to reality. And one more thing—Hitler must undoubtedly have been in a room of some kind because he says with strong emphasis:

"Like tortured ... im Gefändezimmer."

Maybe he means Gefängsniszimmer (prison cell) or possibly Pfändezimmer, a derivation of Pfandzimmer (mortgage office). Next, he exclaims with movement and regrets: "I could not save the life of Kersten! It often cuts into me! Children are naked. Phu."

A sleepy female voice interrupts him and says softly:

"Ich schlafe" (I sleep) or maybe "ich schaffe" (I create) ... in Berlin.

Hitler takes the floor again. Overall the voice sounds serious and searching.

"Mein Kopf ist tot ... Tod ist der von oben gekommen" (My head is dead; death has come from above.)

"I see... my blood in the world that can cleanse and relieve ... technology?"

Without waiting for an answer, he continues in a loud and trembling voice:

"First away with a bunch, the state contemplated ... there is a way for you ... for me? Shucks! Can you walk on your belly? Stop! You call ... thank you!"

"Did Hitler become evil?" asks someone.

"Are you trying to understand him?" Hitler says quickly and ironically adds:

"Wouldn't you be Hitler yourself?"

There are interferences in the radio, electrical discharges, whistling sounds. After a while Hitler's voice infiltrates again and you hear him say: "I'm poor. By God in heaven!"

"The radio is on," someone says.

"Thanks to Lena, thanks to Pelle," whispers Hitler. Suddenly he says in Swedish:

"It was Hitler."

The remote call is switched on and a male voice is heard quickly saying:

"Wicander, wake Reinfeldt!"

Hitler's voice trembles with indignation as he exclaims loudly:

"Lie down (!) In my house. Mr. Wicander how can the (ordlek) ... Have contempt in me. In your heart you peel yourself for usury! Tig! Tig!"

In his outraged speech, one can clearly recognize the Austrian accent.

"One day we will arrive in Austria! If someone falls for it."

The effect of this line strikes like a bolt of lightning and Hitler gets a real outburst of rage: "Megaphone! Mesrach!" he shouts in a trembling voice.

"Watch out with Myrdal! Mr. Freud! It is not at all ... it is not a question of Israel. Who's hitting me? First you know my dear... now you are evil! ... I am very pleased."

A dull bang follows. It sounds like someone slamming a door. Once again, the sound penetrates step by step; the music now overpowers all other sounds. This is how we hear Hitler say in a subdued voice: "Often suffer from the cold ... the dead."

Suddenly he adds very loudly and with movement: "Where is there justice? ... Defamers."

Silence returns. Only Mozart's pearling sounds flow like a rippling spring stream. The concert is coming to an end.

"How beautifully he plays," Hitler remarks but then suddenly adds solemnly:

"Oh God what a far sight!"

"Don't be arrogant," a male voice interrupts him. But Hitler does not allow himself to be disturbed.

"Wolf, and there at the inn?" (Asking him). "What kind of host is it? What is a remote city? Which port is it? Bremen, Scholten."

When a female voice comes into the Norwegian radio broadcast, I accidentally touch the knob and for a few seconds the wavelength disappeared. I quickly turn back to the previous wavelength but can only perceive a few detached words.

"Don't talk ... you have to give signs," I hear Hitler say. His voice seems tired and subdued.

"Also Lenchen?" asks a deep female voice.

"What do you say to Freddie?"

There are disturbances and I cannot understand the answer. I only manage to pick up the voice of what seems to be a female robot that ends the broadcast a bit monotonously:

"Radar goes bad here ... he just says travel with Bojewski's ship ... Federico, Mälarhöjden."

Here the transmission seems to be interrupted.

It is fascinating and dreamlike—this is the "psi language" of the dead. But how can one understand its hidden meaning?

The great difficulty lies precisely in the fact that the dream-like language cannot be understood through the associative thoughts of our everyday consciousness. Its center of gravity is hidden beneath the surface of the "iceberg." It is the same as with certain dreams which, with their own symbolism of image, seek to express what is moving in the subconscious. In such cases, one must find oneself at ease without being disturbed by the interpretations of others. The world of dreams is still rather unexplored and, above all, it is very difficult to distinguish between the images of the subconscious and the real events in the other world.

"Once, once," begins Hitler with a noticeable glow:

"That which we experience in the dream always happens, what once existed. The world goes its own way and finally spring blooms ... The world brings new!"

"It's really, really! Does anyone agree."

Hitler takes the floor again just before the concert's final chord fades away.

"The new hope ... the new judgment. Wake up! Wake up!"

The concert is over and the Norwegian host's voice is heard with complete normality.

I assert that there should be no misunderstanding regarding Friedel's relationship to Hitler. I reproduce his subsequent comments in which he also asks if physical death causes some mental change after one wakes up in the fourth dimension of life.

> Would this man who speaks to me on the band, be really Hitler? Why did he choose me—I who have always been an irreconcilable opponent of violence and was against his regime, also?
>
> Psychologically speaking, we now know that most tyrants are dominated by fixed ideas, respectively greatness and madness. This situation is not changed by the fact that we learn that some of them have suffered from progressive paralysis, syphilis—it's just that it seems to me that we must look with different eyes at crimes committed by an insane man rather than by a healthy one. That Adolf Hitler suffered from progressive paralysis was first learned through Felix Kersten's book *Totenkopf und Treue* (1952). Nowadays this relationship is also widely known through other sources, as well as the fact that Lenin died of syphilis. Felix Kersten writes the following about Hitler's disease in his book (p. 209):
>
>> Himmler then took from a fireproof safe a black briefcase and took out a blue journal that he left me with the words: 'Read yourself here! It is a classified journal over the Führer's disease.' The journal was 26 pages long, as I could see at a glance. Apparently, they had used the medical record from the time when Hitler was blind in Pasewalk. It was from this time that this journal was published and it established that Hitler, as a young frontline soldier, suffered from gas poisoning and was inadequately treated so that there was a danger of temporary blindness. In addition, there were symptoms of syphilitic disease. He was discharged from Pasewalk as healthy. In 1937, symptoms appeared again, which indicated that the syphilitic disease continued its eerie destructive work. By early 1942, similar signs showed that there could be no doubt that Hitler suffered from progressive paralysis of which he showed all the symptoms except the pupil's stiffness and language disorders.
>
> The history of mankind abounds with cases of insane people in power, not only in politics but also in religious life. In both situations, it is a matter of ideologies, of new principles, which are said to save the world, but which, in reality, have brought with them only misery, war and slavery.

As far as Hitler is concerned, I am interested to know the extent to which physical death can bring about any psychological change. Since Hitler as a paralytic suffered from brain softening, the disease should have been cured by death. If this could be proven, one would, thus, have gained a deep insight into the soul life of a sick person—an insight that has not been possible for us so far—but not only that because, at the same time, the problem of guilt and responsibility would appear in a completely different light.

The question of whether death can change a person's soul life seems to me to be of the utmost importance, because if that question can be answered, we would, thereby, be able to get to know the impact of a new life plan, i.e. an area which to this day, has been inaccessible for objective research.

How, then, do these lunatics experience the awakening on the other side? If the disease is removed by death, the awakening on the other side must be experienced as a liberation. But the memory of their misdeeds, how is it experienced? I must inevitably think of the sentence I received during the night: "My head is dead ... death has come from above."

If these were indeed Hitler's words, the answer seemed to have been given already.

And the same man's broken voice had said on New Year's Eve: "We lived in the deepest confusion."

I had never before heard Hitler speak resignedly and calmly. His voice sounded melancholic; I could not recognize it as Hitler's. I followed the recording closely until the point where a woman with a Jewish accent announced that Hitler was present.[21]

11

FRIEDEL AND THE POPE

In 1965 Friedel had the honor, together with archaeology Professor Alfonso de Franciscis, to choose a house in Pompeii to expose snapshots of the dramatic events 1889 years earlier, when hundreds of residents who had failed to escape the eruption of the volcano Vesuvius, burned and choked to death in a few minutes.

Plinius the Younger described the Vesuvius eruption after an eyewitness account of his uncle, the Roman admiral by the name of Plinius, who witnessed the eruption and devastation from his ship at sea. It began with a series of earthquakes and then continued with a violent explosion. Tons of huge boulders were torn away from the top of the mountain, stones were thrown in all directions and a mushroom cloud shot up 33 kilometers into the stratosphere, according to scientists. Liquid magma spewed from the Earth's interior with glowing dust particles, ash and pumice and engulfed the city into scorching darkness.

Here Friedel was at the goal of his dreams. He said that there he would meet the people who, in the middle of their everyday life, according to his way of seeing it, in an instant went over to the other side.

But meet them? When he spoke of this, it was as if he was convinced that they were there in some form—perhaps as spirits—maybe physically in the form of animals or flowers or people finding their way there. Perhaps even himself who, by his strong enticement to seek Pompeii, had once existed there and now returned. Maybe it was not a meeting but a reunion. He smiled at the thought, and probably would have liked it to be true.

But, as far as I understand it, he had not clearly learned through his contacts on the other side what happened to people who had died a very long time ago, like the inhabitants of Pompeii. Were they still there in the fourth dimension of life? His answer was that he interpreted what he had heard that all living beings are repeatedly reborn back into the third dimension of life. Since time does not exist in the fourth dimension, he had no idea of how long it takes for a human being to be reborn.

From my side, I believe that during his first visit to Pompeii in the late 1940s, he recalled his memories of violent and rapid deaths during the war in Odessa. That probably laid the foundation for his conviction that death was not the end. A spiritual being who went out of his physical existence could not just be extinguished and enter eternal darkness. Not even all the religions with their gods, which man invented in his despair, believed in this. So, perhaps that made him very receptive to what was to come: to try to make contact with our physical world from the spiritual world in an incomprehensible fourth dimension of life.

When it came to finding the right place for an excavation of Pompeii, Friedel told me that he tried to get help from his friends on the other side. In the 1965 visit, he had gone around, alone, with his portable tape recorder in the not yet excavated district. But he heard no voices that wanted to give him guidance. However, he said he was hit by something that reminded him of how everything began—a telepathic message. He stood in front of a green hill where some sheep were grazing. It was a fairly central part of the city and on the partially excavated street Via dell'Abbondanza. He said the sound around him faded away, much like with a tape recording, and he sensed a whisper in Italian that sounded like: "Scavare!" Simply an invitation: "Dig!"

He had a strong feeling that he had come to the right place. He consulted with the archaeologists and was told that a façade was hidden in the greenery of the hill, which had been exposed during a small excavation in 1913. Alfonso de Franciscis, who did not do any excavations in Pompeii, but for several years was the leader of the restoration of buildings previously excavated, had now got the job as the head of upcoming excavations and he became enthusiastic. It was known that under one of the hills there would be a house, which belonged to Gaius Julius Polybius, a member of the judiciary related to Emperor Claudius. The house was supposed to be one of the most magnificent buildings in Pompeii. And that was what happened.

The house got the working name of Casa Svedese—a tribute to Friedel—but when it became clear that they had really found Julius Polybius house, it acquired its present name, *Casa di Polibio*.

Friedel told me that the excavation was his life's greatest adventure. It took nearly a year before they found the bodies of Julius Polybius and his family. They were gathered at the back of the house. According to a group of volcanologists, they had probably first stayed in the house in the belief that they were protected there. When the roof collapsed, there were twelve people and they rushed out to the back of the house to take shelter. And there they were discovered, 1889 years later, three men and three women of different ages, four boys, two girls, one of which was in advanced pregnancy.

Three exciting films were shown on the Swedish television in 1968. Then they were sold worldwide and the SBC made a profit. But Friedel was largely ignored. He had signed a contract in which he would be reimbursed for travel and living expenses while the SBC accounted for all production costs. Not a word about any royalty on sales. It is incorrect to say that he was not disappointed but he explained: "I do not think about the money. The most important thing is that I get to do these things in order to gain credibility when it comes to the voices." And that he would definitely get.

While he was working on the 1967 film about Pompeii, some Italian friends told him about the cruel hunting of birds, and since he had access to a film crew, asked if he could make a movie about this. He could, and did it in great anger! There were facilities where the Italians with giant nets caught migratory birds while they were on their way home to us in the Nordic countries. They ate them in Italian cuisine in all different ways, including pasta, of course.

The film was broadcast on the Swedish television and aroused strong feelings. An independent Italian television channel had the audacity to do the same and it caused an even stronger emotional outcry in the ruthless bird hunters' homeland. A heated debate broke out in the Italian Government and, almost immediately, a change in the law banning this form of hunting happened.

Friedel had become a recognized filmmaker and several doors opened, particularly in the Vatican. Actually, all the doors all the way to the Pope's private apartment opened.

Right after he finished his film about Pompeii, he took the film crew with him to another ancient city, Paestum, which is located approximately ninety kilometers from Naples. He had stayed there many times and was impressed by the Doric columns standing directly on the ground and the almost intact defensive walls surrounding the temples, dating from the sixth century before Christ.

The documentary *The Temples at Paestum and the City of Temples and Graves* also became good business for the SBC. This time Friedel got a reasonable honorarium, so he and Monica were able to extend their stay in Italy. And more would follow.

On September 19, it was time for the second show of the year: the performance of San Gennaro's blood in which thousands of people crowded in Naples Cathedral to witness the unlikely miracle of what was considered to be coagulated blood from Naples' patron, San Gennaro, change to liquid for a while. This happens three times a year.

Friedel wanted to film the event—something that had never been done before—but to get papal permission was considered impossible. But not for Friedel.

It was time to go for a walk with friends into the Vatican again. And this time he was lucky. Archbishop Bruno Heim, who had paid a visit to Mölnbo and listened to the voices, was there on a visit. At the time, he was the envoy of the Catholic Church in Finland. He had great influence in the Vatican and was even considered a possible future Pope. I met Bruno Heim in Rome in 1970. At a good dinner and after several glasses of Fernet Branca in a restaurant next to Piazza di San Pietro opposite the Vatican, I tried to find out why Friedel, the man who believed neither in God nor in the Devil, could walk freely through closed doors in the Vatican.

There is no doubt that it was Pope Paul VI who personally gave Friedel the go-ahead to film the blood miracle. Friedel told me later that he had been very careful not to convey the impression that he, with the film, wanted to reveal it as humbug. Among other things, he refrained from tight close-ups. I never knew what he thought about this phenomenon, which is still unresolved.

During the ceremony, those who are close to the glass container can see that something inside suddenly becomes liquid when the priest twists it. This can also be seen on the film. Then the miracle happens and the congregation rejoices because they know that their city will not suffer an accident.

In the film *The Miracle of the blood of St. Gennaro*, there was even a clip for the SBC. In the United States it appeared on several TV channels. It was particularly acclaimed in New York, in Little Italy, where about one million people celebrate San Gennaro in Lower Manhattan. It is an eleven-day event starting September 12, with religious processions and colorful parades, free musical entertainment every day and a wide variety of ethnic foods and delicatessen. On September 19, San Gennaro himself comes out of his home in the church and joins the festivities in a procession through the streets of Little Italy.

Friedel returned to Sweden and we had little contact because he was extremely busy. While he was in Italy (1967), he published his first book in German under the title *Sprechfunk mit Verstorbenen*. It would prove to be the international breakthrough in the voice phenomena. And then he published his second book *Radio and microphone contacts with the dead* in Sweden.

On the occasions we talked with each other he sounded happy and relaxed. He had reached where he always strived to be, i.e., getting to publicize his discovery, which he, without modesty, felt was one of the most important events in the history of mankind—objective physical evidence that the soul lives on after death.

He was constantly busy with guests from different countries, Swedish and foreign media, answering letters and talking on the 'phone. And he told me that, at that time, when he made recordings, he seldom received messages of interest. It was as if his friends on the other side were watching the attention that hit him when it came to what he called the construction of the bridge. "They do not want to disturb me, now that I have a platform to stand on, and they know that I concentrate on spreading knowledge about the voices and the bridge," gladly repeating how important his credibility was: something that would unexpectedly get a real boost.

The head of SBC, Nils-Erik Baehrendtz, asked Friedel if he was able to make contact with his friends in the Vatican for yet another filmmaking mission. They had heard that Pope Paul VI and the Vatican were ready to grant complete transparency related to the discovery of the relics of Apostle Peter in St. Peter's Basilica. The excavation was known but the secret that Peter's bones were missing had been hidden ever since archaeologists in 1939 thought they had found the crypt through a hole in the wall. World War II had halted the continued excavation, but in 1949 Pope Pius XII decided that the excavation should continue. He wanted to obtain an absolute answer to the essential question of the Catholic Church: are Peter's tomb and relics in St. Peter's Basilica?

Yes, it was certainly Peter's tomb, but the archaeologists found that the Apostle's body was not where it should be. They pointed out exactly where in the crypt the relics of the Apostle should have been placed, but not as much as a tibia was found.

The mystery caused mild concern in the Vatican leadership. What happened if they did not find them? Had Emperor Constantine the Great laid the foundations of the main Catholic Christianity church at the wrong place?

Soon, a young archaeologist found a skeleton, while digging, placed on a ridge about ten meters away from the burial site. And it was Peter's, but why was he there? It would take more than ten years before these questions could be answered.

The excavations went on and became known, so Pius XII decided that during the Holy Year 1950 it would be announced that they had found Peter's tomb. It was there, right under the Papal altar and the huge baldachin of bronze in the church. But they kept quiet about the discovery of the skeleton.

It was then that Friedel, the artist from Sweden, was given the unimaginable task of reconstructing and painting the historical people and events that his colleagues had impressed upon the walls one thousand six hundred and forty-eight years before, in the room where Jesus' foremost disciple relics would rest forever.

Through historical documents and some free deductions, the conclusion was that Constantine the Great had moved the relics when the burial site began to be covered by water and there was great risk that the holy bones would be destroyed. And there they lay when the church building began and the crypt was eventually cemented into the foundation of St. Peter's Church.

Finally, it was accepted and agreed that the archaeologists had carved out of clay and concrete Peter's relics. His successor, Paul, had the same view. However, there were, and probably still are, those who believe that this has not been fully clarified.

In 1968 Paul VI decided that Peter's bones had been excavated and he intended to hold a ceremony, which would have the character of a funeral. It gained momentum in the media. Then, the leadership of the Catholic Church courted major TV companies to get access to the crypt and the relics. According to Archbishop Bruno Heim, the BBC offered a symbolic sum of £25 000 to get exclusive rights to make a film about the discovery of Peter's tomb.

The SBC was also in the queue. Nils-Erik Baehrendtz, who was happy with Friedel's filmmaking success in Italy, decided that if anyone could persuade the high lords of the Vatican to allow the filming of the crypt, it was Friedel.

Friedel again contacted Bruno Heim, who was then at home in Helsinki. He promised to give it a try. Shortly afterwards, he called Friedel with the astonishing message that "the Swedish television that has shown its capacity under the direction of the Swedish artist, who painted in the crypt, now knew it may make the film." All Rights Reserved. Free!

Considering this situation and what happened later, Friedel's wishes must have gone straight up to the pope who had given his blessing. And maybe he had an ulterior motive.

In 1969, the documentary "The Fisherman from Gallilea: On The Grave and Stool of Peter" appeared worldwide. Of course it was well received in the Catholic countries. Friedel himself was in Rome when it was aired on Italian television and obviously he enjoyed the attention and praise he received.

One morning after Friedel had breakfast at his hotel, a delegation of three men led by the Pope's secretary, Archbishop Pasquale Macchi arrived to see him. They had met a few times before and relations between them were good. Signor Macchi expressed His Holiness' congratulations on the film and the Pope's desire to have a conversation with him.

A private audience with the Pope? Friedel began thinking of what he had accomplished. This was something which was the privilege of bishops, diplomats and kings only. No, said Don Macchi, it was not about an audience. His Holiness wanted to have a private conversation at his home.

Friedel told me later that his thoughts ran away with him as he and Don Macchi walked through the mighty corridors that led to the Pope's own Holy of Holies. Was it about the voices? Had Jesus Christ's representative on the Earth whose word is law for around two billion followers, had thoughts about Friedel's discovery of a fourth dimension of life that had nothing to do with religion and faith?

The 73-year-old Paul met Friedel in the hall and asked him to join in the work room which was furnished with well-stocked bookshelves and a large imposing desk cluttered with files and papers, a sofa and a couple of armchairs. They sat down. The pope's skinny body was wrapped in a simple white robe. On his right finger he wore a gold ring with a symbol of Jesus, and a crucifix hung around his neck.

He expressed his congratulations on the work Friedel had done in Pompeii and Rome. According to the story I did about Friedel's first meeting with the Pope, he said initially: "We think a lot about Sweden and the Swedish king."

Popes say "we" and "us" when they are talking about themselves. He also thanked Friedel for the paintings he had done at Saint Peter's Basilica. Friedel reported about the encounter:

We talked about everything and I had a feeling that he had something on his mind. I was sure that the voices would come into the conversation. We talked a little about the Catholic Church's openness and that it was meant to show the world the willingness to adjust to the requirements of the present. I said he should show people how he lives. I had previously thought of trying to make a more personal film about him and that was probably the track I connected to. Actually, I took it rather freely and said I thought there was not a satisfactory contact between the Pope and the people. He answered: "It is not us but our mission that is important. It is our desire to meet every human being who wants to meet us. But we know these are fantasies."

I persevered and said again that he should show the people who he was and how he lived. "The little man on the street must know who you are. But the contact with you is important. You only get it at the audiences; they are always the same. People see Your Holiness coming; you speak to them; you bless them. A few people get a few words with you. That's all."

Friedel could not have prepared the presentation of his desire to be able to make a film about the pope in a better way. Throughout my reasoning, Paul sat quietly. He just looked at me. He probably thought about what I had said. I could not trace any grudge against my impudence on his face.

Suddenly, he took my hand and said: "You are right. We need all the contacts we can get. We need to get out to the people from this area where we now sit. If only we had time. We popes may not have time for ourselves. But it's true, misunderstandings occur by not coming into contact with people."

I wondered if he would say something about the voices and my message about the possibility of establishing contact with another life dimension after death. And as if he had read my thoughts, he said: "Tell me something about your research."

I knew through Bruno Heim that someone had conducted research in parapsychology at the Vatican, and he had indicated that Paul was interested in the subject. But I had not in my wildest dreams, imagined that I, a total atheist, would sit alone with the pope and tell him about my discovery. There was no further explanation, but I talked mostly about the scientific tests already done and the future research that would be done and the positive results attained. Paul listened with half-closed eyes, and I was afraid that the tired man had fallen asleep. But he had not. I finished my presentation with a question:

"How would your Holiness and the Catholic Church perceive these electronic voice phenomena and my assertion that they come from a life dimension after death?"

Paul opened his eyes and said:

> We are following your research with great interest. We have also our own research on this topic. This is not contrary to the Church. We know that between death and resurrection there is another sphere of existence, a post-Earthly existence. You have found an opportunity to establish contact with deceased people who live in this life dimension. It is highly interesting. We have decided not to ban a dialogue between us and the deceased, but the condition is that these contacts are made with religious seriousness and for scientific purposes. We have an open mind on all issues that are not contrary to the teachings of Christ.

I must admit that when Friedel reported on this meeting and the talks with Pope Paul VI, I did not know if I would fully believe his story. It was almost unlikely. I did not want for a moment to doubt his sincerity, but the whole thing seemed so improbable considering that the pope was involved!

My earlier doubts disappeared a few years later when I read the book *Voices from the Tapes: Recordings from The Other Side* (1973). Under the title *The Vatican and EVP*, British psychologist and EVP researcher Peter Bander wrote:

> Pope Paul VI was well aware of the research on the EVP (Electronic Voice Phenomena) discovered by his friend Friedrich Jürgenson in 1959. He wrote about this in the Vatican newspaper (*Osservatore Romano*). He awarded the Swedish artist and filmmaker who, among other things, made a documentary about the pope's life and activity, the Order of Commendatore of San Gregorio Magno (Commander of the Order of Saint Gregory the Great).

The book was yet another confirmation that Friedel in no way exaggerated. A letter from Friedel to Peter Bander stated: "I have found a "sympathetic ear" to the Electronic Voice Phenomena in the Vatican … I have got many friends among the leading figures in the holy city. Today's 'bridge' stands firmly on its foundations."

There was no doubt about who had the sympathetic ear. A year later, at dinner with Archbishop Bruno Heim, I managed to find out more.

Surprisingly, Friedel's private meeting with the pope ended in the following way:

Suddenly Paul said: "Do you want to paint our portrait?"

"I must admit I was perplexed: another pope who wants to sit as a model for me. But I found myself quickly and answered:

"Yes, *we* want to."

The pope smiled, understanding the joke.

The conversation lasted for about half an hour. This laid the foundation for Friedel's permission, a year later, to make the film *Everyone wants to see the Pope,* about Paul VI and his activities and about Giovanni Battista Montini who became Jesus' deputy on Earth. So my friend sat there with sketchpads and sequins and portrayed yet another pope; he could now be considered a famous artist from Sweden!

Friedel painted three portraits of Paul during thirty sessions. During several audiences he sketched and spent most of the time at the pope's summer residence Palazzo Pontificio in the small town of Castel Gandolfo outside Rome.

He told me:

> I came to Castel Gandolfo in July and was courted by papal servants. I had a great time there. I could work in the pope's own studio where he usually sat and wrote his own speeches. In the summer after a day at the Vatican, he wanted to withdraw to Castel Gandolfo.
>
> Palazzo Pontificio di Castel Gandolfo is a medieval palace where many popes have lived: a very inspiring environment to work in. It is wonderfully accommodated at beautiful Lake Albano near Rome. The building is nestled in a garden in ancient Roman style with stunning floral displays, pines and cypresses. It has elegant furnishings. The walls are lined with fabrics and fine antique art. The furniture is mostly in Baroque and Renaissance style; much has been inherited from pope to pope.
>
> Don Macchi was always close to Paul and myself. I was not invited to any kind of socializing. They always ate breakfast alone when Don Macchi informed on what the world media had to report.
>
> He showed me around and we had many interesting conversations about the pope and his situation. Sometimes I thought he almost became too intimate in the small revelations about Paul's failing health caused by the fact that he never had time to sleep properly. When I retired, he sat there in his office, and, according to Don Macchi,

continued until 2-3 o'clock at night. He begins each new working day with his own mass. Don Macchi declared: "Being Pope is a martyrdom. He is very lonely even though he meets so many people."

I understood when he was sitting as my model in Castel Gandolfo, what Don Macchi meant. Paul sat quietly with short breaks. He seemed very shy and eager to please. And he talked to me like an ordinary person, just as if he needed to talk casually with a friend. His voice was soft and friendly. He spoke slowly and calmly, without for a moment changing his complete calmness. He talked a little about his predecessor Johannes XXIII who, after four years as Pope, died on June 3, 1963. He was the one who wished that Cardinal Montini would be his successor. It took just 18 days before the white smoke curled out of the chimney of the Sistine Chapel and it was announced that a new pope had been designated.

I understood that John was his idol. He conducted a democratic reform within the Vatican. He deliberated that the issues that the Pope would personally decide on were first discussed by the Church's cardinals, bishops and priests. Paul said on one occasion: "We try to do everything to follow in John's footsteps. He was open and spontaneous; we are more reserved and shy. It is difficult for us."

It was a confession that I could not comment on.

Friedel returned home to Sweden with the promise that the next year he would come back with his film crew and follow the pope in his work. But perhaps what was even more remarkable—he wished to show to the Catholics all over the world that Pope Paul in his exaltation of Jesus' representative on the Earth, was a man of the people.

On the last days of the month of October 1970, my photographer Jerry Windahl and I traveled to Rome for a few days following Friedel in his work with the film. It was, to put it mildly, bingo for the reportage team from Sweden!

On one of the days we spent there, we had agreed to meet Friedel in the Piazza di San Pietro. With Friedel's enthusiasm and conviction that all the doors all the way to the pope's private apartment would be opened to the "Saint Gregory Commander" and his companions, he told us: "Come along now, you should meet with the pope!"

Bruno Heim met us up on the stairs and we passed the first Swiss guards who jerked their lances a little when they saw Jerry with several cameras hanging on his chest. But when they discovered that we were in the company of Archbishop Heim, they went on guard duty. We now

FJ with Paul VI

FJ and Paul VI

FJ at the Vatican

FJ with Paul VI

FJ with Pius XII and Vatican paintings at the Vatican

H Bruno Heim, Fj and Anders Leopold, Vatican

walked through the magnificent halls and towering corridors. In the end, we were so deep inside the holiest area of the Vatican that we far exceeded the limit of what was allowed for the media. We winked at each other and suspected that with the help of this escort, we would be part of a real scoop. In front of me, I saw how Friedel and Paul the pope, inside the latter's private apartment, posed in front of Pius' and Paul's portraits that Friedel had painted.

We finally entered a hall where the walls were decorated with historical pictures and paintings of what must have been Jesus' disciples. In the middle of a long wall there was a door, with a carved image of Christ, and there was no doubt about who lived inside it.

There were, unfortunately, also two buffoon dressed men, in red-striped puff trousers and sharpened lances. They lowered them threateningly. They stared, shocked, at Jerry's cameras. He hung his arms around the sides to indicate that no illicit images would be taken.

Heim had a short conversation with them and then with Friedel who turned to us with a face as if he had just received a death notice, and whispered what we suspected, that we were not welcome, but we were allowed to sit down on a pair of chairs worthy of royal buttocks.

Among the cameras, on Jerry's stomach, there was a small Leica that he used to sneak around with. He touched it but withdrew his hand when one of the lances moved.

We sat like patients in a waiting room hoping that the doctor would confirm we were healthy. We exchanged a number of whisperings to each other and could hold back fits of laughter with difficulty.

Then the door opened and Friedel came out and beamed as if he was a new believer. Under one arm he carried a large folder, which would prove to be the Pope's private photo album. He walked quickly towards us with his right arm outstretched in a strange gesture he might have borrowed from the Pope. And he said, "My friends, the Pope has blessed you through the door!"

This was to thank and receive. To this day I do not know if there was some irony in the message he brought forth from his Holiness. But the thing that made him shine was that he had permission to let us copy the images in the album and send them out into the world. It was the scoop!

We could not wait to sit down on a bench in the Piazza and begin leafing through the album. We saw photos of Giovanni Battista Enrico Antonio Maria Montini during his early childhood and as an elegant civilian student wearing a suit and hat.

I really do not know how these pictures were received in the Catholic world when we wired them from the *Aftonbladet*. But they must have shaken up some circles and attracted enormous attention because it was the first time a pope stepped down from "the Holy See" and showed his human face. Some believed that by showing himself as one of us he lost much of his magic, while others believed that he strengthened his position among the people, which, of course, was his intention when he stood in front of the movie camera.

Unfortunately, we missed a special event. When we went home, Friedel was called to a small ceremony at the pope's private audience chamber in the Vatican. Bruno Heim and Don Macchi were there along with some archbishops Friedel knew. Pope Paul declared that "Il Professore Friedrich Jürgenson" had developed a large and valuable work for the Vatican and the Catholic Church as an artist and filmmaker and therefore, would be awarded the Order of Commendatore of San Gregorio Magno.

According to Bruno Heim, there were only a few non-Catholics who had been honored with this Order since it was instituted in 1831. It is in gold and enamel and consists of a sword and a cross. With this around his neck, Friedel would in principle, if he so wished, have access to all Catholic homes. In the past, it also meant the right to have a time of sex across St. Peter's Square. A use that, to Friedel's disappointment, it is not allowed today.

On the day when Friedel borrowed the Pope's photo album and we had been blessed by His Holiness through the door, while we were still the center of attention, we celebrated in the evening with Archbishop Bruno Heim. We ate and drank and Heim told me that his Holiness was not a teetotaler and drank a few glasses of wine with dinner.

Then I came to the question that had troubled me since I became aware of how the man of the spirit voices, an absolute atheist, had gained such influence in the Vatican.

I do not remember exactly how the Archbishop expressed himself, but first and foremost it was, according to him, Friedel's captivating personality that had opened the doors.

Nevertheless, the voices were not in Friedel's life when in 1952 he had close contact with the Vatican for the first time. It was only his artistry, drawings and paintings of the Old Town in Stockholm that drove Ludwig Kaas to offer him to paint under Peter's Basilica. In doing so Kaas fulfilled his desire that the work should not be performed by a Catholic artist for fear that in their enthusiasm and euphoria, they would exaggerate the imagery.

Here, Heim revealed something very interesting. Although Friedel was the one who officially discovered the possibility of electronic contact with the deceased, parapsychological research in the Catholic Church, via the *International Society for Catholic Parapsychologists,* was already going on. And in that year of 1952, strangely enough, perhaps even as Friedel was sitting there in the moisture-dripping crypt, two Catholic priests received an anomalous voice that was identified as Father Dr Agostino Gemelli's deceased father.

He and colleague Pellegrino Ernetti were recording Gregorian chants. During the play, they heard a strange male voice interrupt the song. They had the recording tested at the laboratory of physics of the University Cattolica del Sacro Cuore in Milan. They could hear the voice very clearly. Gemelli was shocked. It was his father's voice that addressed him by the nickname he used during his childhood. The voice spoke in Italian: "Zucchini, it is clear, don't you know it is I?"

They became alarmed and deeply concerned about what this could mean for the Catholic Church, to contact the dead, and they turned to Pope Pius XII and reported on what had happened. According to an article published in the Italian newspaper *Astra* in June 1990, the Pope told them:

> Dear Father Gemelli! You really do not need to worry about this. The existence of such voice is a strictly scientific fact and has nothing to do with spiritualism. The recorder is totally objective. It receives and records the sound waves from wherever they are coming. This event may become the cornerstone for a building of scientific studies that will strengthen man's belief in an afterlife.

It was like hearing Friedel. But it came from a Pope.

After the sensational recording with Professor Hans Bender and his team in May 1970 at Friedel's house, and the conclusion that EVP was a fact, that the voice phenomena exist, the research took off in many parts of the world. Since then, the Vatican has continued to sponsor all areas of parapsychology including Electronic Voice Phenomena.

12

FRIEDEL ON LIFE ON THE OTHER SIDE

In this chapter I will let Friedel tell us what emerged during his contacts with what he believed were people in the fourth dimension of life; how they live, and his interpretation of how they describe what happens when a human being dies on Earth and wakes up on the other side.

Friedel's narrative is sometimes dreamlike and surreal, the way we usually perceive our own dreams. Perhaps it is only a dream and for us, the living, difficult to understand or to believe that there is a reality beyond death. But in the light of the actual recordings of the voice phenomena that you can enjoy throughout this book, it is easier to understand and believe in Friedel's interpretation of how life manifests in the fourth dimension.

He candidly admitted that sometimes, he may have been mistaken about certain voices in his collection of approximately 6000 recordings. Disturbances and unclear recordings may have led him to misinterpret some messages. But he also affirmed that even if he reduced the number of clear recordings by two thirds, 2000 messages remained in which anyone with normal hearing capacity should be able to perceive the voices.

Friedel was not interested in "believing." He saw the messages on the tape as objective phenomena that often spoke for themselves even in his absence. Of all the things he heard, especially during long recordings from the radio, he formed his strong philosophical view of life in the fourth dimension and the activity that his friends were carrying out to try to build a bridge to us here in the third dimension.

I have picked out selected passages from his first book *The Voices from Space*. He writes in the imperfect, i.e. past tense, which creates a feeling that this occurred during his time but no longer exists. I do not share this view and certainly others who conduct their own research on the voice phenomena don't either. I know that Friedel himself did not see the voice phenomena as a closed chapter when he moved to the other side. I am sorry I did not bring this up with him when I had some input in what he wrote in his second book, *Radio and Microphone Contacts with the Dead*. He described what happened in the past even though he was always in the middle of the action. So, when I now reproduce his words, I do sometimes change the tenses and I think he would happily accept it.

I quote from Friedel's book:

> What we perceive with our senses of space is only a limited reflection of a transition to another dimension, i.e., a boundary area that cannot be grasped with the frequencies of our five senses, at least not as long as our observation ability cannot be put into another swing. In the same way that radio and television waves cannot be perceived with the senses, even though they penetrate the brain, so other frequencies, oscillations, substances and phenomena should also permeate ourselves and our world without our becoming aware of their existence.
>
> In fact, we are not only surrounded by tones, colors and shapes that we cannot observe, but also by living beings, who, despite other life fluctuations, are no less real than ourselves, albeit with the difference that they are independent of space and time that exist only for us. Accordingly, such freedom of movement must first have triggered an inner freedom of the ability to observe, the effects of which we cannot yet fully realize. Just like all great discoveries that firstly have to break laboriously through obstacles, but then when the right time comes, are perceived as natural and obvious.
>
> Life usually hides her big secrets just where we, least of all, believe we can find them, and it also appears that their solution is through an ingenious simplicity, constantly overlooked by us. We have not managed to become aware of the cause of our failure.

In spite of all our religions and in spite of all philosophical and materialist doctrines, we have thoroughly misunderstood life and, therefore, have not been able to solve the mystery of death. But since death, whether we understand its meaning or not, cannot be separated from life, and since we have undoubtedly misunderstood its meaning, the pressure of this unsolved riddle has been turned into a heavy burden from which we cannot free ourselves. Therefore, no other problem has tormented and persecuted us as much as this unsolved mystery of death. It is apparently in the essence of human nature to face everything new, inexplicable and unknown with doubt, mistrust and ridicule, and it takes a deep inner conviction and not little courage, to disturb the ingrained dogmas and doctrines.

When, in October 1960, I wrote the introduction to this book and was engaged in the testing of my tape recordings, all started to get fixed outlines. I must frankly admit that these contours grew into a gigantic mountain whose dizzying heights I alone, would climb. It was a depressing realization of my own insignificance, which for a long time deprived me of the joy of the work and drove it to an almost complete stop. Rather than indulge in the joy of my contact with this higher dimension, I became ever more painfully aware of my own limitations. I think I could resemble the tragicomic situation of an enchanted portrait in which suddenly the ears grow out of the canvas. Because, like a static oil painting, I could not, despite my strange contacts, step out of the frames of time and space. Again, I felt compelled to start all over again.

At first, I managed to regain my self-confidence by understanding my task. To this end, I did not have to exceed the limits of my natural capacity because the task that fell on me corresponds entirely to my innate qualities such as perseverance and patience and the concentration without which a tireless listening cannot be performed. But the most important thing is that despite all the difficulties, fortunately, I am full of enthusiasm for the cause. Quite apart from the constant internal reconfiguration of my thought processes, it seemed then very difficult for me to divide my time rationally. The day is not enough. To listen to the kilometer-long tape recordings requires a tremendous amount of time. There are recordings which I must control a dozen times from beginning to end, number them and write down the text [my transcript of the communicators' words].

My invisible friends had used the word *communication department*, a connection line to their central research station, for the first time.

They talked about a multilingual research team of selected employees in all countries, about tests, about common actions, about phonetic difficulties and disruptions, and so on. The whole broadcast could be considered a hint, a preparation, and only the end was real.

However, interesting as such contacts may seem, certain conditions are required to address them. If they are missing, the recipient is subjected to severe psychological pressure. To be mature under such supersensible tensions, one must, above all, have a constantly vigilant transformative power of self-knowledge. As long as we are not aware of our weaknesses, repressed desires, fears, superstitions, masked ideals, taboos and defense mechanisms, our unconscious turns, with all its spooky arsenal, towards ourselves. Because, in fact, the danger does not lie in the supersensible contacts and experiences, it lies exclusively in ourselves. That is why the fate of most media, seers, clairvoyants and other occult aspirants is all too often connected.

At first I received a description of the lowest level, which actually comprises the result of a frightful deformation of the human spirit. One can define these mistaken paths as a direct result of the general (human) crudeness whose blind power has created cavern-like hollow spaces in the delicate, easily deformable lighter spheres. My friends refer to these as caverns (from the Latin word for caves). Negatively charged thoughts and emotions, primarily fear, envy and hate, create an astral environment geared exactly to the character of these emotional impulses because the astral substance is very easily formed and deformed by desire and imagination. The process itself—the creation of the environment—seems to work nearly automatically, that is to say, independently of individual volition. Criminals and sinners of all kinds that have been excluded or sentenced to death by the living, generally slide into these dark caverns of the astral level.

My friends report further that the transmission of radio waves has caused a major change among the inhabitants of these lower regions. This has to do with the substance of the radio waves that somehow invigorates those who are enclosed in these dark caverns. However, because the mechanical and impersonal nature of the radio transmissions brings about a merely accidental and transitory invigoration, a group of helpful souls (that is to say, my friends) decided to transmit a special carrier frequency that can create a better connection with these isolated spirits.

The "awakening of the dead" plays a very special role within the context of this great liberation activity. It may sound strange, but it seems that most of the dead in these lower astral regions are in a condition of deep sleep, especially those that have suffered a violent death. The "awakening" is basically similar to a psychic intervention designed to liberate the sleeping individuals from their nightmares and obsessions.

The sleepers experience the astral dream or paralysis condition as a kind of "plastic imaging process", in effect as objective reality. Their "awakening" eliminates a portion of the most difficult obstacles because the "dead" are now able to gain access to the community of human souls in their new sphere.

It seems plausible that only after the conditions in this "purgatory", as one might call the lower astral regions, are changed, a regular connection can be established with our three dimensional world.

It was obviously the intention of my friends to demolish this fatal vicious circle, which consists of the continuous and automatic repetition of the same imaginative and emotional processes. In this connection, it seemed that this extensive liberation action could not be accomplished without the cooperation of those still in the body; that the realization of this plan was dependent on collaborators "in the flesh" who could dedicate themselves to this task based on their insights and determined helpfulness without being misled by wishful thinking and emotional daydreaming.

As far as I am personally concerned, I had first to gain an extensive insight into, and become familiar with the otherworldly sphere and the psychic changes that humans experience with death.

When I finally mastered the practical side of the connection after many months of hard work and countless setbacks, there suddenly emerged another large obstacle that proved extremely difficult to overcome because of its subtle nature.

At that time, I had reached a border region that could be called the "border crossing to the beyond." Rather than having to deal with a tooth-gnashing Cerberus, I had to confront another, much more dangerous adversary who threatened by stealth and inattention to degrade the clarity of my insights.

The frightening element of this opponent was the fact that he resided within me and was most difficult to recognize. Speaking allegorically, one could describe him as a "Guardian of the Past" trying like a robot to continually assess all that was new with a traditional yardstick limited by old concepts of time and space, to the point where everything new would be shoehorned, crippled and deformed into the archive of our experience.

This robot's activity and vitality were admirable and tireless, and that was where the greatest danger lay. Even understanding and describing the striking phenomena of a new life dimension was difficult as I, like other people in living life, got used to looking at my own world and myself day by day with the eyes of the past. The events of this new life plan are incomparable—they cannot be interpreted, recognized or classified. They transcend the boundaries of our experience; they are literally new, nameless and unique. But how should one then be able to observe and understand them? Is not the whole thing *a priori* hopeless and insoluble?

If you want to do further research herein at all, you must become aware of your own inadequacy and accept your lack of knowledge. But such an understanding cannot be reached without humility.

The deeper insight I gained into the unknown plane of life, the more clearly the events in our own world emerged. It is amazing that, in reality, the distinction between the two worlds seems to be only imaginary; boundaries have been established as a result of space and time in our consciousness.

Much like ice and steam differ from each other even though they are both water, the difference between our world and the beyond consists merely in the difference of the vibration frequencies requiring a specific degree of consciousness in order to be perceived by us.

The daily pursuit of the magic bridge initially forced me to the greatest vigilance. Even the slightest deviation from the course specified with the utmost accuracy, immediately results in a setback, which, under certain conditions, can be highly perceived. The whole experience proved to be a very hard learning process. Three possibilities were open to me in order to get a clear and detailed picture of this new life plan:

The first path was using the tape recorder via the microphone, a provisional way, and the other via the radio, the direct way. Since everyone can listen to tape recordings, they represent, from a scientific perspective, repeatable and controllable evidence for the existence of a postmortem human condition.

The mechanical-technical character of the tape recorder eliminates, from the beginning, any relegation of the phenomena to subjective experience, especially since there is always the possibility of making new recordings in the presence of new witnesses.

Path number two consisted of my capability of entering the otherworldly sphere by "myself" without having to die first, no matter how fairytale-like this may sound to some readers. I know that with this statement I am directly provoking the suspicion of the reader, but if he or she will concede me just a little more patience, then the reader will surely understand clearly what I have in mind.

The path of the personal crossover once again consists of three separate methods. The first takes place in a fully awake state in which I am able to witness what is happening in the fourth dimension as if I were looking into a television screen. I see what is going on in living color, however without hearing any accompanying sounds. The second method takes place in a semiconscious state. I am no longer a passive observer, but a participating "traveler" who takes part personally in the processes going on around me.

The third method, finally, is my astral out-of-body experience while I am in a deep sleep.

In the case of these rather rare, but fully awake and conscious instances of my presence in the other world, I was able to make detailed notes, whose accuracy would be confirmed by tape recordings immediately upon my return.

Let us now turn our attention to the activity of the so-called "copyists" and "popsers" who have been made responsible for a significant as well as interesting liaison task. The word "copyist" is meant here as "imitators", whereas the English word to "pop" has been rendered into German as a "popser", but one could also say someone who 'pops in,' glides into (the conversation).

The work of the copyist centers on linguistic technology, i.e., the modulations of the human voice. On the other hand, the popsers are masters of oscillation in song and music. Basically, both are using the enormous advantage of their location beyond and outside of our own time environment. They are able, by means of a certain contracting and stretching of time, to change unnoticeably the syllables and words used by radio announcers or the sounds of any musical instruments.

These vocal changes and metamorphoses are taking place completely unnoticed and without any interruption of the song or spoken word. They only change the text and not the sound of the speaker or singer. In these cases, the radar performed a kind of text filtering function in which the exchange of text would by no means extend throughout the entire broadcast band but only include my receiver whether located in Stockholm or Mölnbo.

I wish to emphasize that these word transformations can hardly be spotted without the assistance of an operating tape recorder. In the course of "listening" to a transmission, one is unable to detect the lightning fast changes even if one listens very carefully; besides, the copyists prefer to make use of exotic languages to which one rarely pays any attention.

In spite of my many years of training and Lena's indispensable assistance, I only succeeded on rare occasions to detect such word changes in the course of an original transmission. Even today I am irritated with myself about this, but I also have to admire the virtuosity of the copyists and popsers who succeeded in a masterful way to carry out these textual changes imperceptibly. Unfortunately, I only discovered later that I ended many of these superb text exchange transmissions prematurely because I was convinced that they were ordinary radio transmissions.

In most cases the actual wording of the communication could only be picked out after numerous repetitions. Once I understood it correctly there were no longer any difficulties.

But then it could happen that, for instance, an Arabic announcer would begin speaking in German, Swedish, Estonian, Italian and also Russian without any change of emphasis in his voice! Suddenly he would call me by name, bring me personal news, mention Mölnbo, Maelarhoedjen and the names of my friends that had passed on, mix in a few Arabic words again, and once again quickly, casually, send words of greetings to my wife, Monika, and our poodle Carino and then end his commentary in the original language.

Occasionally it even happened that the copyists delivered themselves of invented commentaries in exotic languages using their own voices, but actually spoke German or Swedish. The changeover could be detected more easily in these cases, especially when the voice of the copyist was familiar to me.

Such direct imitations were often voiced at normal strength using the so-called "radar" (connection), which acted like a kind of loudspeaker. The same exchange technique was used by the popsers in the case of songs and instrumental music.

In the case of comedies, operettas or classical oratorios wherein spoken and sung words, recitative segments and music alternated, the copyists and popsers worked together. The popsers are masters of improvisation; they know how to use every appropriate occasion in a flash and they always sound innovative because they consistently avoid the stereotype.

Whereas the copyists cause surprise with their amazing voice imitations, the abilities of the popsers seem to be pure magic. The musical inserts of the popsers are always filled with rapturous joie de vivre that one could describe most appropriately as Dionysian. It really is admirable how spontaneously and easily these unseen human beings are able to present humor and drama, high spirits and poignancy in iridescent variations.

As the virtuosity of these artists knows no bounds, it is sometimes difficult to determine in which case we are dealing with imitation, text-exchanges or original presentations. I am convinced that no normal radio listener could detect these contact attempts without the help of certain keywords, the transmission of personal communication or, most of all, the multilingual confusion.

One time I received a transmission in which the popsers had exchanged the voices of a Czech male choir in such a way that a personal communication to my wife and myself was clearly received in four languages. At the same time, they maintained the orchestra and the applause without any change.

These multilingual song presentations were textually put together so unequivocally and personally that any doubt as to their intent would have to be completely excluded. Our first and family names were often called out or sung to clarify even further the personal character of these transmissions.

All of these cases involved sizeable groups of trained musicians, singers and actors who used free improvisation to display their artistic talents. There were also certain performances that were given by amateurs as well as children, involving smaller comedies, dialogues, and choirs presented informally and with lots of humor.

All these countless transmissions that were captured by me in the course of around eight years, undoubtedly represent a highly interesting, invaluable and, above all, an objective basis of evidence for my contacts.

Just the fact that these mostly luxurious presentations were transmitted on Europe's strongest radio frequencies is of decisive significance. One hardly needs to make the point that no radio station in the world would dare to broadcast such completely senseless and incomprehensible transmissions to the general public without triggering an immediate avalanche of protests.

However, despite my irrefutable evidence, I have to assume the determined resistance of certain circles who deny the existence of a higher dimension or that of another worldly sphere, and since my tape recordings obviously could not originate with a legal radio station, I will probably be suspected of operating my own, secret private radio transmitter. Of course, such allegations could easily be refuted because which private person would be able to broadcast such curious transmissions over a period of several years without causing notice or opposition, not to mention the huge costs that would be associated with such a risky enterprise. And it would be impossible to realize such a pirate radio station with its varied program, without numerous technicians, artists and well-equipped studios. And how would one make sure that all of these fellow conspirators would keep their mouths shut? No, the idea of accusing me of organizing and operating a secret radio station is plainly absurd.

No matter how strange and fantastic it may all sound, it is certain that what we are dealing with here are the voices of dead people who seek from their own perspective, and on their own initiative, to bridge the abyss between their sphere and ours.

For this purpose, the organizers on the other side are not only using a radar-like installation, but evidently they are in control of their own electromagnetic carrier frequencies that they know how to "fade in" at will, with our short, medium and long wave frequencies.

All contacts started with our sphere are subject to the supervision of a so-called "Central Investigation Station" and, evidently, cannot take place without the latter's mediation.

For instance, if the copyists and popsers exchange words within radio transmissions or put new texts into more extensive performances by means of their radar, this takes place exclusively in my radio receiver or tape-recorder, either in Stockholm or out in the country in Nysund near Mölnbo. However, the radio transmissions of the "Investigation Station" are crossing the ether unchecked and can be heard simultaneously in the entire world. This fact is of decisive significance because it presupposes the creation of an ongoing future connection between the two worlds.

The radio transmissions of the Investigation Station differ substantially from the radar contacts of the copyists and the popsers, not only because of their special strength (loudness), but also because they can be recognized by the special security measures that are drastically enforced.

These security measures are based on the following considerations: Since the planned connection with our world is intended to create a new mental attitude, the general public will have to be confronted gradually with the undeniable facts. Inasmuch as this entire action is intended to create an easing of tensions, "the organizers" are concerned to avoid as much as possible all elements of surprise that could cause confusion or shock. This is the main reason why all announcements over direct transmissions took place in a camouflaged fashion. One who does not recognize the different voices and their multilingual expressions, gets the impression that it involves some ordinary radio interference. In the case of these transmissions, my family name and location was never mentioned, a security measure that was deemed essential for the peace and quiet of my work. I owe it to my invisible friends that I did not have to prove to representatives of the Swedish security services that my radio contacts had nothing to do with the Fifth Column, but only with the Fourth Dimension.

As mentioned, the electromagnetic waves of their "Investigation Station" could be inserted into the radio transmissions of all our stations. Sometimes when I listened to an ordinary musical program of the radio, I heard faint voices in the background that brought me pieces of information. On those occasions, the pauses or the endings of a pianissimo were cleverly used for this purpose.

While these notices were generally transmitted in discrete tones, the investigation center has the means that permit the amplification of sounds up to deafening fortissimo. I received samples of such maximum sound strengths, sometimes only a few words, but so enormously loud that I winced in surprise each time.

Once I received a broadcast where the popsers had exchanged voices in a Czechoslovak male quartet and suddenly began to sing in four languages a personal message to Monica and me. But, at the same time, they had kept the orchestra and the applauding audience unchanged. Such multilingual performances of song were so unambiguously and purely personally composed that any doubt was absolutely ruled out.

Prominent personalities from the Antiquity, the Middle Ages or the time of the early Baroque have never signed up for me. I guess most of them have already been reborn and died several times, and, under other names, are here or on the other side.

Already the striking fact that people—like Hitler, Stalin, Trotsky, Lenin, van Gogh, Eleonore Duse, Annie Besant, my mother, D'Annunzio, Chessman, Göring, Himmler, Felix Kersten and many famous Jews and Christians, theologians, musicians, composers but also simple workers and craftsmen, i.e., people from the "broad layer of the population," with whom I have had and have contact in various ways—perform together and work on common tasks in the contact search with us in the third dimension, is of utmost importance to me.

So when, on the other hand, a real reconciliation has taken place between the executioners and their victims, I can only greet this with joy. I see and understand that here is the first real testimony of a universal human community in which the idea of universal brotherhood has been realized without exaltation or preaching morality.

For me, there can also be no doubt that these dead have seen through the true meaning of cause and effect and discovered the secret of death.

However, those on the other side also have to face connection difficulties and, over time, I realized that we, here in this world, could make a contribution by means of technical improvements, better directional antennas, filters and amplifiers that would lead to a substantially clearer and more flexible connection.

During the night between Friday and Saturday, June 30, 1961, I had a dream that can be counted among my most peculiar and interesting visits to the other side. I woke up around five in the morning and wrote down my experiences.

I was outside in the open, in front of a wide underground entrance that led into the deep like a gently sloping incline leading to what seemed to be a parking garage. A curious greenish yellow light shone from a clear evening sky, strangely dark and light at the same time. Many friendly people surrounded me. They were working at the entrance, improving and widening the way into the deep for the so-called dead, who are really alive even though they sometimes cannot free themselves for quite a while of the notion that they are dead. I am surrounded by well-meaning people who are willing and pleased to fill me in on the conditions of the hereafter.

It is strange, but with every shift in my feelings, my situation changes with lightning speed. Suddenly, without any transition, I find myself in a very large hall that is constantly expanding in front of me. It represents a curious combination of train station, church and public baths or swimming pools. Adjacent are countless waiting halls, storage rooms, public restrooms, shower stalls and swimming pools.

I enter a large room that is illuminated by unseen sources of warm golden shining light. I understand immediately that this room is very special and that it is connected somehow to something important.

I view this curious place with amazement. It reminds me in one way of a funeral chapel, in another of a decorated funerary chamber, and yet it hides something else of utmost significance. The place is filled with people who stand in small groups, softly conversing. There is a happy, yet somewhat solemn mood. Most are smiling quietly and contentedly, and all the faces exhibit the same certainty: it is done, we made it!

New people arrive unnoticed, and suddenly it became clear to me: this room represents a place of transition, a portal through which the dead pass after a burial.

The scene changes again. I meet an artist, a stonemason and a known museum director from Stockholm. I am told that the upper floors comprise numerous studios, which can be used by all the artists.

Yet most of them prefer to take part in collaborative work down here that includes a change in attitude and orientation. It is becoming increasingly clear that I have found myself in a sphere that is suffused by human feelings where our emotions not only bring about changes in the external space, but that reflect our inner drives visibly on the surface of our bodies. Here nothing could be hidden for it was precisely the nature and purpose of this place to bring to the surface and work through everything that was suppressed, hidden, incomprehensible and displaced. This would not reach the point of total exhaustion but only up to where the role they played in the human life that just passed was fully understood.

I came upon three women that were sitting across from one another and were occupied with a curious "emotional demonstration." The women were visibly changing the shape of their bodies. They obviously competed with one another with the goal of outdoing certain movie stars in the grotesquely exaggeration of their female curves, which were visible temptations, too. This performance seemed repelling and ridiculous. However, it revealed the urgent necessity to relieve an obsession. Perhaps these women were lonely in life, or ugly and deformed. In the next moment I find myself in the middle of a very luminous reception room that is connected to a mysterious burial chamber by a broad, open entrance. A man is standing in front of me and is speaking to me eagerly. I can clearly see his body, but I can't make out his facial features; they seem dissolved or erased.

"My name is Hugo F. I was a cavalry officer when I was young," he introduced himself. I was surprised, for I didn't know that my friend Hugo F. had a relative with the same name. The man led me to a kind of monument that had a metal emblem.

"This is our family crest," he said with emphasis. I looked at this curious thing, which reminded me of a decorated brass wreath, and tried in vain to comprehend its symbolism.

In the next moment the scene changed again. I am walking past a long row of rooms, corridors and hall that claim my full attention because of their curious appearance. I come closer to what looks like the main hall of a train station with many doors.

I stop in front of a large storage room. A faint smell of flowers, pine needles and palm branches flowed towards me. It was the typical smell of a funeral chapel for it also smelled like corpses. This depositary is filled to the rafters with funeral relics and utensils, fresh and partly wilted wreaths, bouquets of flowers, funerary ribbons, stuffed suitcases and the like. All these are things that convey the sorrow expressed towards the deceased. These are surely ether representations that follow the deceased, impressed by them into the afterlife. With that I mean certain astral copies and replicas of physical things that like the astral body of the deceased, continue in the fourth dimension. All these things were lying around in profusion.

Who was supposed to pick them up and what was the purpose of it all? This question occupied me for a long time; only much later did I find an answer.

Initially I understood that, in all, there are three types of physical dissolution:

1. The usual burial; 2. cremation; 3. the destruction of the body by accident, (this wasn't all that clear to me then) for example, by drowning, massacres, explosions of various kinds and so on.

One could ask the question: Isn't death, death, and what does it matter in what manner our body is destroyed? This argument is only partially true, because the mode of dying influences the transition into the next life. Certain laws apply in this process and the deceased have to undergo different cleansing procedures, although these proceedings are done during deep sleep.

It became also clear to me that certain deadly illnesses, such as various cancers, leprosy and so on, somehow affect the astral body of the deceased, i.e., they continue to exist in the imagination of the disembodied mind. Anyway, all those illnesses must be cured and eradicated completely. Special bathing facilities exist for this purpose; also semicircular shower niches, odd looking massage and cosmetic salons, and various treatment rooms in which the deceased are delivered from the remnants of their illness.

It smelled badly in these rooms. I don't know if these smells were brought upon by the fixed imagination of the deceased. However, I left the unpleasant smelling cleansing rooms and found myself in an adjoining swimming pool hall, which has left me with the deepest impression of all the experiences during the astral walk.

In reality, it wasn't only a swimming pool, but a whole row of pools that lost itself in the distance. The light was reddish yellow and a little dim; it reminded me of candlelight, the source of which I could not detect. On the floor of the hall were rectangular bathtubs, hundreds, maybe thousands of them. I was unable to overlook them all.

I stepped closer to the tubs in which charred human shapes were lying motionless. The bodies were totally black and mostly shapeless; one could recognize only the contours of the head, the shoulders and the chest that protrude from a dark, to me unknown, liquid. Here it smelled also like flowers and corpses.

In the hall were a few tall nurses who somehow reminded me of visiting social welfare nurses. Strangely, they led small black dogs around on a leash, which reminded me of Scottish terriers because of their scraggly fur. The most curious thing, however, is that the dogs seemed to be smiling at me and wagged their tails affectionately. The nurses were carrying on a subdued conversation; they looked kind and content.

In my notes from that night, I had marked this spot with "normal deceased." Unfortunately, I cannot recall the actual meaning of this notation. I can only remember that the majority of the deceased had to go through these cleansing baths.

As I approached the bathers, I discovered that under the black charcoal crust of the bodies, that delicate childlike pink skin would shine through here and there. Some of the faces had regained their normal skin color. I understood that some of the deceased were being bathed to health again after some kind of cleansing procedure involving fire.

The dead were all sleeping; that is to say, they were unconscious. In another friendly illuminated room, hundreds of waiting people stood around. A somewhat solemn, religious mood seemed to pervade these premises. I was told that these people were waiting to cross over after the cremation of their bodies. The important condition was that the deceased had to discard many of their ways of thinking and feeling, after which their crossover to the astral plane would gradually take place. This, however, applied only to those who had died "a normal death."

Others had different passageways available that were unknown to me.

I awoke with the clear feeling that I had received an important glimpse into a particular sphere of the hereafter, a kind of reception center maybe, which had to be passed by most of the deceased.

The meeting with Hugo in the dream had a remarkable resolution. We had a neighbor in Mölnbo named Hugo who often visited us. The following day after my dream, Hugo came visiting with some relatives.

I told Hugo about my dream. "Curious, very curious," said Hugo puzzled; "I don't have any relative named Hugo F., but I myself was a cavalry officer when I was young." We also spoke about the dream with Hugo's relatives; however, no one could explain the mysterious relative.

13

PICTURES FROM THE OTHER SIDE

During his lifetime, Friedel claimed that in the future it would be possible to send images from the other side to an individual recipient and that messages would appear directly on the recipient's PC.

In the 1990s his prediction came true. Many researchers reported both pictures and texts of those "who had passed away" a long time before. Nor has it been technically possible, purely from a scientific point of view, to rule out the possibility that the messages, images and texts have a paranormal origin, i.e., that they come from another life dimension.

As I wrote earlier, I vouch for photographer Claude Thorlin in Eskilstuna as a very credible person. I have described some of his recordings, which were presented at Friedel's international press conference in 1964. He attracted a lot of attention when, in 1969, he took a picture of a spirit with a feminine appearance that suddenly hovered over the tape recorder in connection with a recording.

But he got even more attention with the picture of Friedel that flashed on his TV screen at the same moment that my dear friend was being buried in Höör's church on October 19, 1987.

In March 1969, Ellen and Claude Thorlin were visited in their home by an engineer, with a keen interest in electronics, who was curious about Claude's experimentation with tape recorders and also the voice phenomena. They listened to Claude's recordings, some of which are described in Chapter 7. Since Claude was a photographer, the visitor wanted to show him a couple of strange photographs on which, quite inexplicably, some mysterious lights and lines had appeared. There is something called "supernormal photography" which some perceive as supernatural phenomena. Claude emphasized that as a photographer, he had seen an innumerable number of photos of various kinds but never encountered anything that could be designated, "supernatural."

He was skeptical. There were so many ways to manipulate photos. But the conversation aroused his curiosity. He had not previously linked the voice phenomena with "supernatural" images. Ellen, as I mentioned earlier, was mediumistic and on the morning of March 20 became a little disturbed. She said that she had a definite feeling that something "was going on:" that something would happen; that she felt "under the influence" from the other side. Claude saw this as a sign that they should start the tape recorder and make some recordings. Then Ellen suggested that they should do an experiment on what they had previously talked about: supernormal or mental photographing while they recorded on the tape recorder. He agreed but decided that they should have a witness present during the recording.

He contacted his friend Sten Warghusen in Eskilstuna, a managing director with a very good reputation in the town. He accepted and promised to show up in the afternoon.

Ellen's concern had increased and she felt tired. Therefore, she lay down on her bed for a relaxing break but immediately fell asleep. When Sten Warghusen arrived, he and Claude went to wake up Ellen. She told them that at first, she was wide awake, but suddenly got the feeling that someone was touching her head. She felt as if invisible fingers were gently massaging her scalp and then she must have fallen asleep.

Ellen could not recall what she had dreamt of but she had experienced a sense of presence, as if someone was close to her.

They went into the living room and it was decided that they would put a dark cloth on the table to eliminate any glare from the glossy surface. They placed the tape recorder on the middle of the table and next to the microphone. Claude attached the camera to a tripod and pointed it so that all three were in the picture, including the tape recorder and microphone. There was a distance of three meters between the camera and the tape recorder.

The camera was a thumbnail and SLR camera of the brand Practika. The design was such that it effectively ruled out double exposure. In order to be able to open the mirror and tighten the shutter, it was required that the film be fed to the next box at the same time. The camera was loaded with black and white film (Kodak plus X). A "ball type" remote trigger was connected to the trigger mechanism. Aperture 2.8 and time 1/5 second.

The window blinds were down and the room was sunk into semi-darkness. It was twenty minutes past five. Claude Thorlin wrote in his book *The dead Speak on Tape* (Larsson Publisher, 1972):

> We, three people, sat around the table. The tape recorder was running and we talked quietly. The atmosphere was good and pleasantly relaxed. Suddenly, Ellen pressed the rubber ball and a faint rustling from the camera announced that exposure had occurred. After a short time, we stopped the tape recorder. Then Ellen said that just before she pressed the ball, she had a strong sensation of something like hair tickling her face. When the tape was played, we could all hear a strange and unusual sound. It sounded like someone with his mouth right next to the microphone making a strong exhalation and emptying his lungs of every ounce of air.

Later, Claude told me that the sound strongly reminded him of Friedel's recording of his yoga friend Boris Sacharow's deep inhalation and exhalation.

The unexpected sound that none of the three present had heard in the room, increased the tension when Claude went into the apartment's quick dark room to develop the film. He opened the back of the camera, cut off the exposed film stub and put it in the fixing bath.

After a while, he turned on the red darkroom lamp and examined the developed strip. The negative was quite dense and slightly over-exposed. What immediately caught his interest was a dark spot that was clearly visible on one corner of the negative. By examining the mark more closely with the help of a watchmaker's magnifying glass, he seemed to be able to distinguish the features of a human face, but upside down in relation to the three in the picture.

Astonished, slightly shocked, he hung up the rinsed film to dry over an element. When it dried, he immediately printed a paper copy with great excitement. Then it seemed clear. There was no doubt that it was a face. All three could see the head of a girl next to the tape recorder. It was upside down near the microphone, which loomed like a round ring through her hair.

The questions piled up: who was she? Where did she come from? Was she the one who breathed so hard in the microphone? The spirit girl was given the working name "Olga" but would soon introduce herself with her real name.

Berndt Hollsten, former chief editor of the popular weekly magazine *Såningsmannen*, who gladly spread ideas that were often at odds with the establishment, worked to collect material about paranormal phenomena. He had received a copy of "Olga's" image and stated that it was the strangest phenomenon he had faced in his research.

Hollsten did not mistrust Claude Thorlin in any way but wanted to get an expert opinion about the picture and he managed to get the world-famous photographer Lennart Nilsson interested. Nilsson was known in the world for his stunning images from inside the human body; among other things, he photographed the development of a fetus.

They both came to visit the Thorlins and listened to a detailed account of how the stunning image had appeared. Lennart Nilsson examined the negative and could immediately tell that it had not been tampered with: for example, some kind of double copy. He also promised Claude to inform, when requested by the media for his opinion, that there was no cheating. But he would not otherwise express an opinion on how the image had originated.

The day after, Claude and Ellen made a recording and seemed to hear a faint whisper, which they interpreted as: "Caimy ... Do you think my image is good?"

The Spirit girl, therefore, was named Caimy and Claude and Ellen rejoiced on the fantastic event!

Från vänster till höger: Claude Thorlin, Sten Warghusen, Ellen Thorlin, som tog bilden med en fjärrutlösare, samt Caimy, andeflickan. Bilden togs den 20 mars 1969.

The Spirit girl Caimy upside down at the right side of the image.

Claude Thorlin commented on the recording with Caimy in his book *The Dead Speak on Tape:*

> I am absolutely convinced that we have witnessed here a paranormal phenomenon of rare magnitude. Trying to explain the whole thing is extremely difficult. We move in the border area of an unexplored country and are, for the time being, constrained to guesses and hypotheses. The most immediate idea, however, is that negative and tone bands are affected according to some common principle. Maybe we dare guess at electromagnetic wave motions in some form. Undoubtedly, Ellen played a key role in the context and served as some sort of catalyst, which made the phenomenon possible. Her experiences before, during and after the experiment speak also for this: falling asleep, the feeling of hair that tickled her face, nausea and strong fatigue.

The photo on page 245 was taken with a Polaroid camera and, therefore, there is no negative. This Polaroid photo was sent around to several different technical photographic laboratories for inspection and somewhere along the way, it disappeared. Fortunately Claude had photographed the image.

On 14 September 1998, shortly after Claude's death, his wife Ellen sent me the only copy she could find in her husband's photo collections and indicated that I could dispose of it freely. I posted it on my website and now the photo is available in all occult contexts all over the world. The last time I saw it was in a Spanish TV show about the paranormal and other occult phenomena, wherein the picture was included in the vignette itself. Suddenly, it faded when I accidentally was tuned to that channel, probably much like when Claude saw it.

During all the photo-technical tests, nothing emerged showing that the image was a forgery of any kind. And, as I wrote, Claude's credibility was above any suspicion.

The original Polaroid copy reveals a little more about this image, widely published in newspapers and online. Admittedly, the image is almost black but one can still discern the lines from the TV screen. Friedel died on October 15, 1987, and was buried four days later. If we accept everything he told me about what happens after death, he must have woken up in the fourth dimension of life almost immediately and an image was sent over to our life dimension while his body was buried. The bright spot on the image is his left shoulder and he is wearing a light shirt; the collar above his right shoulder appears on the original.

The burial at Höör's church took place at 1.00pm on October 19. The Thorlin couple wanted to be at the burial but did not manage to make the long journey between Eskilstuna in Södermanland and Höör in Skåne.

But they were well aware of the time when the funeral would take place and had intended to start the tape recorder to perhaps, get a greeting from Friedel.

Ellen said that when she woke up on the morning of October 19, she still had fragments of the memory of a dream in which a voice had told her to turn on channel 4. They pondered this at the breakfast table and Ellen had a feeling that it was related to Friedel's funeral. But what was meant by channel 4? Swedish Radio (SR) had three channels and, at that time, Swedish Television (SVT) had only two.

Claude had read about the Harsch-Fischbach couple in Luxembourg who, in the early 1980s, declared that they had captured paranormal images on a TV screen. Inspired by these thoughts and Ellen's strange dream, he decided to keep his Polaroid camera on standby in front of the TV and turn on the TV channel 4 a few minutes before 13:00. He loaded the camera with a black and white film.

The TV flickered because there was no broadcast on this channel and the sound was annoyingly sharp. They muted it a bit but still started the tape recorder.

I interviewed Thorlin and his wife on January 15, 1988.

Ellen reported:

> We were a bit tense and expectant, but the flicker on the TV became tiring. It also felt boring and my interest waned. I had doubts. What did we expect? To see the funeral?
>
> After about a quarter of an hour, Ellen went up to the attic to pick up the laundry.
>
> **Claude:** had almost given up hope, and was about to turn off the TV when the screen slowly blackened. My first thought was that a technical error had occurred, that the picture tube might have been subjected to too much stress. Then I saw a point of light that slowly increased in intensity and size. Somewhat excited, I raised the camera and pointed it at the bright spot. Then suddenly, the bright spot expanded all over the frame and in the light I thought I saw a face and pushed the camera shutter. The whole thing developed for about five seconds then the black in the picture disappeared and the flicker returned. I remember staring at the TV for a long time and then at the camera and I promise that I was so excited that my heart was pounding out of my chest.

Claude shouted at Ellen and wanted her to be a witness when the image was produced in the camera for a few seconds and slowly turned out. Ellen heard in Claude's voice that something startling had happened and came crashing down from the wind.

Together they looked at the Polaroid image, which slowly changed from white to black shadows. They saw a faded face, blurred but clearly a face. After a few seconds, Ellen exclaimed: "Oh my God! It's Friedel!"

The picture on page 245 is a copy of the Polaroid picture—a picture that was tested for about four months before Claude dared to show it in public. He had good memory of what a fuss it had been about the picture of the spirit girl Caimy.

Since no manipulation could be detected, there were comments insinuating that the picture may have been in a TV program about Friedel.

Friedel was the protagonist in SVT's program "This Is Your Life" in 1985 with Lasse Holmquist as host. Was the picture possibly there? Claude got an SVT technician to run through the entire program and he could not find anything reminiscent of Claude's picture. He himself did the same without detecting any sign that the paranormal image was included in the program.

Friedel was also the main character in the film *Last Gate to Eternity* by the German director and filmmaker Rolf Olsen, in which I participated, along with other episodes, in Friedel's interviews at his home in Nysund. When Rolf heard about the amazing and unlikely photo, he went through the entire film to try to track down an image reminiscent of Claude's Polaroid image. No frame or movie sequence could be mistaken for the image.

In my interview with Claude, he declared: "We do not care if people do not believe in what we have told. It was the same with Caimy."

After Friedel's death and all the commotion caused by the picture, they tried many times to make contact with Friedel via radio and tape recorder, and once managed to obtain a weak voice that was not directly reminiscent of Friedel's. They thought they heard a deep male voice that uttered: "I was so skinny!" This was a fact. Leading up to his death, Friedel's body had become emaciated.

14

OTHER RESEARCHERS OBTAIN GOOD RESULTS

1964 was a turbulent year in Friedel's life. The big events were the international press conference and the tests in Freiburg and at Nysund and the publication of his first book *The Voices from Space* (Saxon & Lindström, 1964), which was published in the spring.

News of the voice phenomena spread around the world via the media and just the idea that it might be possible to get in touch with the dead in such a simple way as connecting a microphone to a tape recorder was mind-boggling.

Even before the press conference in June, Friedel had attracted attention in Germany. *Die Andere Welt* published an interview with Professor Hans Bender who declared that "the voice phenomena recorded by a Swedish artist are probably paranormal." Bender confirmed that the voices were examined by his group (as mentioned earlier) at the University of Freiburg and the Max Planck Institute in Munich.

Mr. Kirner from *Die Andere Welt* and Mr. Geisler from *Hermann Bauer Verlag* in Freiburg visited Friedel. According to my dear friend, several microphone and radio recordings with the German publishers were carried out with surprising results. Kirner wrote and published two extensive articles about Friedel in *Die Andere Welt* in March and April.

Geisler wanted to do a German translation of the book and publish it with *Hermann Bauer Verlag*. Friedel agreed, provided he was allowed to proofread and make some corrections. Ideally, he would have done the translation himself but he was busy writing his new book, *Radio and Microphone Contacts with the dead* (Nybloms Publishing, 1968).

He had also begun planning his big Pompeii adventure and longed for the paintbrush and palette. Despite not wanting anyone to comment on what he wrote prior to publication, he let me read part of the script.

The first German edition was published by H Bauer Verlag in 1967 under the title *Sprechfunk Mit Verstorbenen*. The Swedish edition of *Radio and Microphone Contacts with the Dead* was released in 1968.

When *The Voices from Space* came out in the spring of 1964, Friedel, for the first time in at least five years, felt that he had begun something that others would be involved in and ready to develop.

I think I can set a date for the day when Friedel thought that he could proceed with his research in a more relaxed way, while at the same time plan for the promised excavations in Pompeii. It was on Friday, May 28, 1965, when we had made some recordings without much success. He avowed that same day, "You know, I've handed this over to the scientists. This is a development that I was hoping for, that there would be more people besides me doing research, and Europe's leading scientists in parapsychology have now become involved in this matter."

Actually, the tests with Hans Bender and his team had been very positive and Bender stood by his opinion that, very likely, the voices had a paranormal origin. And Friedel received reports from various parts of the world about people and groups that replicated his work and made successful recordings.

Friedel affirmed that about a dozen Swedes had heard about the subject and had received very clear voices without his participation. I contacted two of them.

Ture Feldin, forester from Sundsvall, reported the following:

> We did a test on the evening of the thirteenth. We talked around the microphone and were not immediately prepared for anything. So during the playback, we all heard a paused voice that said very clearly:
> "Ture hear!"
> Unbelievable. But the voice was there. Of course, there are also some dubious sounds on my tapes. But there is a voice that anyone can hear which says:

"Contact Ture! On the radio ... contact quickly! We are waiting ... we help."

In addition, we have received a voice that my family and I firmly believe is mother's. She died in 1953. Her voice says:

"Ture. Welcome ... mom."

I do not know what to believe. These voices have appeared entirely without Jürgenson's intervention. They are on the tape. That thing is done.

Among the people that Friedel mentioned was a colleague of mine, Stig Söderlind at Eskilstuna-Kuriren, who lived in Eskilstuna where Claude Thorlin was also doing his experiments.

Söderlind confirmed in my interview published in the *Aftonbladet*:

I have received a lot of dubious quality. But a female voice as clear as my own has come through. We were three men talking. There was not a woman in the apartment. On the tape, you hear how I describe the voices and say: "The voices not only speak in Swedish, they can also appear in Aramaic ..." Suddenly a female voice is heard saying very clearly:

"Yes, it can be any word"

And shortly thereafter:

"Sentimento."

Söderlind played part of the tape to me on the phone. Men's voices were clearly heard and then a very clear female voice. The quality of the voice surpasses several that I heard at Friedel's house. I wrote in my article:

"It's there on the tape, you can hear it yourself," said the editor Söderlind. But what is that voice? And how has it come in?"

Friedel himself admitted that it was perhaps the most compelling microphone recording that he had heard: better than most of his own. And it was directly related to the ongoing conversation.

Shortly before, Friedel had received the visit of Konstantin Raudive as mentioned in Chapter 1. Raudive had studied in Sweden and he mastered Swedish well enough to be able to read Friedel's book *Roesterna fran rymden*.

Friedel thought that he could have a very serious collaborator in him. But it took time before Raudive became convinced that the voices really came from another dimension of life. He often recorded short words in German, French and Latvian, that he mastered well from his homeland and later his studies in France. Then, one night, something occurred that fully convinced him.

When he played a recording, he clearly heard a woman's voice that he could identify. The voice uttered in Spanish:

"Va dormir ... Margarete" (Go to sleep ... Margarete).

He wrote about this in his book *Unhoerbares wird hoerbar*, [Inaudible become audible] which came out in 1968, the same year that Friedel's second book *Radio och mikrofonkontakt med de doeda* was published: "These words affected me greatly" said Raudive, "because Margarete Petrautzki had died recently, and her illness and death had been very hard on me."

Raudive's life changed and he was equally devoted as Friedel to the voices. Until his death in 1974, he recorded around 100,000 audio tapes. He collaborated with Hans Bender and several German electronics experts. For a while around 400 people were involved in his research work as described in his book. Simultaneously with the book, Raudive released a gramophone record. Neither Friedel nor I were particularly impressed by the recordings presented. Raudive made the mistake of mixing in too many dubious tape recordings, which minimized the impression caused by those, which were indeed, of a higher class.

In his book he wrote: "We now have proof that the soul lives on after death. Instead of mere faith, we have gained certainty that is provable through objective physical facts."

Raudive had strong support from various scientists. One of them was Professor Alex Schneider in Switzerland who participated in Raudive's experiments. He felt that the book should be translated into English to reach a wider international audience.

Several publishers were interested, and one suggested that he come to England and take part in experiments under strict test conditions. As a result, he made several trips to London where recordings were made under strict control. The results were impressive and the book was published in English in 1971 under the title *Breakthrough: An Amazing Experiment in Electronic Communication with the Dead*.

Friedel released his third German language book, which was a summary of the two previous books.

One day in May 1965, Friedel was in an especially good mood because the negotiations with SR and SVT were going well, meaning the financing issue of filming in Pompeii was solved. He could now plan his Pompeii projects. He would soon, together with his TV team, document the decay of the ancient city and, at the same time, together with the Italian archaeologists, decide which house would be excavated.

He told me: "I feel that the voices are with me. It is in Pompeii that I will build the bridge. All of this is important for me to gain credibility so that people do not think I'm just a crazy artist who is great."

I thought his record was already convincing: even then he had reconstructed paintings from St. Peter's crypt under St. Peter's Church in Rome and, in addition, had become Pope Pius XII's portrait painter; he was the first artist to paint and have an exhibition in Pompeii. I felt this was just the beginning.

The film *Pompeji: en kulturell relik som måste bevaras* (Pompeii: A cultural relic that must be preserved) was shown on the Italian television the following year and the heated debate that followed, forced the Italian government to invest millions in the restoration of the ancient city.

The Voices Solve the Mystery!

In the summer of 1966, the archaeological excavation was due to begin but was delayed when a tragic event occurred that hit Friedel very hard, which meant postponing the trip to Pompeii and resulted in his spending all his time with the recordings. I had a role in this drama, too.

I was *Aftonbladet*'s national editor in Örebro and covered most of central Sweden. Every morning, I called the police in the larger towns to hear if anything of interest to us had happened. And on Saturday, June 4, 1966, something dramatic happened. A 17-year-old girl from Köping, just a few miles from Örebro, had been missing since Wednesday, June 1. She had never been away from home or work before without notifying her family. All her personal belongings and money were in the house. The reason why she was not declared as missing until Friday was because her father had been away. This was very alarming. In the last couple of years, two women had been murdered in the area and both cases were unsolved. My photographer, Jerry Windahl, and I set out to take part in the reconnaissance. We received the name and pictures of the missing girl, Rigmor Andersson, at a press conference.

I remembered the name. One year before, Friedel had been visited by a man, Berndt Andersson, from Köping, and one of his three daughters, Rigmor. Friedel had enthusiastically spoken about the visit, and above all, about the girl. She had a special charisma and he saw her as almost mediumistic. She had excellent hearing and could concentrate. And she had a great desire to try to get in touch with her mother Eivor, who had passed away two years earlier: not least because it would help her father, who was having a hard time recovering from the loss of his dear wife. He found life completely meaningless.

He had read about the man of the spirit voices in a magazine and then delved into the book. But it was Rigmor who persuaded him to contact Friedel.

This was the kind of visit that Friedel had a hard time saying no to. As usual, he was reserved, in case the recordings would not yield anything. He explained that one cannot reach everyone on the other side immediately after death. The person you sought contact with may not have been awake or aware of the change.

Once he also said that most people who visited him were not prone to hearing voices other than those he himself recorded. But they were still happy just by meeting him and talking about their grief. Most of the time they left with the promise to try on their own since they had now learned how to do it.

But the unexpected could also happen—an immediate contact. According to Friedel, even during the first recording, Rigmor and Berndt Andersson had heard a faint, almost whispering female voice say: "Det vet vi ... Eivor ..." (We know that ... Eivor ...).

"It was my wife ... her name was Eivor!" said Berndt Andersson, overwhelmed and in tears. "Yes, it is mother's voice," said Rigmor very moved.

Berndt Andersson and his daughters visited Friedel on several occasions. Berndt Andersson also started to make his own recordings and, according to Friedel, with very good results. They were so compelling that Friedel copied them to have them in his own collection.

Now, a year later, the missing girl was Berndt Andersson's daughter, Rigmor. When I got the name at the press conference, I called Friedel. He was already informed by his sister Elly, who lived in Köping and knew the family. He was very upset and said that he would not go to Pompeii until he found out what had happened to Rigmor. I told him that we were out on several occasions and participated in the search for her. I had talked briefly with Rigmor's father but I did not mention that I also had contact with Friedel.

Friedel had always argued that his friends on the other side, in different contexts and through their comments, showed that they were aware of what was happening in the circle around those who were looking for contact. But he also pointed out that they did not function as some sort of information center, which, with a request, could provide information about a missing person and what had happened to that person. At this point, there were barriers and constraints when it came to those living beings in the other life dimension. Still, some messages could be interpreted as looking into the future and cryptically suggesting that they knew what was going to happen. It is called precognition, which Friedel gave examples of in some of the earlier recordings.

Friedel spent all his time trying to make contact with his friends on the other side to possibly get information about Rigmor's fate. He told me when we spoke on the phone, that if Rigmor was murdered it was a police matter to find her and to find the killer. But as long as she was gone, and perhaps even if she lived, it was important for him to try to clarify the matter.

He had previously recorded her voice when Berndt Andersson and his daughters were visiting. Now he played over her voice on a tape to help identify it if it suddenly appeared. The voice was soft and broad, a typical dialect from the middle of Sweden.

Meanwhile, we followed the search closely with the police, the military and hundreds of volunteers. And, in the classic evening newspaper style, we reconstructed her last hours before disappearing from the time she left her workplace—a goldsmith's shop—to the kiosk where she showed up at around 8:00pm but did no shopping. I was given a hint by the kiosk assistant that the police had not given us: "she looked as if she was waiting for someone."

Since Rigmor was described as a well-behaved and cheerful girl, we assumed that if she had decided to meet somebody at around 8:00pm, it would be someone she knew. Maybe this was also the last person to see her before her disappearance, and perhaps that someone was the perpetrator.

On June 11, I read on a local newspaper that Rigmor had been engaged at the beginning of the year and that her fiancé was doing military service at Falun, a little town north of Köping, and had been home on Wednesday, June 1, the same day that Rigmor had disappeared. I contacted the journalist who had written the article and he gave me the name of Rigmor's fiancé. We decided to go to Falun the next day and try to make contact with him.

I called Friedel. He was very distressed, and this according to his later explanation, made him miss the message since he had gotten his assistant Lena on the tape the day before, in the follow-up of a question asking if she could say something about Rigmor's fate. He recorded his question at the normal speed of 7 ½ i.p.s. (19 cm / sec). A moment after the question, he stopped the recording and listened to it at the lower speed of 3 ¾ i.p.s. (9.5 cm / sec). This was the way he had tried his hand at microphone recordings and contact with Lena. In the distorted sound he could often hear her whispering voice.

Lena whispered: "Heute Abend durch die Radio!" (Tonight through the radio!)

Throughout the evening and well into the night, he recorded with the radio but heard nothing. He felt a painful insecurity and that made him miss the message.

On the afternoon of June 11, Rigmor's body was found in a forest glade about a mile from Köping. There was no doubt that she had been strangled to death.

The police had apparently reached the same conclusion as us. We were halfway to Falun when we heard on the car radio that a man in his twenties had been arrested on suspicion of the murder of Rigmor Andersson. Thus, we had nothing else to do and returned to Örebro.

Six months later, when Friedel was in Pompeii and a powerful storm hindered the work of excavation and filming, he completed his book with an additional chapter on the assassination of Rigmor Andersson. In the meantime, he had overheard the tape from June 10. He found nothing at the normal speed and listened to his question and Lena's response at the lower speed. There, in the bit on the tape that he had failed in his excitement after Lena's message, he heard a male voice say clearly: "Rigmor Tot!" (Rigmor dead!)

OTHER RESEARCHERS OBTAIN GOOD RESULTS

I have listened to this recording several times. The voice says her name clearly. It came up the day before the girl's body was found. But Friedel did not hear it until he listened to the recording again six months later. The title of the article is: Rigmor is dead!

Friedel said that the voice reminded him of Felix Kersten's. I could not decide about that and neither could Kjell Stensson. He admitted that he heard the voice and that the phenomenon of a clear voice recorded at the wrong speed was completely unknown to him.

Apart from Lena's whispers, Friedel had never perceived a voice when he switched on from the higher rate to the lower one. If a voice is recorded at the rate of 7 ½ i.p.s. and listened to at 3 ¾ i.p.s., it is a lower octave; a soprano becomes a tenor, a tenor becomes a baritone and a baritone becomes a base. But the voice that said: "Rigmor tot," recorded at the higher speed and reproduced at the lower one, was a clear male voice. "A technical impossibility," said Stensson. And so it was. This is yet another example of the inexplicable ways of the voice phenomena.

Police headquarters in Köping were right next to the church. When Rigmor Andersson was buried, her fiancé collapsed and confessed that he had killed her. He admitted that he had lost his temper when she ended their relationship.

A few weeks later Friedel went to Pompeii. His film about what he called "Pompeii's second destruction" had been shown earlier in the year and the clearance work had begun. He was now a celebrity and was hailed almost as a hero of archaeologists and of all those who worked in Pompeii.

15

FRIEDEL'S AND ANDERS LEOPOLD'S JOINT RECORDINGS

Friedel and I made a lot of recordings together, during nightly sessions in the late 60s. Many were hard to interpret and of poor quality and I often needed his help to make a possible interpretation. But there are some, which I like to reproduce in text and sound before I talk about them. In my opinion, they are astounding microphone recordings which I made when I started writing this book. Some are better quality than some of Friedel's recordings.

Readers might think that because I met Friedel often and experienced some successful recordings with him, I must have sat by my tape recorder at home frequently and sought contact. Actually, I was interested in existential questions about life and death, and perhaps about the fantastic discovery of a connecting bridge between two planes of existence. But even if I was happy with what happened in Mölnbo, unfortunately I did not have Friedel's patience. And I did what Arne Weise did: that is, after all, he experienced what were perhaps the most significant recordings with Friedel but did not make any of his own. Furthermore, I did not have the time required because I was in the middle of a journalistic career that required most of my interest and energy.

My wife Mona was probably more inclined to experiment with the tape recorder, but she also had a lot to get involved in as a fashion journalist and a mother of two. There are some tapes from the 1960s-1970s that I have now listened to but refrain from mentioning here due to their questionable quality.

Since I had the responsibility for the *Aftonbladet*'s editorial office in Örebro, I had to commute often between Örebro and Stockholm. It was almost certain that I would visit Monica and Friedel on the way home from the big city.

I have not dated the recordings that follow and I was not involved in some, but I have heard them several times. A few are mentioned in Friedel's notes that I attach as documentation, and, when I listen to them, they bring back memories of that time.

Monica and Friedel were vegetarians and she could transform food dishes without meat into delicacies. That evening I had a hamburger with onions. But a hamburger that was made of beetroot and as good as the "original."

We sat down at the table for a long time and drank good Italian white wine (with hamburgers!) and I think it was the first time I managed to get Monica to talk about the voices. She never participated when journalists, or people who wanted help to get in contact with relatives, visited Friedel. She spoke rarely of their own experiences and, when it came to voices, Friedel never made any attempt to get her involved. But she watched over him like a mother over her child. In spite of the fact that she was a very engaged and busy dentist in Stockholm, and commuted between the capital and Mölnbo, she managed the so-called ground services, which, among other things, included answering the phone and thoroughly informing herself about the caller before handing the phone over to Friedel or promising that he would call.

A journalistic memory is often a short memory. An interview or a conversation, when you do not have access to a notepad or a tape recorder, can linger until shortly, and afterwards you throw memory posts on a typewriter (as it was then) or a computer (as in the present) or make some marginal notes on the pad (always). It is enough to recall essential parts of the interview.

I felt that the conversation with Monica during the dinner was so important to me that when I got back to Örebro, in the evening, I made notes which I was going to use at any convenient time.

The occasion arrived when we shot the film *The Gate to Eternity* and I would make a filmed interview with Monica: a reluctant Monica. I used my notes in order to lay the foundations of my questions. She asked to read the questions and then decided to write down the answers, which

E 1

1

Anders Elmkvist:
Fru Jürgenson, Ni har ju från början
varit med om Eder makes märkliga band-
inspelningar. I femton år har Ni del-
tagit i röstfenomenens utveckling och jag
skulle gärna vilja veta, vilken upp-
fattning Ni har av denna kommu-
nikation och vilken betydelse den har
haft i Edert liv.

Manna J.
Den insyn jag fått i en dold livsdimension tack vare bandinspelaren är
för mitt liv så betydelsefull, att det nästan
är svårt för mig att i korta fraser
ge uttryck åt den. Om man betän-
ker att den dolda verkligheten, som
varit helt omöjlig att uppfatta och som
plötsligt genom en bandspelare rycker
fram och blir hörbar, så hanske
man kan förstå att man ovillkorligen
måste ändra sin tidigare inställ-
ning till livet och döden.
Det faktum, att vi haft kontakt
med många familjemedlemmar och

Friedel would translate into German. But even though Monica spoke almost perfect German, she wanted the interview to be in Swedish and subtitled in the movie.

After quite a far-reaching discussion, I got her answers in Swedish. She was very careful and corrected both questions and answers. I simply received a finished script.

The recording became a little chaotic because Friedel constantly wanted to intervene in everything. But Monica's decision was implemented and it was edited out of the final version of the film. When she saw and heard the first version, she firmly said no. We could not persuade her, not even with a few changes. She later explained that when she heard her own voice talk about something that was very personal and private to her, it was so unreal that she felt it would cause more harm than good regarding Friedel's case.

I do not have the cut-out section of the film, but kept the text and have reproduced the introduction below as documentation.

> (Anders): Mrs. Jürgenson. Initially, you have been involved in your husband's remarkable tape recordings. For fifteen years you have participated in the voice phenomenon development and I would love to know your opinion about this communication with people on the other side and what impact it had on you.
>
> Monica Jürgenson: The insight I gained into a hidden dimension of life, thanks to the tape recorder, is so important in my life that it is almost difficult for me to express it in short sentences. If you consider that the hidden reality, which was completely impossible to perceive and suddenly, through a tape recorder, advances and becomes audible, maybe you can understand that you must necessarily change your earlier attitude toward life and death.
>
> The fact that we had contact with many family members and numerous friends among the so-called dead, who after their death have participated in our lives with practical information and psychological advice, is the proof not only that these people live but also that their specific individuality is intact after physical death.
>
> A: Can Mrs. Jürgenson give an example of information from these dead people who have had practical significance for you?
>
> Monica J: We all know that in everyday life, events, which are seemingly small and insignificant, may play a major role. Actually our everyday life consists of a series of trivial commonplaces. Like when I could not find a pair of my favorite glasses which, despite thoroughly

searching for a couple of weeks, I could not find! Subsequently, during a tape recording, a voice came up that revealed where they were: namely under some cloths in a cabinet where I put them when I sorted out some tablecloths.

On another occasion, the day before a trip abroad, we found it impossible to find Friedel's wallet with travel funds, train tickets and passports. The atmosphere was almost hysterical when Friedel turned on the tape recorder and asked friends to help him to find the wallet. We received an exact statement from them that the wallet was in the jacket sleeve. It had happened that when I brushed off his suit jacket the wallet had slipped out of his inside pocket and got stuck in the sleeve.

On several occasions, I have also received good advice to prevent the development of an incipient disease.

A: Can Mrs. Jürgenson give me an example of psychological advice?

Monica J.: First of all, I must remark that all people have more or less psychological difficulties preventing them from spontaneously experiencing the reality that exists behind our beliefs and the adequate and creative way to express themselves. I understand that the most important thing is that every person develops self-knowledge and becomes aware of his limitations.

The psychological help that I and many others have received through these contacts has been outstandingly constructive. The so-called dead have never urged anybody to do whatever but have tried, instead, through parables and images, in a humane way, to make the person understand where the knot is. In an amazing new way, they try to provide our daily limited mind with an insight into our subconscious.

Among other things, the psychological help I received consisted in the fact that I was burdened by fears that the so-called dead have proven to me to be imaginary and which were, thereby, dissolved.

Through such personal imaginations and also through all generally erroneous notions, for example about life and death, man becomes psychologically bound to a relationship that creates disharmony and hinders free personal development.

These were statements by Monica Jürgenson, under the influence of Friedel. Eventually, Friedel and I got started with the recordings.

As always, he wore headphones because they gave him the opportunity to hear Lena's whispers informing about something. I could also hear the whispering sounds but, not being acquainted with the phenomenon, perceived them mostly as disturbances. I also heard how a happy and powerful male voice sang, but I interpreted it as a radio broadcast. But Friedel did not because he suspected that something would be revealed during the play. And it was.

Here, a bit of technology is required to listen to what has nothing to do with the song. In other words, a German radio voice and also some other weaker voice disturbances.

TAKE 25

The singer not only shouts Friedel's name but also mentions "die Toten" and ends powerfully and clearly with the words "on B-A-A-A-A-ND !!"

"Hört på band ... die Toten lieben band, där steht Friedel und hört på B-A-A-A-A-ND!"

(Listen to tape ... the dead love tape ... there stands Friedel and listens to T-A-A-A-A-PE!)

Of course, this recording made us cheer. I do not remember if we got something else that evening. This was significant enough and I heard at the first playback Friedel's name, and of course, the powerful words, "on tape!"

Friedel used to be quick to identify a voice, especially when it came from a singer. But this time he was completely satisfied with the recording and did not speculate on whom the voice belonged to.

When, on another occasion, we received another voice, I was at first very hesitant about Friedel's interpretation. The one we heard claimed to be Vincent van Gogh. But with a little practice, one can hear him mention his name. It is unlikely that this is a radio recording, not least because the voice in the introduction throws a Swedish phrase after a short German phrase: "now it gets better." The last word is emphasized and has a bit of a break. Later on in the tape, Adolf Hitler also mixes in.

TAKE 26

Even in this case it is important to "listen out" for the German radio voice.

"Kannst du hoeren? Nu blir det batter ... ich heisse van Gogh der arme ... wann Adolf Hitler klein und Franken war wir also foedd i skranken har Nietzsche, Adolf, Petsch ..."

(Can you hear? Now it's getting better ... my name is van Gogh the poor ... when Adolf Hitler was little and [in] Franconia we were born in the closet? /counter? Nietzsche, Adolf, Petsch ...).

Next, a girl choir sings and, according to Friedel's interpretation, they sing about "Die Tote" (The Dead) who live in "Frieden." Probably he would like "Frieden" to be an allusion to his name, but it also means "peace."

However, the chorus is clear and you can hear that the piece really starts with "Ja die Toten." This does not seem to be a radio broadcast but what about the ending? Carefully follow the rhythm as you listen and you will notice that the interpretation is correct.

TAKE 27 (LISTEN)[22]

"Ja die Tote siehe sie leben, siehe sie leben in Frieden, ja die Tote siehe sie leben in Frieden."

(Yes, the dead, see they live, see they live in peace, yes the dead, see they live in peace).

When we got the following recording I could not believe my ears. I heard what must have been a radio broadcast: a jazz song in which a woman goes to the so-called "scat singing," wordless improvisation, such as the one Ella Fitzgerald was an expert in. Perhaps it is she who sings. At the first playback, I heard "papa Friedrich" and after several playbacks, both Friedel and I noticed that actually she sings three times "Friedrich." This is a powerful recording.

TAKE 28

A jazz singer sings "papa Friedrich" on three occasions and uses Italian, Swedish and German words.

"Papa Fried(rich) molto trött. Papa Fried papa trött. Papa Fried hört bra. Hey! Aah bacio"

(Daddy Fried(rich) very tired. Daddy Friedrich tired. Daddy Friedrich heard well. Hey! A kiss.).

These are two powerful recordings from 1963, when I did not yet know Friedel. But I have heard them several times. You can see his own notes in the image below.

I am always amazed at how clearly you can hear the voice, even if some words are difficult to interpret. It sounds a little desperate. It is a woman who simply welcomes Friedel home after his visit to Italy and a place called Serapo. The voice breaks through in a piece of music that fades away. The woman shouts out her name, Hilda. There is no doubt that she mentions Friedel by name twice and the voice is clear. And she talks about his contact with dead people. According to Friedel's transcript, she speaks Swedish, Italian, Russian and German in a temperamental and slightly tragic voice.

TAKE 29

"Hilda ... tack! No, notsche, no schete notsche non tschera ... ob sie tala ... wenn du pratast so hoeren dalige menschen ... pall ju fallen tief ... out... Friedrich kontakta sterben menschen in atmosphaera ... vaelkommen Friedel aus Serapo!"

(Hilda ... thank you! No, notsche, no schete notsche non tschera ... whether they talk ... when you talk people hear there ... pall you fall deep ... out ... Friedrich contact dead people in the atmosphere ... welcome Friedel from Serapo!).

When Friedel wrote his second book, he ruled out the first phrase, "No, notsche, no schete notsche non tschera" because he found no way to translate it.

The following recording is one of the most powerful I witnessed with Friedel. A woman singing with a thin, slightly mournful voice to "kleine Pappi" as Friedel was most often called.

The voice is very clear and suggestive: quite similar to the voice of recording 29. The story is that she wakes up and sees "Fritzi ... Fritz" face. She does not sing to the music as a vocalist would. Instead, she goes into the rhythm with short breaks. First, she accompanies a pianist who plays some kind of cocktail piano that suddenly tunes into another station with a jazz song and solo by a guitarist. She does not disappear but remains with her rhythmic slightly monotonous song. That is, to a completely different radio broadcast and to a completely different piece of music. It is a fantastic example of how the voices make use of a carrier wave that is not directly tied to a particular sound, a human voice or music. The important thing is the carrier wave.

TAKE 30

"Jag beratta kleine Pappi ... a Busserl Fritzi ... Hallo! Da bin ich erwacht Fritz ... und will zeigen endlich dein Gesicht ... wir wollen euch gefallen ... und zwar in einem Wort ... Du einziger von allen ... und so komm ... nimm mich beim Wort."

(I tell little daddy ... a kiss Fritzi ... Hello! Then I woke Fritz up ... and finally want to show your face ... we want to please you ... in one word ... you are the only one of all ... and so come on ... take my word for it).

Interesting Happenings

One might ask why I, in Friedel's presence, did not receive any message directly addressed to me. Maybe my nagging doubts about the voices' origin made the doors not open fully to me.

A remarkable recording, which had to do with me, still occurred in my absence. I was invited by Friedel to come and listen as soon as possible: "Now, you've made contact!"

I came as soon as I had the opportunity, and was obviously excited about what he had received. And perhaps, as usual, I was a bit skeptical. Thus, I told him to keep quiet because I did not want to hear any comments from him until I overheard the recording once or twice and conveyed what I heard. If there were something I could identify, it would not, in all cases, be with the help of Friedel's suggestion.

The tape played. He sat there with his arms crossed and a triumphant smile. Suddenly, a piano concerto could be heard faintly but with increasing amplitude. It was Beethoven's Moonlight Sonata. A few seconds into the piece of music, the sound becomes weaker and a rough male voice utters:

"Elmquist!"

No more, no less. I heard my family name mentioned clearly, in the middle of the Moonlight Sonata.

Friedel rejoiced after my first spontaneous reaction when I without hesitation stated that I heard a voice speak my family name. But that was nothing compared to his reaction when I told him that I was sitting at home, practicing a relatively simple introduction to Moonlight Sonata on the piano. I had even made my oldest daughter Pernilla practice the same piece under my leadership.

That evening we drank an extra bottle of Italian white wine and, of course, he had an LP with Beethoven's compositions in his extensive record collection, of which the "Piano Sonata no. 14 Quasi una fantasia, Op. 27, no. 2 in C-sharp minor, Moonlight Sonata," is perhaps the most beautiful. So we enjoyed alternating his recording and the disc, and I played without much success the little I had learned on his old piano, which was tuned to perfection.

Besides Claude Thorlin, Lizz Werneroth in Skane, south of Sweden, also experimented with the voice phenomena (see: Lindström, 2007). One of her recordings impressed Friedel. It was late one night and she was quite tired but, still on the radio, she called her friends on the other side. Suddenly, a female voice came up uttering loud and clear:

"Lizzy ska sova" (Lizzy go to sleep!)

TAKE 31

Here is Friedel interviewing Liz and asking her to play the female voice urging her to go to bed. You hear her voice when she calls, and the answer sounds as if in her own voice.

"Lizzy ska sova!" Hello!

But then there was the issue about the voices' origin. There were very few of us in Friedel's circle who could identify a deceased loved one, and thus obtain evidence that it was a message from the dead, which appeared on the tape recorder. Those who got over their doubts were obviously Friedel and Monica, Claude Thorlin, Irmgard Kersten, Martha Anell, and others. Friedel sometimes said jokingly, although in all seriousness, that I should wait until a close relative died, so that the opportunity would arise to get in touch and identify the voice. In fact, during this time I did not have a close relative who had left the Earth, apart from my grandparents, whose voices I would never recognize from when they spoke to me in my childhood.

Although I have occasionally, over the years, considered writing a book about Friedel, I had not made any serious attempts to record voices until I started this work in September 2012. It felt almost necessary that I should try now and then. My tape recorder is a small compact, advanced recording device: a Handy Recorder H2-200m with built-in stereo microphones, which I use primarily to record lyrics and music for my movies, which I then transfer to the PC. I have received some voices of varying quality and have selected the best that readers can listen to.

Convinced at last! It's the Dead Who Speak

And here is what I have aimed at, an overwhelming proof, to me, that the voices come from the dead!

On Friday, September 7, 2012, I received a greeting from my wife Mona who passed away on July 15, 2010. I identified the voice immediately but took several safety precautions straightaway to avoid the worst trap: self-suggestion and wishful thinking.

For me there is no doubt that the voice belongs to Mona. It is unbelievable and it hit me very hard when I heard her. She had been close to Friedel and participated in several recordings in Mölnbo. This microphone recording was done one week after I took the decision to get all my material about Friedel in order and write the book. This was the second recording a few days after a very impressive recording which was directly addressed to me.

But I play Mona's greeting first. According to my interpretation, she utters in a tired and whispering voice: "Jag finns ... jag aer med dig." (I exist, I am with you). I saw it as both an answer to getting in contact and a kind of support for the decision I made to write the book.

The recording was done next to the large sea pool in Largo Martiánez in Puerto de la Cruz, Tenerife.

On the original recording, several minutes before the weak voice gets into the roar of the Atlantic waves behind my back, you can hear me asking Friedel and Mona to get in touch. I have shortened the recording and amplified the sound as much as possible.

I wanted to avoid self-suggestion and sent the recording to Chester Serrander in Karlskoga, a good friend who, at the time, was researching the subject of Spiritualism, and incidentally, inspired me to write this book. I asked him to listen carefully through the recording and, in the sea roar, try to identify a female voice. This was all he was told. This was his e-mail response:

> I have now listened to the audio clip many times. I have put it away, come back, listened. Waited overnight, listened again in the morning. Then, I listened one last time and I always hear this: "Jag finns haer med dig" (I'm here with you). It is only "finns" that seems less clear, it starts clearly with a consonant, but "finns" is good because then it all becomes logical. It also seems that the female voice has a significantly distinct dialect. Clearly, I feel a strong sense in the message.

I warmly thanked Chester because had he not done his listening and interpretation for me, perhaps I would fear of becoming a victim of wishful thinking and self-suggestion, as Friedel constantly warned against, and my level of ambition would have decreased. And perhaps I would not have completed this story of "my friend on the other side." Furthermore, Chester's observation regarding a distinctive dialect reinforces the message. Mona was born and raised in Eskilstuna and still kept a little of the typical Eskilstuna-dialect.

In this example, it is important to pay attention to the sea noise in order to clearly perceive the weak voice.

TAKE 32

I clear my throat and, shortly afterwards, a Spanish voice from someone who is nearby is heard faintly and, directly on this, a female voice, very faint but clearly says in Swedish:

"Jag finns ... jag aer med dig" (I exist ... I am with you).

Those who are reading this, and hear the voice, cannot identify it because of not knowing Mona. But what matters is that you hear it. If you do, it serves as proof that this voice cannot come from someone who is beside me but rather emerges out of nothing with the help not only of the Atlantic Ocean waves but also of the carrier wave. It is an authentic voice phenomenon.

My first recording during this period had occurred unintentionally a few days earlier and had driven me to turn on the tape recorder at appropriate times from then on. I was not trying to record any alien voices from space; I sat and edited a small documentary about the people behind street names and busts in Puerto de la Cruz, in Tenerife. Naturally, people, who in that case, were on the other side. My film was finished and I intended to voice dictate the text.

But firstly I will cite a comment by Oerjan Bjoerkhem (1946-1996), religious psychologist, author, journalist, and son of the famous parapsychologist John Bjoerkhem who participated in Friedel's recordings along with Arne Weise. Oerjan Bjoerkhem was one of the guests in Lasse Holmquist TV program *This Is Your Life*, with Friedel as the protagonist.

He had replied cautiously to a question by Holmquist about the credibility of the recordings, which many people had started doing on their own. Orjan Bjoerkhem affirmed:

> These recordings are made in most cases without any special control. Whoever recorded the voice can describe how it happened and who was present, but the only thing you can finally count on is the person's credibility. In Friedrich Jürgenson's case, scam is excluded. But this is going on today in the world and the media tell us about sensational recordings of voices from famous people speaking from the other

side. As long as such recordings are not carried out under controlled conditions, they have no scientific value. However, I would argue that some apparently anomalous recordings would require great technical knowledge to achieve a trick replay of that kind.

Several of Friedel's recordings were done under scientifically controlled conditions. But what I reproduce here are some of my recently recorded voice phenomena, which, therefore, lack scientific value. The only thing I can offer is that you hear what you hear and rest assured that I lack the technical knowledge to manipulate a tape recorder. And, although readers do not know me, I appreciate it that you grant me some credibility.

What you are going to hear is actually the clearest voice you have heard so far, including Friedel's "Tanner" and "Grekola." And it is addressed directly to me. Also, I think I can identify the voice, however unlikely it may seem. The rough male voice is reminiscent of the one that pronounced my family name Elmquist at Friedel's recording almost 50 years earlier.

I placed the microphone on a small table tripod as I usually do when I read the lyrics while I run the movie on the PC. The tape recorder was switched on, even though at that moment I didn't do a voice test. Therefore, you hear how I move the tripod. I say nothing. You will hear me clear my throat and cough, which is a recurring nasty habit because of a wheezy throat, which sometimes forces me to repeat an audio recording. I shut off the tape recorder and pick up the manuscript. I click on the latest recording in order to check if anything has come through. Immediately when it started, a hovering female voice shouting in English: 'Who are you?" can be heard in the distance, and directly after that, a powerful man's voice asking the same question but in Swedish: "Vem aer du?" (Who are you?). The strong man's voice seems to abort the female voice but, just when he stops, we hear her finish. When I heard the strong male voice with a direct question to me, I was pretty shaken up and did not perceive the much weaker female voice.

Thus, from the beginning, I heard only the strong man's voice, which we can all hear, and it was so shocking that I sent the audio clip over to my daughters who always followed the recordings with great interest.

Petra emailed back: "But Dad, don't you hear that there is also a woman who shouts in English?" Only then did I discover the whole thing and the phenomenon was even more impressive.

TAKE 33 (LISTEN)[23]

You first hear a distant female voice shouting in English and immediately afterwards, a rough man's voice asking the same question in Swedish.
"Vem aer du?" Who are you?

Another interesting case happened to me because on September 20, 2012, around 23:30, I was visited by a woman from the spirit world. I cannot think of any other description. Simply because she greets with the same expression as people do when they say hello to each other in Spain, where I live: "Hola ... buenas!" which translates as "Hello!" Good (day or afternoon)! But she was not physically present. That night I had a hard time sleeping.

When I started doing the recordings, sometimes I used to start the tape recorder and put it by my bedside while I prepared myself for the night. I definitely didn't have a female visitor in the flesh.

She sweeps like a spirit through the room and must have been close to the microphone because her voice can be heard more clearly than my own. I was in the kitchen getting a glass of water, and continued on my way through the living room to the bedroom. As usual, I muttered a little to myself. Just before I mumble, her voice comes in. It is as if the female voice used my voice as a carrier wave.

TAKE 34 (LISTEN)[24]

"Hola! ... Buenas!"

The medical doctor and psychiatrist Nils-Olof Jacobson, whom I have been quoting, is perhaps the person who knows most about the parapsychological phenomena represented by these alien voices. He listened to these recordings and told me that some were among the clearest he had heard. He wrote me an e-mail advising me to devote myself to recording for a little while each day:

> I hope you find the time and the inspiration to do other recordings. I have a feeling that you might be lucky enough to find yourself on a geophysical favored place, just like the Harsch-Fischbach [Maggy and Jules] who received a message stating that the reason they managed to get such clear recordings was the special geological conditions in their area. It might have something to do with the Earth's magnetism.
>
> This is one reason; the second one is that I get the impression that waves from the sea should be particularly suited as background

noise for contacts: a natural, harmonious sound that rhythmically changes character and intensity. It would be a shame not to explore these possibilities.

If I were there, I would probably try to take a moment every day, or at least most days, to attempt recording. It will not be necessary to take too long every time. And please, if possible, the same place and the same time of the day, so that the channel, so to speak, can stabilize. Experience from elsewhere suggests that it may be significant.

I took Nils-Olof's advice and did several recordings at roughly the same spot by the large sea pool where I recorded Mona's voice. I have not had the patience to do some longer recordings and in ninety percent of them I did not receive anything of value.

But on one occasion I received a voice that can be difficult to interpret, but one that I take as a direct message to me, and in which my name is mentioned.

It is a strange recording. Someone says something very quickly and it triggers a happy, slightly artificial laugh from a woman; after this, a male voice half-sings and seems to say my name, quickly and a little carelessly, sounding almost like "Anners." Then a longer pause, and at that point the voice comes through: "… life is Dorsey!'

The natural sounds from the sea roar are present before and after the recording, and differ markedly from the alien voices.

If the voice really says Dorsey, which I believe it does, there is a point here. It can be an example of the so-called precognition, which I described in connection with Friedel's recordings. A little over a week later, I finished a film for a good friend who had turned eighty, and who, during a visit to the USA, managed to sing at the jazz musician Tommy Dorsey's orchestra. And then I recorded several songs by Tommy Dorsey. Of course, life can be Dorsey!

TAKE 35

"Anders (Anners)… livet är Dorsey!" (Anders (Anners) … life is Dorsey!)

During a visit with friends in Puerto de la Cruz, in Tenerife, in July 2013, I had the tape recorder with me and let it record my conversation with the Swedish artist, Per Lilliestroem. His wife, Elizabeth, and my girlfriend Sigrunn were present.

FRIEDEL'S AND ANDERS LEOPOLD'S JOINT RECORDINGS

When I listened patiently through the rather long recording, something happened. We talk about Libya's leader, Gadaffi, who had finally been silenced, and Per tells the story of Libya, a small Arab state. He says "And what the hell was Libya?" and quickly a voice is heard, implying "you tell that!" The mumbling, muffled voice that is heard right afterwards is my own.

TAKE 36

The conversation is conducted in Swedish and right after Per said "And what the hell was Libya?" a voice clearly whispers in English.
   "You tell that!"

At the time of writing, this is the last of my recordings that I will reproduce. Hereby, I do as Friedel and Thorlin and others; I ask for an answer, some kind of answer to confirm the communicators' presence. It was September 6, 2012, at 22:45. A voice points out "you can get it now!" Unfortunately, perhaps I turned off the tape recorder too soon.

TAKE 37

I ask for an answer and a female voice comes in and says in Swedish: Det kan du få nu (u)! (You can get it now!)

16

THE VOICE PHENOMENA SPREAD ALL OVER THE WORLD

The German physicist Fidelio Köberle (1915-2007) read Friedel's book *Sprechfunk mit Verstorbenen* and, in the foreword to his third book (1981), he wrote: "This book has changed my life. It marks a turning point."

Hanna Bushbeck (1906-1984) had the same experience in 1968, when she read *Sprechfunk mit Verstorbenen*. She lived in Santa Barbara, California, between 1953 and 1964. There, she associated with people engaged in experimental parapsychology. The news of the EVP phenomena had not yet reached them.

Hanna Buschbeck returned to Germany, and, after reading in the German newspapers about the tape recordings and the alien voice phenomena, her interest was piqued. Shortly afterwards, she lost her husband, her mother and two sisters. In 1968 her life changed when she read Friedel's book. From that moment until her death in 1984, she focused totally on psychical phenomena and particularly on the electronic voices. Her own experiments led her to claim that she had had contact with her mother.

Hanna Buschbeck visited Friedel in 1970 and told him that she intended to start an association in Germany and that its members would actively research the voice phenomena and exchange experiences.

Friedel promised her that he would come to lecture and support her new project.

I remember that Friedel was very happy after her visit. He thought that he had yet strong confirmation herein that he had succeeded with his bridge-building.

In her home in Horb am Neckar, Hanna Bushbeck promoted meetings and conferences and in 1972 she aroused a lot of attention in the media in connection with an international convention in Koblenz, in which many senior scientists participated. Of course Friedrich Jürgenson was there as well as Professor Hans Bender, Alex Schneider, President of the Parapsychological Association of Switzerland, Argumosa from Spain, Professor Walter and Mary Jo Uphoff from the United States, Dr Buckard Heim from the Max Planck Institute, Dr Konstantin Raudive, Fidelio Köberle and Rector Leo Schmid from Switzerland.

At this meeting, Hanna Bushbeck and Fidelio Köberle formally decided to form an association to gather all EVP researchers under one roof. The Verein für Tonbandstimmen Forschung (VTF) became a reality in 1975, and was widely distributed mainly in Germany and Austria. They were also in close contact with Italian colleagues, who had organized an EVP conference in 1973, probably inspired by the Vatican's involvement in parapsychology.

Köberle published the magazine *VTF-Post* in which researchers and research groups from around the world posted their experiences.

The VTF received a lot of publicity but the research had not yet been taken seriously in the media. It was easy and tempting to dismiss people who claimed to have contact with the dead. Nevertheless, the interest persisted, since trusted scientists considered it proven that the voices existed. Their origin, however, was shrouded in obscurity. The most common theory was that the voice phenomena occurred through living people who participated in the recordings and acted as a kind of unconscious electronic medium. However, that did not make the whole thing less interesting.

In 1977, a congress was held in Recanati, Italy, and Friedel and some of the famous scholars were present including some Vatican priests. That conference received a lot of attention in the Italian media, precisely because the Vatican showed a great interest in the voice phenomena. Perhaps the uproar was also caused by the participation of the famous Count Mancini Spinucci from Fermo who took the initiative to form an association for EVP researchers, Associazione Italiana di Scientifica Psicofonia (AISP). At the same time, he made his property and land available to the association. The institute joined the University of Fermo.

Friedel was particularly pleased about this because it was the result of a visit Spinucci had paid to Friedel when he was in Rome. The count was devastated when his son passed away. He had read in the Italian newspapers about "the man with the spirit voices" so he visited Friedel for a couple of days in a row and they made recordings. According to Friedel, a voice came in, which the count identified as his son's. From that moment on, he began experimenting with recordings and claimed to have had contact with his son several times. This was the background to his commitment and the creation of the association and the institute.

The real breakthrough for the VTF and EVP research happened on January 25, 1980, in the German TV show *III nach Neun*. [3 after nine] The host Karl-Heinz Wocker gathered a large number of people who were engaged in the recordings. They reported about their contacts with relatives who had died several years before, and illustrated this with their own recordings of varying quality. The response from the public was enormous and it did not take long before the TV station's switchboard was overloaded with calls.

FJ appearance on his burial day at Claude Thorlin TV

FJ by Uher

FJ in Höör

FJ press conf, Höör 1980s

FJ with favourite dog in Höör

FJ Höör Swedish TV promo

The main forum for VTF has been, and still is, the annual convention held in Germany since its beginning in 1975. And there is no doubt that interest in the world is large, as shown by the VTF's contacts with several sister organizations and, in this context, it may be worth mentioning a few:

Germany: The German Association For Transcommunication Research, Arbeitsgemeinschaft für Jenseitskontakte (AFJ) in Berlin, Tonbandstimmenforschung (TBSF) [Tape voice research] in Darmstadt, Verein Tonbandstimmen-Forscher in Hamburg, [Association of tape voice Researchers] Gesellschaft für Psychobiophysik. [Society for Psychobiophysics]

Italy: Associazione Italiana di Scientifica Psicofonia (AISP) founded in 1977, which has a research institute associated with the University of San Fermo; And Interdisciplinary Laboratory For Biopsychocybernetics Research (IL Laboratorio).

Brazil: Instituto de Pesquisas Avançadas em Transcomunicação Instrumental (IPATI) – Institute for Advanced Research in Transcommunication Instrumental (IPAT), Brazilian Association for Transcommunication.

USA: American Association of Electronic Voice Phenomena, Association TransCommunication (A Trans-C).

United Kingdom, EVP & Transcommunication Society of Great Britain and Ireland, The Norfolk Experiment, EVP Research Associates UK.

France: Infinitude – Association Française de TransCommunication; Instrumental Transcommunication: EVP and ITC, Transcommunication, John and Maryse Locke – Transcommunication Group.

Mexico: KARINE – Asociación Mexicana de Transcomunicación Instrumental.

Austria: Verein für Tonbandstimmen Forschung in WIEN, Verein für Transkommunikations-Forschung (VTF).

Russia: Russian Association for Instrumental Transcommunication (RAIT).

Canada: Canadian Association of Electronic Voice Phenomena.

Israel: Israel Group of Paranormal Investigators (IGOPI).

Netherlands: ITC experiments by Hans F. Kennis

Spain: Sociedad Española de Parapsicología

International: ITC Journal.org

Köberle and Buschbeck devoted the rest of their lives to the voice phenomena and spread Friedel's work around the world.

Back to Köberle's meeting with Friedel in Koblenz in 1976: According to Friedel, he spoke warmly about the book *Sprechfunk mit Verstorbenen* that had changed his life. But, since the release of the book, a lot had happened and, in 1968, Friedel had published his second book.

From all that Köberle had heard Friedel talk about, both privately and at conferences, he concluded that a new book summarizing his research, preferably written in German, with the focus on the recordings and voice phenomena was necessary.

In September 1977 Friedel and Monica separated. Later, he contracted heart disease, which, ten years later, would take him to the other side. He refused to go to the hospital, even though he sometimes was so ill that he would have needed intensive care. It was as if he did not want to prevent the natural progression in his body, and it was clear that he felt strong curiosity about what would happen to him after death.

Friedel moved to Höör in Skane, where a friend of his and Monica's, Martha Annell, joined him. Martha had lost her husband and contacted him with Friedel's help. He moved into her house, which was perfect for his activity. There was an annexe connected to the old building, not unlike Nysund, where he made a studio for painting and for the voices. Here he devoted himself mainly to writing his third book: this time in German, as Köberle had suggested.

Friedel followed the advice that some caring friends had come up with when he wrote his first book, not to convey all his subjective experiences to the public but to stick to the objective tape recordings. Thus, a lot of his philosophizing about the voices was not included in the new book, *Sprechfunk mit Verstorbenen: Praktische Kontaktherstellung mit dem Jenseits*. It was published in 1981 by Goldmann Verlag in Munich. The book was also translated into English under the title *Voice Transmissions with the Deceased*.²⁵ Eventually, also in Italian, Dutch, Portuguese and probably a few more languages.

The book published in 1981 includes a foreword by Fidelio Köberle, which I have reproduced here, together with Friedel's introduction titled "May I introduce myself" as both say a lot about him, his discovery and how it affected his life and others.

Fidelio Koeberle

This book has changed my life. It marks a turning point. Today, I know that it has answered questions and offered solutions for which I have unconsciously waited for a long time. Firstly, however, I had the same skeptical objections as everyone. Because, after all, the author is claiming in all seriousness that with the use of an audio tape recorder, you can talk with the dead. That such contact can be made anytime and, above all, that it can be done by anyone, which, nevertheless, seemed to be a daring statement.

Remarkably, my doubts vanished after reading the first pages. In an inexplicable way a spark connected and I believed the author's honest intention not to deceive himself or others. I have lived and suffered with him through the high and low points of this journey into the unknown. The book did not release me from its grip. While it reads like a gripping adventure novel or good science fiction, it is a true autobiographical presentation. Jürgenson has proved his admirable courage by admitting publicly to his discovery and confronting its consequences, even though he knew that he would encounter rejection and make many enemies. His courage impressed me and I decided to follow in his footsteps.

Firstly, I worked with a borrowed and very old piece of equipment, which proved to be a mistake, because the amplification left much to be desired and this was, most likely, the reason why I experimented [for] six months with no results. I assume that this would not have happened with a more modern recorder—I was then mostly working with the microphone method. I'm still amazed over my endurance back then, which I credit to my strong motivation that came from reading Jürgenson's book.

Finally, I got my first results, which increased rapidly with the better recorder. Now, I know for sure, the paranormal voices on tape exist! And, besides that, I obtained unique evidence and experience that cannot be denied by any discussion that I was dealing with real personalities with each of these voices. I asked questions and received sensible answers, which, at times, were highly surprising. I was addressed by name and was given evidence that they participated in my life. Now I could no longer abandon this project.

For many years I experimented alone and had only Friedrich Jürgenson's book as a guide. Later, I joined with other colleagues who, on account of the book, got involved the same way I did and were also conducting their research alone. Today, thousands are experimenting all over the world, either alone or in groups. A colleague, Hanna Buschbeck from Horb, created a working group of interested people that could exchange their experiences by mail and at conferences. It was from this circle in 1975, that the VTF: Association for Tape Voice Research evolved; it publicly promotes and coordinates research and provides information for those interested.

This work has already borne fruit, especially since Friedrich Jürgenson gave it his full support. Early on, in the mass media (press, radio and television), almost all comments had been ironical. Today, the tape voices are debated with greater substance and objectivity.

They are very well known among the general public, particularly in the German-speaking countries. A German television broadcast in January 1980 (Talk show "Three after Nine") brought 2,500 letters to the VTF with requests for information. I was able to attend many courses at schools, where I lectured participants on how to record the tape voices. This created some attention and excitement and has contributed to the tape voices being taken seriously.

Jürgenson's book has directly or indirectly touched countless people in the entire world that responded by breathing an understandable sigh of relief: "So, it is true, there is life after death!" This had always been assumed, but it is a decisive step to actually know. Even many people, who consider themselves believing Christians, shrug their shoulders if asked on their honor and conscience if they believe that life continues after death. Much that was previously taken as an article of faith became demystified, so that one no longer knows what to hold on to, anymore. But the knowledge of life continuing after death is part of humanity. If man ever loses this, mankind will lose a decisive part of being human.

In this day and age of conceptual uncertainty, Friedrich Jürgenson makes his epochal discovery. And it is nothing less than technology that is lending a helping hand. Here it would be hard not to think of some kind of providence by a higher power. Interestingly, it was not Jürgenson who was trying to establish contact; on the contrary, the initiative came from the deceased. They addressed him and called his attention to their presence. At first, he was totally surprised and absolutely confused. But he did not allow himself to be diverted, because he could clearly feel the importance of this breakthrough from another world.

He was no ignoramus; from the days of his youth onward, he was aware that contacts with the hereafter existed. He was only baffled by this new means of communication through a tape recorder. Now, for the first time, a technical piece of equipment was being used as means to relay the connection between both worlds. He recognized the crucial advantage, which consisted in the elimination of the subjective factor, which can never be excluded completely when it comes to living persons.

And if the interpretation of the voices manifested on the tapes is influenced by subjective factors, it is easy to protect oneself by letting others check and confirm them. For the first time in the history of mankind, we now have an information channel to the other side free of subjective influences. Something very important is yet still added: nobody has to "believe" anyone anymore; that is to say that we don't have to rely on the integrity of the reporter. The method is so easy that anyone can get at least some information firsthand. Today, almost every household owns a cassette recorder, which, with a little "know-how", can be a completely adequate tool for successful recordings.

It is clear to me that the tape voices still pose a challenge to common sense in most people. The thought of an existence beyond our material body is difficult to conceive because of the triumphant advances over the last two centuries in natural science and technology in the western and eastern world. For the materialists, the soul is like an organ of the body, which ceases to function at death. One of the arguments preferred, is that once your body dies, you won't have a larynx anymore, so how can the deceased still talk? When someone speaks like that, it is clear that they have never been involved in the broad field of parapsychological research. Besides the voices on tape, there are other indications toward an individual postmortem existence of the human personality.

The authenticity of paranormal voices on tape was accepted surprisingly early on by the "official scientific community." Unfortunately, that is as far as it has gone; that is to say, they have not accepted that many new developments have happened over the past twenty years. Some parapsychologists who do not conduct experiments of their own will explain the origin of the voices by saying that the experimenter is producing them subconsciously. The theorists would not be able to uphold their hypothesis if they only knew all the information from the spirit world that we know today. Luckily, the researchers in the field are free of such biases. They think it absurd to accept that they are talking with their own subconscious via a tape recorder. It is about time that the universities acknowledge the results of the widespread amateur research, so they will not miss the connection and repeat what they said twenty years ago, which was forgivable then because they did not have all the facts but which is inexcusable today.

After Jürgenson's book, there has been a whole series of valuable publications (Dr. Konstantin Raudive: *The Inaudible becomes Audible and Do We Survive Death?* Minister Leo Schmid: *When the Dead Talk*; Hildegard Schäfer: *Voices from Another World*), but it was his book that opened the door for the first time. Since then we can listen to a world that up until now was closed off to us. His book has historical significance. Without exaggeration, his discovery can be compared with that of Columbus. Both have researched a new world and consequently both discoveries had unforeseeable effects on our lives. As in the case of Columbus, there were forerunners whose activity, however, did not lead to concrete results.

Only when someone devotes his entire life to the service of discovery does a breakthrough occur. Jürgenson neglected his profession and forgot all about earning money because he felt responsibility towards these communications.

He did not just receive them for himself but, because the time was right, he was to pass them on. It showed how Jürgenson was prepared for that task. It was the time in his life to be awake, open, and alert for whatever may confront him, because it must be checked and confirmed for authenticity and true contents. He intelligently kept a distance from any solid conclusions. For him it became a question of clarity and self-knowledge, which is why illusions and self-deception had no chance. Every reader feels a total involvement when he or she grasps the authenticity of the argumentation. But for those who know Jürgenson—and I consider myself very fortunate to be his friend— they know that the enthusiasm for these tasks never slackens once it has seized you. Today, at 78, he is still working tirelessly to construct a bridge to the other side.

He speaks with his friends during daily recording sessions. Like him, many others have devoted their whole life to the service of this significant task, and the work gives them a great deal of satisfaction. When we experience almost daily how happy people are when they hear from family members or friends who have passed on, and when they exclaim excitedly "they are really alive!", then we know that with this work we render an immeasurable and priceless service that has a great future. The Catholic Church, which raises no objections to the sincere research of the paranormal voices on tape, also acknowledges this. Many people have found a way back to religion after finding out about the voices on tape.

Since the beginning of the latter, there have been interesting new discoveries. For instance, the late engineer, Franz Seidl of Vienna, developed a 'psychophone' which transmits well-modulated voices and which deserves to be investigated more thoroughly than has been the case until now. Hans Luksch in Vienna obtained success in solving crimes by asking murder victims on tape about their murderers. Jürgenson already noted that paranormal voices played backward also contained statements.

The systematic evaluation of different voices also showed that the reverse voices should not sound at all the way they do which continues to confound physicists and electronics experts. Undiscovered treasures are to be expected with the use of variable speeds and filters, which can sometimes eliminate irritating interference. Research is underway to determine whether phase conversions at around 180 degrees would bring improvements. These are just a few indications concerning the variety of individual aspects that still need to be researched within the 'voices on tape' phenomena.

I see it as my life's mission to bring the voices on tape and their message to as many human beings as possible; on one hand, to help them to orient their worldview, and, on the other hand, to reach professionals with specialized knowledge who can support the diverse areas of research. Therefore, I welcome that this pioneering book by Friedrich Jürgenson is being published as a high volume edition, and offers the chance to involve many people in this fascinating research. There are hardly any adventures left in our modern world, and, when they exist, their objectives are often senseless. The research of the voices on tape represents the greatest adventure of our day; its risks are calculable and controllable. It is probably the most meaningful activity to be engaged in for oneself and for our fellow human beings. May a spark of the enthusiasm with which this book was written leap across to the reader and cause him, as so many before, to be able to raise his gaze with confidence and gratitude to the stars with the certainty of knowing that we are not lost even though we must die.

May I introduce myself?

Since all the facts described in this book are new and unique and have involved my person and my family, it is necessary for me to first introduce myself to the reader. You should know that I do not belong to the type of people who lack self-criticism and whose fantasies and dreams easily take over.

Instead, I am fully aware of the importance of what I present to the public and the responsibility it entails.

I begin with some important biographical facts and then a truthful, sensational, and factual report on the construction of a bridge between this world and the hereafter.

I do not belong to any political party, secret fraternity, religious sect, or any "ism" or similar movement. I was born at the beginning of the century in Odessa by the Black Sea. My parents originated from the Baltic region; my father was a physician. At present I am a Swedish citizen. Before this I had to change my citizenship twice because of the political changes that occurred in 1917. In my childhood I attended a German school in Russia and my childhood was happy and harmonious until the First World War delivered a violent blow to the security of our home and hearth. Even as a child I felt the consequences of this World War.

The really violent storm, however, only started with the subsequent Russian revolution, which showed its true face during those three years of civil war. Without burdening the reader with the terrible details of those events, it is enough to mention that our daily life was constantly subjected to waves of terror, starvation, grinding poverty and outbreaks of typhus, followed by a cholera epidemic.

But, despite all that, life went on. Necessity forces one to be objective and teaches one to live in the present. In the short breaks, when we were not being shot at, we bathed in the sun at the beach. We were constantly hungry, froze pitifully in the winter and danced ourselves warm in unheated rooms; despite all deprivation and danger, the human being can tolerate a lot more than we think, especially in our youth.

In the course of three civil wars, Odessa was "liberated" fourteen times in bloody street battles. The consequences of these alternating "liberations" were always the same, and they affected all levels of society with the 'intelligentsia' suffering the most. I can only describe it as a merciful fate that my family made it through intact. In 1925, we even managed to emigrate and settle legally in Estonia.

As I traveled with my voice teacher to Palestine in 1932 to further my vocal training, I was about to be pulled into warlike unrest again, as Arab terror flashed against the Jews. Terror is terror; and it is rather inconsequential to those who are suffering under it, whether it is in the name of freedom, in the name of religion or is executed by some racist ideology, on a large or small scale, to the left or to the right.

When I then returned to Estonia after seven years living abroad, I was caught by the Second World War, and this at the hour when the three Baltic States were in the process of freeing themselves from Russia. Once again, history was going to repeat itself, only in a somewhat more modern version. The subject still was dictatorship, war, terror and "liberation." The variations corresponded to the respective rulers and were implemented depending on the circumstances, including devastating bomb attacks, mass deportations, concentration camps, gunshots to the back of the head or gas chambers.

Thus, from my youth, I was surrounded by misery and danger: never any real peace, relaxation or any feeling of confidence, which is needed especially by a young person. One was never capable of remedying the many miseries. Only one thing did I understand, and that was that I would never, under any circumstances, take part in a military service: it didn't matter if during war or peace, regardless of the dangers to which I exposed myself. From my early days, I have what amounts to an allergic reaction and intensive dislike against everything that has to do with uniforms and weapons, with military training and the use of force, murder, or mass butchery; it doesn't matter if it applies to humans or animals. That is why I became a vegetarian.

The professional occupations that I have chosen corresponded to my natural abilities. In my youth I was a singer; in my later years I became a painter. Although my voice training took nine years, I was able to follow my singing career for only two years. A problem with my gall bladder, but mainly chronic colds, prevented me from continuing with my performances on stage.

Fortunately, when I was young, I also enjoyed my part time training as a painter, and, with that, the transition to a new occupation went naturally and smoothly. Since my new occupation included exhibitions and traveling abroad, I could make closer and varied contacts among people of all social levels, since artists are easily welcomed into most homes. In the summer of 1958, leaving Italy once again, I returned to Stockholm, my permanent residence at the time. I had spent a productive, beautiful "fairytale like" time at Pompeii, and was in the process of turning an interesting work plan into reality, which was likewise connected to Pompeii. By the way, this buried city has exercised a magical attraction on me since my childhood, and has always been the target of my longings.

Something happened in the spring of 1958 that really exceeded my silent hopes by far. I had quite suddenly succeeded in organizing an exhibition of my paintings in Pompeii, in the heart of the ancient city, in the airy "palastra" of the forum-bath.

At the same time, I was occupied with the completion of a painting, which, because of its interesting motives, gave me much joy; in addition, a strange circumstance came about. I was allowed to enjoy working in the delightful house of the so-called "Tragic Poet" that was located diagonally across from my exhibition; its moody, reflective surroundings became my studio. A large room was necessary since every picture that I painted was 9 meters long (29.5 ft.).

I was busy with my paintings from dawn until darkness set in, but I enjoyed the dreamlike atmosphere of the ancient, excavated house. Sometimes I left my work and walked through the narrow alleys, and was able to gain an in-depth knowledge of the excavated city since I was in possession of the master keys to all the houses.

An offer was made to me at the end of the official inauguration of my paintings exhibition, to take part in the excavation of a house in Pompeii, the following spring. One can understand what this offer meant to me. Undoubtedly, I had reached, then, the top of my career as an artist and it seemed incomprehensible to think that the dream of my life, taking part in an excavation, should be so easily fulfilled.

As I arrived in Stockholm, and in the intoxication of my success started preparations for my Pompeii plans, something happened that would dampen my ambitions. Slowly, but consistently unfolding, it brought to a halt my artistic activity and all of my future plans. At the same time something different, unbelievable, came upon me and my thoughts and feelings: yes, my whole consciousness was changing and allowing me to experience a new reality step by step.

In *Voice Transmissions with the Deceased*, Friedel shares much about his life.

He empathizes with Pope Paul VI's words: "It is not we who are important, but our mission." The first chapter of this book is important because therein, he makes a very rhapsodic account of what happened before the voices. He does not write a word about his acclaimed films and meetings with Pope Paul, both topics that would make people realize that this was not "a drunken artist" who took advantage of people's fear of death and made money from it, as others did.

At the time, after the move to Höör, Friedel was disturbed by the fact that in his footsteps followed charlatans, quacks, fanatical occultists and the like, which utilized his discovery and just minted coins from it. He received reports from serious friends in different parts of the world about radio and TV programs in which so-called voice researchers presented untenable claims and astonishing contacts with the deceased in spectacular forms. Actually, despite investing in Italy, he was sometimes depressed on account of his hopes and ideas about the building of the bridge to the other side, which had begun to be occupied by imitators who did trick recordings and manipulated and copied his own results and other serious researchers' dedicated work.

Media created sensation and there were many ironic jokes about the mysterious voices from space in various entertainment programs. But I'll point out that fortunately, in the Nordic countries, they chose a different path—they remained silent.

After thirteen years working in the second largest newspaper in Sweden, the *Aftonbladet*, I went over to the largest one, *Expressen*.

There they had, for obvious reasons, not granted great interest to "the man with the spirit voices", even though the topic "Is there life after death?" often appeared in different forms in the feature pages. The problem was that the *Aftonbladet* had a reporter "near the source" who could deliver material that generated a number of selling headlines. Since that was impossible to match, they were silent, except on one occasion.

The journalist and writer Anders Ehnmark, who was then a correspondent for the *Expressen* in Rome, wrote a crushing article about the spirit voices after reading exuberant reports about Friedel and the voice phenomena in the Italian newspapers. However, he did not contact the source, Jürgenson or the Catholic priests, but drew his own conclusions and presented them in his own skilled journalistic manner as the truth. Thus, one would think that Friedrich Jürgenson and the spirit voices were excluded from the *Expressen's* columns. But this was not so.

And a former *Aftonbladet* correspondent with first-hand information from the other side was now in the newspaper. So why not use him and give readers the true story of Friedrich Jürgenson and the spirit voices and what science had come up with?

I had the background material, but I needed to put in extensive study to get a current and credible picture of what the research had come to. In a way, I also did it for Friedel, with the hope that I would produce material that cheered him up. At the time, Friedel was working on his book in German and decided not to travel to more conferences to give lectures that had taken a heavy toll on his efforts. His last trip was to the great Congress of Recanati in Italy. One Sunday in early January 1978, the *Expressen's* leaflet was topped with "Has he hit a bridge to the dead?" and Friedel's picture. My article was based on a number of comments from scholars and Catholic priests and it had a very positive effect on Friedel, who thought it was time for a new press conference.

I reproduce, below, some comments from the article. Firstly, another repetition by Professor Hans Bender, University of Freiburg, which was also a confirmation that he stood by his position regarding the sensational recordings at Friedel's in May 1970:

> We have evidence that the voices exist. In our experiments in Sweden, which are already several years in the past, we concentrated on trying to prove the existence of physically unexplained voices on tape. I believe the paranormal hypothesis about the origin of the voices is highly likely.

Professor Peter Bander, Cambridge Institute of Education in England, whom Friedel wrote letters to and told him that he had a "sympathetic ear" in the Vatican, thus from Pope Paul VI, avowed:

"The voice phenomena cannot be explained away as the influence of the subconscious".

Professor Alex Schneider, University of St. Gallen, Switzerland: "This can give humanity more than science can."

When Konstantin Raudive's book *Breakthrough, An Amazing Experiment in Electronic Communication with the Dead* was published in England, a hot debate erupted. This meant that a group of English scientists began their own research, led by Peter Bander, which was reported in his book *Carry on Talking, how Dead are the Voices?*

The Catholic Church and the Vatican continued their research in parapsychology and EVP. In the book Bander presents some church comments—the prominent Catholic priest, Professor C. Pfleger, says much the same as Pope Paul VI told Friedel:

"Facts have helped us understand that there is a state of existence between death and resurrection."

At the time, the Pope's Nuncio (emissary) to EEC countries was Archbishop Igino Eugenio Cardinale who declares in the book: "Of course, all this is mysterious. But we know that the voices are there for all to hear."

And the Anglican Bishop Buthler: "I am definitely impressed by this phenomenon and, moreover, this experiment is only the beginning."

On January 26, 1978, media once again gathered at Friedel's, now at his new home in Höör. There was no significant international support nor any TV broadcast. Friedel's message this time was that several experiments had been done which showed that in the near future we would get images from the other side on our computers and on TV screens. He did not know that ten years later he himself would manifest on computer and television screens—after his death.

He had no concrete examples of such image transfer and, probably, that diminished the impact of his presentation slightly. In addition, at least I, who had followed him during these years, could state that the best voices included in the demonstration were those he received in the 1950s and 1960s. It seemed that in the late 1970's and until his death he had lost his grip on the recordings. On the other hand, he was very involved in different places and, of course, that deprived him of the time he needed to listen, stubbornly and patiently, over and over again to his recordings. Friedel had also embraced John Björkhem's idea:

"It is enough if only one word is taken up on the tape in a quiet room. Several empirical evidence is not necessary because subjective elements are precluded in such tape recordings."

Friedel had thousands of good quality words and sentences recorded under the conditions Björkhem had hinted at. Perhaps he considered that was enough for the time being. He leaned also on the scientific tests performed, which confirmed the existence of the voices.

After this press conference nothing was written in the *Aftonbladet*. It was the *Expressen*, which, with the usual exaggerated headlines, presented my article under the title: "Swedes warn the world. Promise TV images from the other side."

I do not really know what the Swedes warned about. But it was probably the shocking effect that would result from seeing deceased people, perhaps close relatives, on the computer screen or on TV.

I think that in later years it was more important for Friedel to reach out with his message to the people than to get new contacts and messages from the other side. He said at times that he knew that his friends in the next dimension of life followed his work and supported him. Their common task was to build the bridge and probably to arouse people on the Earth to the awareness that death was not the end and that they could establish contact with relatives who had left the physical world.

We met not so often during these last years. But we called each other and he was always anxious to know how my family and I lived. When I responded by talking about his illness, he waved it away. He knew his physical body could not cope much longer. And the truth is that he was not concerned about himself. He simply looked forward to death. He did not doubt for a moment that he would go over to the life dimension that he had had contact with for so many years. When he talked about it, I could not mistake his enthusiasm. He was heavily emaciated and Marta told me that he was asleep several times during the day. Mainly, he worked on his new book and painted not so often as before.

The book came out in 1981 and was then translated into English and several other languages. The German version was published in six editions, and, before each reprinting, he had corrections or additions that he sent to Fidelio Köberle, who somehow became his agent. But then everything changed and for a short time he lived again.

It was his own idea to make a film about himself for a change: another dream to come true. I filmed a lot at that time but it was mostly a kind of family documentation. Sometimes we joked that something might appear from the other side in the films.

Friedel hired a Swedish filmmaker whom I had never met. He did some interviews with Friedel that I saw on a video and we could not approve of them. So Friedel asked me if I, with my contacts in the media world, could find someone who wanted to make a good quality film about the voices. I probably knew that but we concluded that he could do it himself with the help of his connections in the Swedish Television.

On that road and with some assistance from Köberle, he reached the actor, director and screenwriter Rolf Olsen who was then active in Munich. Where he got the Nordic name Olsen from was never clear to me. His name was actually Rudolf Knoblich (1919 - 1998), born in Austria.

He usually wrote scripts for his films and they were about farce, comedy, drama, horror films and thrillers. Between 1949 and 1990, he made 50 films. He was also highly appreciated as an actor and sometimes played a role in his films.

He was a very quiet and likable man whom I had the pleasure of working with. We met a number of times at Friedel's and drew up plans for the film work to be carried out during 1987. Rolf wanted to do the first part in the farm in Höör in which Friedel's tape recordings would play a prominent role.

Friedel himself would interview some people who had their own recordings. He wanted to take Friedel with him to Germany and Italy for this purpose. Considering Friedel's health, there was some doubt that he would embark on another journey. But he did not want to listen to us. Now he was full of energy and willing to do what Rolf desired. It was the speech of a man who, without hesitation, was prepared to die at his post.

It was decided that I would do the interviews with Monica and Irmgardt Kersten, in German. Since both spoke Swedish, I suggested that we make use of my native language because my German left a lot to be desired. Rolf tested my pronunciation and found that I spoke as clearly as a beer drinker from Munich, and it worked well. So questions in German were prepared. To get Friedel to speak naturally when he was recording, we wrote down some key questions in German, which I would ask him while I was sitting next to the camera so he looked at me and not at the camera. Then I thought my voice would be edited out.

As I reported in Chapter 15, Monica did not want her interview to be in the film. We noticed how determined she was, although her motivation was unclear. But I guess she was surprised by the emotion she showed and she said something about that when she heard her own voice—the whole thing had become too personal. She was a party to the case and she thought that it would hurt Friedel's position.

I believe that the recordings with Felix Kersten were the ones that mattered most to Friedel. He could identify Kersten's voice and got the support from Kersten's wife Irmgardt and her son Arno. The most important recordings were made when SBC's well-known radio and TV technician Kjell Stensson was present. Therefore, the possibility of any kind of manipulation was excluded. As I described earlier, the recordings were on both sides of the tape and exactly on the same place: something totally unexplainable technically.

Friedel saw his movie dream realized shortly before he left life in this world. We saw the first copy of the video together. I remember how he sat, earnest, tense, and hoped that a greeting on the screen would appear. But it did not.

You can see the video *The Gate to Eternity* on YouTube.[26]

17

RECORD AND LISTEN

It may seem easy to make recordings through the microphone, and slightly more complicated using the radio, but if you do try to make contact with a deceased person, it is in the listening that everything hangs on: particularly after the recording.

I quote Friedel:

> People have often asked me about the best way to communicate with the dead. As I have averred, it depends first and foremost on our motives, but also on our patience and steadfastness. The art of listening requires four conditions: Detente, vigilance, uncoupling from our mental activity and tranquility.

If we start with microphone recordings, we just need a microphone and a tape recorder, or a tape recorder with a built-in microphone. Friedel worked with the old type of tape recorder in which one could regulate the speed. He always played it at the higher speed, which is a good thing to do even with a modern device. It's wise not listen at a lower speed to begin with. If something is on the tape, what you hear at the higher speed is most important.

It is best to be alone when recording. This is not a parlor game where you sit in a group like a séance and hope to make contact. Two people are ideal because then you can carry on a conversation that allows for the modulation phenomenon. The natural voices or sounds, the monologue or conversation between two people, suddenly lose intensity and apparently work as a carrier wave that lifts an alien voice in the form of some single words or, at best, a phrase that may either seem completely incomprehensible or is pronounced clearly in your own language. If you experience that phenomenon, you should be satisfied with anything that comes in. The interpretation of what is said must be secondary and often it requires a lot of listening.

Take your recording work seriously; speak with short interruptions and hope your friends on the other side really exist and can attain the connection with you. Aside from the recording with Arne Weise, who received an answer to his question, I cannot recall accurately that I heard Friedel ask questions that demanded answers. He did not work that way; he just came in with an appeal to his friends to get in touch. And as you have read and also heard, they announced themselves in many different ways with everything from knocks, unexplained noise phenomena to technically impossible messages in the form of songs, phrases, or words.

Recording via a microphone should be at the highest possible volume without overriding. And something very important is to be aware of all the sounds that you hear in the room. Therefore, during the listening, you should know that you took a deep breath just at that moment, you cleared your throat, you were sniffling, your foot scraped on the floor, a vehicle made a noise on the street, etc. All this is important because such all-natural sounds can be interpreted in different ways and can easily lead to pure self-suggestion (pareidolia).

It seems that natural sounds are needed in the room to help create a carrier. Still, the experiment with a short pause and absolute silence, conducted by Hans Bender and his team at Friedel's, showed that alien voices can reach us in other inexplicable ways. However, it is clear that the voice messages can get over the "bridge" with the support of a carrier wave more easily. There are statements from people involved in EVP all over the world, saying that usually an alien voice appears when you let water run from the tap for a short time or when you light a match or record the completely natural sound of a crackling fire or crumple up a magazine and so on. But, here, I again warn of self-suggestion. Feel free to test yourself when you consciously evoke these natural sounds, and you will notice how easy it is to listen to (interpret) voices in these.

When it comes to microphone recordings with several people present, it is also very important to try to remember what each person said.

This is because a word may be spoken by one of the participants that goes unnoticed, which sounds completely incomprehensible. Thus, it will create confusion in the experimenter. The recordings should not be longer than five to ten minutes. This applies to all tape recordings.

Recording from the radio can be done in two ways. Either connect the tape recorder to the radio or place a microphone next to the radio's speaker. Friedel preferred the first option but, nowadays, many EVP researchers have decided that direct uptake via microphone provides better reception. This is known as Direct Radio Voice (DRV). This allows the noise in the room to develop a carrier. Recording from the radio only, means excessive noise which might not allow for an anomalous wave to come through.

In the EVP circles there is something called "Jürgenson's frequency." It is 1485 kHz on medium wave. At this frequency Friedel somehow managed to establish contact with his assistant Lena and her whispering voice. The radio is tuned to the frequency used by Friedel: medium wave, at about 1480 kHz, searching between the Vienna stations at 1475 and Moscow 1484. But it is extremely rare that you can directly hear alien voices from the radio. Perhaps you can get a whispering voice to react. Again, always record in short sequences.

Use headphones and search very slowly upwards. Friedel claimed that he received the best recordings when a broadcast from a station in Vienna around 1475 was clearly heard. Sometimes he did not manage to tune into the station and got negative results when he carried on searching. At around the 1484 bandwidth, there is a station in Moscow that sometimes faded away and, there, Friedel received several messages. At around 1500 there is an Italian station. If after tuning in without success, just start over.

It is possible that during the search you will hear a short message like Lena's whispers, but you must have very good hearing. Each time you think something is happening, for example you hear whispering noises, and the interference decreases for a moment as you start recording. It is not necessary to have the tape recorder on while you search. But as soon as you hear something, turn it on and run for five minutes without changing the setting. You may get a feeling or even a mental message, a sort of whispered command that sounds like "stop" or "contact." At this point, feel free to let your imagination run because a little self-suggestion might motivate you.

I haven't seen any evidence that specifying a certain time of the day or weather conditions increases the possibility of success. Friedel only said that he had a feeling during the full moon and not too late in the evening, and that his best results were via the radio.

Some EVP researchers have opined that the best conditions for establishing a connection are in chilly or cold weather and clear moonlight, not necessarily in the full moon. During violent solar flares when the atmosphere is charged with electricity, for example, or during a thunderstorm, the opportunities diminish.

Microphone recording can be done at any time of the day. For Friedel, a decision to turn on the tape recorder often resulted from a spontaneous feeling, and perhaps a desire that something would happen. Intent seems to be a factor because the recordings flow and connect with a loved one who has passed over.

Friedel always said that the process is not about faith but knowledge; the voices appear in the recorder, which is an objective machine. He gained the recognition of many serious researchers but he admitted that during the recordings the experimenter has the right to intensely believe that there exists an opportunity to establish contact. If you are not open to the possibility, there is no point even in trying.

According to Friedel, do not attribute the premise of good recordings to the weather, but to the desires and the mental attitude of the operator. A large part of the success depends on us, on how we seek contact. The best prerequisite is to be natural. Avoid all pathetic, neurotic, highly inflated grievances. Be natural and friendly, rather than excessively pious.

And, above all, the most important thing is the extremely careful listening. Have a positive attitude when listening to a recording, but also assume that it could take hours—maybe days of patience—and many recordings and thorough listening before something happens. And you should also understand that it is time consuming. Patience and more patience is what counts. The only thing I can say is that if you have a positive attitude and really believe that it is possible to establish contact with deceased people who find themselves in another life dimension—and I can promise you it is not easy—then you have the prerequisite of success. Perhaps some of what you have read in this book will make it easier for you to get that inner conviction.

There are many dangers lurking for the novice listener. The biggest pitfall is self-suggestion as I have emphasized. Self-suggestion consists of personal desires and expectations, combined with poor sound quality of the recording, which can lead to an uncritical ear hearing words that do not exist. If the voices are weak and unclear, then listen again and again; listen fifty times and more. But it is easy to get caught up in an interpretation right from the start. Once it has taken root in your brain, it is difficult to get rid of it. It feels as if what you hear can really be a message of some kind, or just a single strange word, so get help from someone who shares your interest. Let that person listen as intensely as you have done without any direct guidance and then compare your interpretations. Be aware that experience shows, not least Friedel's own, that voices might come in not only when the tape recorder is functioning normally but also just before you decide to turn it off. It is not a rule but it often occurs incomprehensibly. And if you think that the voice uses several languages, you are on the right track. It is the polyglotism that you read about in the examples in this book. Here, language skills can be a great advantage. But do not worry if you are not multi-lingual. Friedel and other EVP researchers have confirmed that the communicator likes to use the language that the listener speaks, but sometimes mixes it up with other languages precisely to establish that it is not a regular radio broadcast.[27] EVP researchers from different countries have sent recordings to each other, which show that, for example, Italian recipients have been notified in Italian mainly; the same with the very active Dutch who hear Flemish words, which, for example, listeners in England rarely get.

Another thing that everyone agrees on is that the messages that come in are aimed at the person who is currently listening and recording. That connection is the bridge itself. These messages cannot be intercepted, not even by the NSA (National Security Agency), the US security service, which, by the way, listens to most of what we send out into the air. If there are several people who jointly record on different tape recorders, the message can sometimes end up on all the devices.

In closing, I will quote Friedel again:

> Listening is a difficult art. It must be learned slowly. You have to practice not only during tape recordings but daily—hourly. How many of us are able, in the hustle and bustle of our time, to muster the time and patience to relax and pay attention to everyone who speaks to us? If possible, seek peace in nature. Listen to the birds, the wind, and the voice of the waves; simply listen to the silence.
>
> The "language of the dead" is the imagery of the subconscious, which, free from all compromises, regardless of whether they are based on false courtesy, stylistic embellishment or double standards, directly conveys the truth of the feeling. If we want to understand

the simple language of the dead, we must be free from the tyranny of our intellect, for, if arrogance and coldness reign, the inclinations of the heart solidify.

Do not expect the dead to preach spiritually. For millennia, here, we have talked so long and so loudly about love and brotherhood, about freedom and equality, justice, and humanity, that we have totally lost the ability either to see or hear reality and truth. It also does not matter if it is our philosophical systems of religion or ourselves that have failed. So, do not expect from the dead political, moral or ethical philosophical speeches. All this "spiritual good" on the other hand has lost its significance.

The solution to the mystery of the secret of life and death lies hidden in the depths of our consciousness, in the darkness of which we cannot penetrate without the light of self-knowledge.

FJ unknown photographer.

REFERENCES

Bander, P. *Carry on Talking, how Dead are the Voices?*

Bender, H. On the Analysis of Exceptional Voice Phenomena on Tapes. Pilot studies on the 'recordings' of Friedrich Jürgenson. *ITC Journal* 40, (April 2011), pp. 61-78.

Bogoras, W. (1975). *"The Chukchee"* (Jessup North Pacific Expedition, Publications, No 7). AMS Press (first published 1909). *The Chukchee*, edited by Michael Dürr and Erich Kasten, 2017: 9 – 45. Fürstenberg/Havel: Kulturstiftung Siberian — Electronic edition for http://www.siberian-studies.org).

Cardoso, A. (2010). *Electronic Voices, Contact with Another Dimension?* O' Books/John Hunt Publishing, Ltd. UK: Ropley, Hants.

Cardoso, A. (2012). A Two-Year Investigation of the Allegedly Anomalous Electronic Voices or EVP. *NeuroQuantology*, September 2012, Volume 10, Issue 3, pp. 492-514.

Cardoso, A. (2017). *Electronic Contact with the Dead, What Do the Voices Tell us?* White Crow Books. UK: Hove.

Cardoso, A. (2021). *Glimpses of Another World, Impressions and Reflections of an EVP Operator.* White Crow Books. UK: Hove.

Kardec, A. (1857). *Le Livre des Esprits.* Paris: Dentu.

Kardec, A. (1864). *Revue Spirite.*

Kersten, F. *Totenkopf und Treue* (1 Jan. 1952) Hamburg: Robert Mölich Verlag.

Jacobson, N-O. (1974). *Life Without Death? On Parapsychology, Mysticism, and the Question of Survival.* London: Turnstone Books. Jacobson, N-O. (2000). ITC and Science. *ITC Journal* 1, pp. 61, 62.

Jürgenson, F. (1964) *Rösterna från rymden*. (The Voices from Space). Saxon & Lindströms.

Jürgenson, F. (1967). *Sprechfunk mit Verstorbenen, Praktische Kontaktherstellung mit dem Jenseits* (Voice Transmissions with the Deceased, Practical Instructions for Contacting the Other World). H Bauer Verlag.

Jürgenson, F. (1968). *Radio and Microphone Contacts with the Dead*. Sweden: Rosterna Fran Rymden, Saxon & Lindstrom Forlag.

Jürgenson, F. (2004). *Voice Transmissions with the Deceased*. Stockholm: Firework Edition.

Köberle, F. https://www.vtf.de/artikel_e.shtml

Leopold, A. (2014). *Min vän på andra sidan: boken om Friedrich Jürgenson som upptäckte röstfenomen från en fjärde livsdimension*. Sweden: Parthenon förlag.

Lindström, G. (2007). Lizz Werneroth, a successful ITC experimenter for 40 years. *ITC Journal*, pp. 65-68.

Raudive, K. (1968). *Unhörbares wird Hörbar*. Germany: Reichl

Raudive, K. (1971). *Breakthrough: An Amazing Experiment in Electronic Communication with the Dead*. UK: Colin Smythe, Ltd.

Raudive, K. (2021). *Breakthrough: An Amazing Experiment in Electronic Communication with the Dead*. UK: White Crow Books.

Senkowski, E. (1995, 2000). *Instrumentelle TransKommunikation*. Frankfurt/Main : R. G. Fischer Verlag.

PHOTO CREDITS

Friedel Art:
FJ in front of Pompeji painting = ©photographer unknown / Friedrich Jürgenson
Foundation; Carl Michael von Hausswolff collection
FJ Painting San Michele Capri = ©photographer unknown / Friedrich Jürgenson
Foundation; Carl Michael von Hausswolff collection
FJ Painting San Michele Capri = ©photographer unknown / Friedrich Jürgenson
Foundation; Carl Michael von Hausswolff collection
FJ Peter's grave Vatican painting = ©photographer unknown / Friedrich Jürgenson
Foundation; Carl Michael von Hausswolff collection
FJ self portrait = ©Carl Michael von Hausswolff collection
FJ with his painting of Pius XII = ©photographer unknown / Friedrich Jürgenson
Foundation; Carl Michael von Hausswolff collection
FJ with Pompei paintings = ©photographer unknown / Friedrich Jürgenson
Foundation; Carl Michael von Hausswolff collection
Jürgenson orkidée = ©Carl Michael von Hausswolff collection
Painting by FJ pompeji = ©Carl Michael von Hausswolff collection
Paul VI by FJ ©The Vatican - photo©photographer unknown / Friedrich Jürgenson
Foundation; Carl Michael von Hausswolff collection
Pius XII by FJ - ©The Vatican - photo©photographer unknown /

Friedrich Jürgenson
Foundation; Carl Michael von Hausswolff collection

Friedels Last Days In Höör:
Archive_Studio = ©1999 Carl Michael von Hausswolff
FJ appearance on his burial day at Claude Thorlin TV = © 1987 Claude Thorlin / Friedrich Jürgenson Foundation; Carl Michael von Hausswolff collection
FJ by Uher = ©photographer unknown / Friedrich Jürgenson Foundation; Carl Michael von Hausswolff collection
FJ Höör Swedish TV promo 2 = ©Lasse Larsson, Eskilstunakuriren / Friedrich Jürgenson Foundation; Carl Michael von Hausswolff collection
FJ in Höör 2 copy = ©photographer unknown / Friedrich Jürgenson Foundation; Carl Michael von Hausswolff collection
FJ press conf, Höör 1980s
FJ with favourite dog in Höör = ©Märta Annell / Friedrich Jürgenson Foundation; Carl Michael von Hausswolff collection
Märta Anell and CMvH Höör 1999 = ©Marietta von Hausswolff / Friedrich Jürgenson Foundation; Carl Michael von Hausswolff collection

Friedel Personal:
F Jürgenson Foundation archive = Färgfabriken Center for Contemporary Art art / Friedrich Jürgenson Foundation; Carl Michael von Hausswolff collection
Felix Kersten receives medal from the Dutch government for saving people during WWII. (the Orangienorder medal by Prins Bernhard of Holland) ©=©photographer unknown / Friedrich Jürgenson Foundation; Carl Michael von Hausswolff collection
FJ = ©Evert Hallin / Friedrich Jürgenson Foundation; Carl Michael von Hausswolff collection
FJ 1960 by Claude Thorlin = ©Claude Thorlin / Friedrich Jürgenson Foundation; Carl Michael von Hausswolff collection
FJ 1960s = ©Claude Thorlin / Friedrich Jürgenson Foundation; Carl Michael von Hausswolff collection
FJ book cover shot 1964 = ©Per Angré / Friedrich Jürgenson Foundation; Carl Michael von Hausswolff collection
FJ by Uher = ©photographer unknown / Friedrich Jürgenson Foundation; Carl Michael von Hausswolff collection
FJ in Mölnbo 2 = ©1970 John Kjellström / Friedrich Jürgenson Foundation; Carl Michael von Hausswolff collection

FJ in Mölnbo = ©Claude Thorlin / Friedrich Jürgenson Foundation; Carl Michael von Hausswolff collection
FJ the film maker = ©photographer unknown / Friedrich Jürgenson Foundation; Carl Michael von Hausswolff collection
FJ unknown photographer = ©photographer unknown / Friedrich Jürgenson Foundation; Carl Michael von Hausswolff collection
Hans Bender FJ 1973 1 = ©Claude Thorlin / Friedrich Jürgenson Foundation; Carl Michael von Hausswolff collection
Hans Bender FJ Nysund = ©Claude Thorlin / Friedrich Jürgenson Foundation; Carl Michael von Hausswolff collection
Hans Bender, Gisela Beckedorf and FJ 1973 2 = ©Claude Thorlin / Friedrich Jürgenson Foundation; Carl Michael von Hausswolff collection
jurgensontape1 = collage ©2013 Carl Michael von Hausswolff photographer Claude Thorlin = ©Claude Thorlin / Friedrich Jürgenson Foundation;
Carl Michael von Hausswolff collection
Press 1962 = ©photographer unknown / Friedrich Jürgenson Foundation; Carl Michael von Hausswolff collection
Swedish Television _here is your life_ 1980s = ©SVT / Friedrich Jürgenson Foundation; Carl Michael von Hausswolff collection
Villa Nysund Mölnbo = ©Claude Thorlin / Friedrich Jürgenson Foundation; Carl Michael von Hausswolff collection
Young FJ = ©1927 Photographer unknown / Friedrich Jürgenson Foundation; Carl Michael von Hausswolff collection

Friedel Pompeii:
FJ in Pompeji 2 = ©Lello Capaldo / Friedrich Jürgenson Foundation; Carl Michael von Hausswolff collection
FJ in Pompeji 3 = ©Lello Capaldo / Friedrich Jürgenson Foundation; Carl Michael von Hausswolff collection
FJ in Pompeji = ©Lello Capaldo / Friedrich Jürgenson Foundation; Carl Michael von Hausswolff collection

Fiedel Vatican:
Bruno Heim, Fj and Anders Leopold Vatican = ©1970 Jerry Windahl / Friedrich Jürgenson Foundation; Carl Michael von Hausswolff collection
FJ - Vatican = ©1970 Jerry Windahl / Friedrich Jürgenson Foundation; Carl Michael von Hausswolff collection
FJ and Paul VI = ©1969 Pontificia Fotografia Felici / Friedrich Jürgenson Foundation; Carl Michael von Hausswolff collection

FJ with Paul VI = ©1970 photographer unknown / Friedrich Jürgenson Foundation; Carl Michael von Hausswolff collection

FJ with his painting of Pius XII = Lars Larsson / Friedrich Jürgenson Foundation; Carl Michael von Hausswolff collection

FJ with Pius XII and Vatican paintings at the Vatican = ©1969 photographer unknown / Friedrich Jürgenson Foundation; Carl Michael von Hausswolff collection

Official FJ with Paul VI = ©1970 photographer unknown / Friedrich Jürgenson Foundation; Carl Michael von Hausswolff collec

NOTES

[1] Leopold, Anders (2014). *Min vän på andra sidan: boken om Friedrich Jürgenson som upptäckte röstfenomen från en fjärde livsdimension.* Nyköping: Parthenon.

[2] Prof Hans Bender (1907-1991). One of the top Parapsychology researchers in the world, founder of the Institut für Grenzgebiete der Psychologie und Psychohygiene (IGPP) in Freiburg, in 1950.

[3] www.itcjournal.org at: http://itcjournal.org/leopoldreport/FJ-voices.html

[4] The phonograph was invented by Thomas Edison in 1877. It was the first machine that could record, preserve and reproduce sound. The sound was stored as a track on one cylinder.

[5] Professor Ernst Senkowski, a German physicist deceased in 2015, is the greatest world expert in EVP and ITC. His book *Instrumentelle Transkommunikation* (1995) is undoubtedly the major work of the discipline. Dr Senkowski compiled from the beginning, in full detail, all the major events that happened in the field, many of which he personally witnessed and participated in.

[6] Throughout the book the word 'alien' is used in relation to the spirit voices not to extraterrestrials.

[7] It seems that in view of the quality of Schreiber's initial transimages, his results were questioned and sometimes doubted. However, the method he developed, allegedly under his deceased daughter Karin's instructions, has been used worldwide since then by many ITC operators with excellent results. I, Anabela, used this method when I started my ITC exploration and obtained good results. I testify to its validity.

[8] Dr Nils-Olof Jacobson died in 2017 and his website is no longer active.

9. I, Anabela, believe that the term 'radar' used by Jürgenson throughout the book, which also appeared often in my own transcontacts, should be understood in the sense of an energy unknown to us. Another great transcommunicator, Adolf Homes, received this explanation via an anomalous computer text: "[Our] 'Energy Radar' has no relation whatsoever to yours."
10. Anabela Cardoso's communicators also spoke of the "Opening of the Path", implying a new way of communicating with the next dimension of life through ITC open to everybody.
11. Readers can find the recordings marked LISTEN at ITCJournal.
12. http://www.itcjournal.org/?page_id=6583
13. http://www.itcjournal.org/?page_id=6583
14. http://www.itcjournal.org/?page_id=6583
15. http://www.itcjournal.org/?page_id=6583
16. http://www.itcjournal.org/?page_id=6583
17. http://www.itcjournal.org/?page_id=6583
18. http://www.itcjournal.org/?page_id=6583
19. http://www.itcjournal.org/?page_id=6583
20. http://www.itcjournal.org/?page_id=6583
21. The complex issue of Hitler's purported monologues recorded by F. Jürgenson must be taken cautiously (chapter 10). I kept to the original chapter of the Swedish version because I agree with Anders Leopold's reasons. But readers must be aware of the fact that although Friedrich Jürgenson was convinced that it was Hitler who communicated, in some of those monologues maybe he plainly made a mistake or an impostor spoke. Or maybe it was indeed Hitler. We have no way of knowing for sure.
22. http://www.itcjournal.org/?page_id=6583
23. http://www.itcjournal.org/?page_id=6583
24. http://www.itcjournal.org/?page_id=6583
25. https://archive.org/details/JurgensonVoiceTransmissionsWithTheDeceased
26. http://www.rodiehr.de/a_36_video_gate_to_start.htm
27. Nowadays polyglotism seems to happen less frequently—perhaps because the communicators know that the discipline is well rooted and thus, they no longer need to use it as often as at the beginning. However, it may still occur.

www.ingramcontent.com/pod-product-compliance
Lightning Source LLC
Chambersburg PA
CBHW020223170426
43201CB00007B/301